The
BLUE
PAGES

A Directory of Companies
Rated by Their Politics
and Practices

PoliPointPress

The Blue Pages: A Directory of Companies Rated by Their Politics and Practices

Copyright © 2006 PoliPointPress, LLC

This edition published in 2006 in the United States of America by PoliPointPress, P.O. Box 3008, Sausalito, CA 94966-3008
www.PoliPointPress.org

Contributors: Chris Colin and Carol Pott
Production Management: Michael Bass Associates

Library of Congress Cataloging-In-Publication Data

The Blue Pages / PoliPointPress / edited by Carol Pott
ISBN: 0-9760621-1-9

Library of Congress Control Number: 2005910605

Printed in the United States of America
January 2006

Published by:
PoliPointPress, LLC
P.O. Box 3008
Sausalito, CA 94966-3008
(415) 339-4100
www.PoliPointPress.org

Distributed by: Publishers Group West

Contents

About This Directory

"Money is the mother's milk of politics," one veteran legislator noted in the 1960s, and it almost sounds quaint now, like pointing out that advertisers use sex now and then to sell their products. But if the acceptance of this depressing truism has spread, so too has an awareness of how we might respond. If money is the problem, we now know, money can also be the solution: We can *choose* who gets ours.

Enter *The Blue Pages*. By summarizing the political contributions and business practices of over 1,000 companies and over 4,000 brands, this directory allows you to see exactly what your cash supports. Armed with this knowledge, you then have the option of redirecting your spending, if you wish—say, to a credit card company that doesn't contribute so much to the wrong political party, or a clothing maker whose environmental record is a little better. In this sense it's accountability this directory seeks to promote. Business leaders may believe that their contributions and labor practices advance their interests directly but if these same decisions begin to cost them at the cash register, it won't be long before their policies change to protect their bottom line.

The practical details of the "conscious shopping" movement can be dauntingly complex. Following the money can lead one in different places, depending on which party is in power, for instance—that reddish tint to a certain media conglomerate may start looking blue next time a Democrat is in the White House. Then there's all the influence that's bought *after* an election, in the form of lobbying: The Center for Public Integrity reported in 2005 that lobbyists have spent almost $13 billion since 1998 to influence members of Congress and federal officials on legislation and regulations. Political influence aside, trying to parse the ethical behavior of a corporation invariably produces wildly mixed results—here an illegal sweatshop, there a progressive hiring policy and a generous donation to hurricane victims.

Even after sorting through all that, there can be endless debate about the very premise of responsible consumption. Some argue that shopping can never solve the world's problems, and that curbing consumerism is the only answer. Others, such as economist Paul Krugman, point out that commerce is the only thing that's ever helped. These discussions are worth having, but endless debate also works in favor of the status quo. The simple truth is that organized consumers have effected change in a demonstrable way over the years, often where government was unable to.

This directory itself is easy to use. The company entries are organized alphabetically within 13 business sectors, and the index lets you locate specific companies and brands even more quickly. Each entry shows how much the company contributed and to which party, and the notes provide additional information about the company's business practices.

The entries have been carefully researched. First, we assembled a list of companies from a broad range of sectors. Next, we identified each company's top three executives. We then reviewed these executives' political donations during the 2003-04 giving cycle by consulting contribution records held by the Federal Election Commission and the Center for Responsive Politics. The Center for Responsive Politics also provided us with details of each company's political action committee (PAC) contributions and proprietary research on the party distribution of the PAC donations. We utilized the comprehensive research done by the Human Rights Campaign to outline company benefits structure. We also looked at companies' labor practices, environmental records, social responsibility and so forth, but the contribution records themselves are based solely on the donations of the top three executives incorporated with totals from the company PAC.

We welcome your comments on *The Blue Pages* and its usefulness. You can contact us at info@polipointpress.org or by mail at PoliPointPress, P.O. Box 3008, Sausalito, CA, 94966.

Clothing, Shoes, and Accessories

"You'd be surprised how much it costs to look this cheap," Dolly Parton once remarked. *The Blue Pages* would tweak that a bit: You'd be surprised how cheap it is to look this good.

At the heart of the U.S. apparel industry's financial and ethical problems lies inexpensive clothing. With cheap clothing pouring in from China—more so now that a decades-old quota has been lifted—domestic manufacturers find themselves in a continuous search for a competitive, politically viable, and high-quality production system. The search has not always gone well.

Eighty years after the Triangle Shirtwaist Fire first drew the public's attention to labor issues among clothing companies, the antisweatshop movement of the 1990s reminded the industry of how far it still had to go. A few high-profile cases sent companies scurrying to better monitor their factories—and marked improvements have been made as a result of this pressure.

But the issue is complex. Ensuring responsible production is not as simple as tracing Kathie Lee Gifford's blouses to sweatshops in Central America. Even in cases where manufacturers have clamped down on labor abuses—a minority, still—environmental considerations complicate the matter further. Harmful pesticides and insecticides are often used in the growing of cotton, and toxic dyes frequently find their way into clothing.

Further complicating the issue is the question of importing. While quota critics argue that U.S. manufacturers have long enjoyed an unfair advantage—precisely the kind of government protectionism conservatives decry when the beneficiary is a poor person rather than a wealthy corporation—the advantage in fact extended to developing countries, too. Under the quota system, nations such as Mauritius, Lesotho, and Cambodia stood a chance of competing against China; without it, some fear, those jobs might vanish.

This sector tends to base its campaign contributions on whichever party is in power and was rewarded recently by the 108th Congress, which reduced taxes on materials imported from other countries—a move the industry considered essential to its competitiveness in the long term.

The years ahead will undoubtedly be marked by debate over the reinstitution of quotas and by struggles over labor practices and environmental concerns. The Gap, an often-boycotted company with links to sweat-shop labor, the violent suppression of worker protests, and even deforestation, showed signs of progress with a recent Social Responsibility report admitting a variety of shortcomings. Even better, the dramatic success of small, ethically run companies such as Patagonia and the recent upstart American Apparel have focused attention on the marketability of corporate responsibility.

In the meantime, responsible consumers can take steps of their own: ask where garments are made, keep an eye out for organically grown cotton and natural or low-impact dyes, look for Fair Trade or Union Made labels, and buy secondhand or hand-made clothes from independent retailers.

Top Ten Republican Contributors

Limited Brands, Inc.	$289,174
J. C. Penney Company, Inc.	163,964
Gap Inc.	161,552
May Department Stores Company, The	113,802
Jones Apparel Group, Inc.	79,270
Guess?, Inc.	52,000
Saks Incorporated	43,515
Children's Place Retail Stores, Inc., The	42,357
Federated Department Stores	20,612
Retail Ventures, Inc.	20,550

Top Ten Democratic Contributors

Gap Inc.	$194,344
Dress Barn, Inc., The	157,000
J. Crew Group, Inc.	118,205
Sean John Clothing	67,495
Limited Brands, Inc.	59,006
Men's Wearhouse, Inc., The	58,000
Levi Strauss & Co.	57,950
Jones Apparel Group, Inc.	39,506
Kenneth Cole Productions, Inc.	34,500
May Department Stores Company, The	33,482

Abercrombie & Fitch Co.

No contributions. Settled multiple class action suits in 2004 alleging racial and sexual discrimination. Settled a derivative suit brought in 2005 by a shareholder who alleged the board breached its duties by awarding a "grossly excessive and wasteful" pay package to its CEO. One of 26 retailers that agreed to a $20 million settlement in a federal class action lawsuit alleging sweatshop practices brought by garment workers in Saipan. Paid $2.2 million to settle charges alleging a company policy required employees to meet strict workplace dress codes and wear company product without compensation. Has sourced from countries with widespread, well-documented human and labor rights abuses. Has been cited for encouraging sweatshop labor with its supplier practices. Has a written nondiscrimination policy covering sexual orientation and offers health insurance coverage to employees' domestic partners. www.abercrombie.com

Adidas AG

See p. 172 in Sporting Goods.

Aeropostale
No contributions. Has sourced from countries with widespread, well-documented human and labor rights abuses and encourages sweatshop labor with supplier practices. www.aeropostale.com

American Eagle Outfitters, Inc.
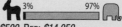
CONTRIBUTIONS: TOTAL: *$14,550* DEM: *$500* REP: *$14,050*

Has sourced from countries with widespread, well-documented human and labor rights abuses. Foundation raises funds and enlists volunteers for projects fostering civic involvement, teen and college education programs, and diversification. www.ae.com

Amer Sports Corporation
See p. 172 in Sporting Goods.

Ann Taylor Stores Corporation
No contributions. Has sourced from countries with widespread, well-documented human and labor rights abuses. Workers in China were paid 12 cents an hour in 1998 and worked an average of 90 hours per week, according to a National Labor Committee report. Also cited for forced overtime in El Salvador, where workers were paid 60 cents per hour and work 13- to 15-hour days, 7 days per week. Has a written nondiscrimination policy covering sexual orientation but not gender identity. Refuses insurance coverage for employees' domestic partners. www.anntaylor.com

Anthropologie

CONTRIBUTIONS: TOTAL: *$250* DEM: *$250* REP: *$0*
Subsidiary of Urban Outfitters, Inc. (p. 29). www.anthropologie.com

Arden B.

CONTRIBUTIONS: TOTAL: *$3,200* DEM: *$3,080* REP: *$108*
Subsidiary of Wet Seal (p. 30). www.ardenb.com

Associated Merchandising Corporation, The
No contributions. Subsidiary of Target Corporation (p. 145). www.theamc.com

AZ3, Inc., doing business as BCBG
No contributions. Privately held. Settled a suit in 2000 alleging the sale of "dangerously flammable" women's chenille sweaters and failure to report the sale in violation of federal law. Agreed to a broad settlement in a lawsuit in 2000 alleging labor, minimum wage and overtime violations at a supplier-held sewing shop in Los Angeles. Has sourced from countries with widespread, well-documented human and labor rights abuses and encourages sweatshop labor with its supplier practices. www.bcbg.com

BabyUniverse, Inc.
No contributions. www.babyuniverse.com

Bad Boy Worldwide Entertainment Group
See p. 150 in Media and Entertainment.

Bailey Banks & Biddle Fine Jewelers
No contributions. Subsidiary of Zale Corporation (p. 30).
www.baileybanksandbiddle.com

Banana Republic
No contributions. Subsidiary of Gap Inc. (p. 13).
www.bananarepublic.com

Barneys New York, Inc.   100%   0%
CONTRIBUTIONS: TOTAL: *$20,276* DEM: *$20,276* REP: *$0*
Subsidiary of Jones Apparel Group, Inc. (p. 15).
www.barneys.com

Bebe Stores, Inc.   100%   0%
CONTRIBUTIONS: TOTAL: *$500* DEM: *$500* REP: *$0*
Settled multiple lawsuits brought by the U.S. Department of
Labor alleging sweatshop conditions as well as wage and hour
overtime abuses. Settled several civil rights cases of racial
discrimination brought both by employees and customers.
Exonerated in a closely watched labor case in 2002 alleging
poor working conditions and labor violations. Has sourced
from countries with widespread, well-documented human and
labor rights abuses. Has been cited as encouraging sweatshop labor with its supplier practices. www.bebe.com

Bergdorf Goodman
No contributions. Subsidiary of the Neiman Marcus Group,
Inc. (p. 21); parent, Texas Pacific Group (p. 168). Company and
executives pled no contest in a case charging price-fixing of
women's clothing in 2000. Has a written nondiscrimination policy covering sexual orientation but not gender identity. Offers
insurance coverage to employees' domestic partners.
www.bergdorfgoodman.com

Bergner's
No contributions. Subsidiary of Saks Incorporated (p. 25).
www.bergners.com

Berkshire Hathaway
See p. 54 in Finance, Insurance, and Real Estate.

Big Dog Holdings, Inc.   0%   100%
CONTRIBUTIONS: TOTAL: *$6,000* DEM: *$0* REP: *$6,000*
Has sourced from countries with widespread, well-
documented human and labor rights abuses. Big Dog Foundation supports efforts helping dogs, children, and dogs helping

people. Donated $100,000 to charities assisting with the September 11, 2001 aftermath. www.bigdogs.com

Bloomingdale's
CONTRIBUTIONS: TOTAL: *$5,000* DEM: *$5,000* REP: *$0*
Subsidiary of Federated Department Stores (p. 11).
www.bloomingdales.com

Boston Store
No contributions. Subsidiary of Saks Incorporated (p. 25).
www.bostonstore.com

Brooks Brothers
No contributions. Subsidiary of Retail Brand Alliance, Inc. (p. 24). One of 26 retailers that agreed to a $20 million settlement in a federal class action lawsuit brought by garment workers in Saipan alleging sweatshop practices. Has donated a percentage of sales, up to $50,000, to the Make-a-Wish Foundation for terminally ill children. www.brooksbrothers.com

Brown Shoe Company, Inc.
CONTRIBUTIONS: TOTAL: *$20,250* DEM: *$0* REP: *$20,250*
Manufactures in, and has sourced from countries with widespread, well-documented human and labor rights abuses. Continues to pay cleanup fees for industrial solvent contamination of a residential area behind a former factory in Colorado. www.brownshoe.com

Bulova Corporation
No contributions. Subsidiary of Loews Corporation (p. 61).
www.bulova.com

Burlington Coat Factory Warehouse Corporation

CONTRIBUTIONS: TOTAL: *$1,250* DEM: *$1,250* REP: *$0*
Settled a suit with the Federal Trade Commission (FTC) for allegedly failing to disclose the origin of textile products in its internet catalog and agreed to pay $11,000 for any future violations. Was sued by the state of California for alleged failure to disclose lead levels in costume jewelry. Outreach supports the Leukemia & Lymphoma Society and offers educational child safety and wellness seminars. Does not have a nondiscrimination policy covering sexual orientation or gender identity. Refuses insurance coverage to employees' domestic partners. www.coat.com

Burton Snowboards
See p. 173 in Sporting Goods.

Calvin Klein

CONTRIBUTIONS: TOTAL: *$250* DEM: *$250* REP: *$0*

Subsidiary of Phillips–Van Heusen Corporation (p. 23). One of 26 retailers that agreed to a $20 million settlement in a federal class action lawsuit brought by garment workers in Saipan alleging sweatshop practices. www.calvinklein.com

Candie's Inc.

CONTRIBUTIONS: TOTAL: *$500* DEM: *$500* REP: *$0*

Pending shareholder class action for overstating revenues and earnings. The Candies Foundation works to educate America's youth on the consequences of teen pregnancy. www.candiesinc.com

C&J Clark International Ltd.

No contributions. Agreed to pay a portion of the estimated $7.4 million in cleanup costs for groundwater contamination resulting from hazardous waste dumping in violation of Environmental Protection Agency (EPA) regulations. www.clarks.co.uk

Carhartt, Inc.

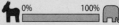

CONTRIBUTIONS: TOTAL: *$1,130* DEM: *$0* REP: *$1,130*

Has sourced from countries with widespread, well-documented human and labor rights abuses. Outreach supports Future Farmers of America; NASCAR driver Matt Kenseth and his crew; the National High School Rodeo Association, SkillsUSA, an educational program for skilled workers; and the Championship Bull Riding series. www.carhartt.com

Carolee Designs, Inc.

No contributions. Subsidiary of Retail Brand Alliance, Inc. (p. 24). Outreach focuses on breast cancer awareness and research, raising over $2 million in the last 15 years. www.securerba.com

Carson Pirie Scott

No contributions. Subsidiary of Saks Incorporated (p. 25). Settled a discrimination case brought by the National Organization for Women by changing a policy that charged women more money for alterations than men. www.carsons.com

Carter's, Inc.

CONTRIBUTIONS: TOTAL: *$5,500* DEM: *$75* REP: *$5,425*

Currently under investigation by the Federal Elections Commission (FEC) for violations in the $8,000 reimbursement of four executives and their wives for eight separate political contributions made to Georgia senator Saxby Chambliss's campaign. Company CEO also made a substantial donation to the National Rifle Association that is not included in our contribution breakdown. Has sourced from countries with widespread, well-documented human and labor rights abuses. www.carters.com

Casual Corner Group, Inc.
No contributions. Subsidiary of Retail Brand Alliance, Inc. (p. 24). Has donated a percentage of sales, up to $50,000, to the Make-a-Wish Foundation for terminally ill children. Currently up for sale. www.casualcorner.com

Casual Male Retail Group, Inc.
No contributions. Has sourced from countries with widespread, well-documented human and labor rights abuses. www.cmrginc.com

Catherine's Plus Size
No contributions. Subsidiary of Charming Shoppes (p. 8). www.catherines.com

Champs Sports
No contributions. Subsidiary of Foot Locker, Inc. (p. 12). www.champssports.com

Chanel, Inc.
See p. 108 in Health and Beauty.

Charming Shoppes
100%   0%

CONTRIBUTIONS: TOTAL: *$250* DEM: *$250* REP: *$0*

Has sourced from countries with widespread, well-documented human and labor rights abuses. Has been cited as encouraging sweatshop labor with its supplier practices. The company's Lane Bryant, Fashion Bug, and Catherine's Plus Sizes stores donated 200,000 units of new apparel and shoes to assist in relief efforts following Hurricane Katrina in 2005. Focuses philanthropic efforts on women, children and the homeless through a grant program. Donates coats to inner-city youth. Donates professional work clothing to a nonprofit program aiding woman exiting job-training programs. www.charmingshoppes.com

Chico's
No contributions. Subsidiary of Chico's FAS (p. 8). www.chicos.com

Chico's FAS
56%   44%

CONTRIBUTIONS: TOTAL: *$27,309* DEM: *$15,358* REP: *$11,951*

Pending class action suit alleging violations of the California Labor Code for its wardrobing policy requiring employees to purchase Chico's clothing as a condition of employment. Has sourced from countries with widespread, well-documented human and labor rights abuses. Has been cited as encouraging sweatshop labor with its supplier practices. www.chicos.com

Children's Place Retail Stores, Inc., The

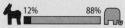 12%   88%

CONTRIBUTIONS: TOTAL: *$48,357* DEM: *$6,000* REP: *$42,357*

Has sourced from countries with widespread, well-documented human and labor rights abuses. Paid $1.5 million settlement in class action brought by shareholders alleging violations of the Securities Act for material misrepresentations and omissions concerning the financial and operating condition of the company at its initial public offering. CEO Ezra Dabah and his family have weathered legal challenges, prison sentences, and bankruptcies, including charges of falsifying clothing import documents that landed two members of his family in jail. www.childrensplace.com

Citizen Watch Co., Ltd.

No contributions. Has sourced from countries with widespread, well-documented human and labor rights abuses. Has an environmental and waste/pollution reduction program. Philanthropic efforts provide official-time precision clocks for major sports venues and for landmarks around the world. www.citizen.co.jp

Citizen Watch Co. of America Inc.

No contributions. Subsidiary of Citizen Watch Co., Ltd. (p. 9). www.citizenwatch.com

Claire's Stores, Inc.

100%   0%

CONTRIBUTIONS: TOTAL: *$18,000* DEM: *$18,000* REP: *$0*

Settled a suit in 2001 filed by the Equal Employment Opportunity Commission (EEOC) on behalf of female employees who alleged pregnancy discrimination. Was singled out by the Labor Department in 1996 as a retailer encouraging sweatshop labor in its supplier practices. Has a written nondiscrimination policy covering sexual orientation but not gender identity. Refuses insurance coverage to employees' domestic partners. www.clairestores.com

Coach, Inc.

 100%   0%

CONTRIBUTIONS: TOTAL: *$11,000* DEM: *$11,000* REP: *$0*

Recently spun off from its subsidiary status under former parent Sara Lee Branded Apparel (p. 25). Pending decision for damages in alleged racial discrimination suit involving violation of the Civil Rights Act of 1971, the New York Human Rights Law, and the New York Administrative Code. www.coach.com

Cole Haan Holdings, Inc.

No contributions. Subsidiary of NIKE, Inc (p. 175). Has sourced from countries with widespread, well-documented human and labor rights abuses. Has a written nondiscrimination policy covering sexual orientation and gender identity. Offers insurance coverage to employees' domestic partners. www.colehaan.com

Columbia Sportswear Company
See p. 173 in Sporting Goods.

David's Bridal 20% 80%
CONTRIBUTIONS: TOTAL: *$2,500* DEM: *$500* REP: *$2,000*
Subsidiary of the May Department Stores Company (p. 20). Has a written nondiscrimination policy covering sexual orientation but not gender identity. Refuses insurance coverage to employees' domestic partners. www.davidsbridal.com

Dillard's, Inc. 61% 39%
CONTRIBUTIONS: TOTAL: *$18,000* DEM: *$11,000* REP: *$7,000*
Agreed to pay $15 million to settle a suit filed on behalf of a five-year-old girl who severed and lost three fingers on a company escalator. As a follow-up there is a pending investigation into alleged negligence in the company's maintenance and repair of the escalator. Two top executives took $1.8 million bonuses in 2004, a year marked by company layoffs and store closures. Has a written nondiscrimination policy covering sexual orientation but not gender identity. Refuses insurance coverage to employees' domestic partners. www.dillards.com

Dockers
No contributions. Subsidiary of Levi Strauss & Co. (p. 17). Has a written nondiscrimination policy covering sexual orientation and gender identity. Offers insurance coverage to employees' domestic partners. www.dockers.com

Donna Karan International Inc. 100% 0%
CONTRIBUTIONS: TOTAL: *$30,000* DEM: *$30,000* REP: *$0*
Subsidiary of LVMH Moët Hennessy Louis Vuitton SA (p. 88). One of 26 retailers that agreed to a $20 million settlement in a federal class action lawsuit brought by garment workers in Saipan alleging sweatshop practices. Settled class action case alleging the company forced union workers in a New York factory to work 7 days a week, 12 hours a day, without minimum wage or overtime pay. www.donnakaran.com

Dooney & Bourke Inc.
No contributions. Has sourced from countries with widespread, well-documented human and labor rights abuses. www.dooney.com

Dress Barn, Inc., The 100% 0%
CONTRIBUTIONS: TOTAL: *$157,000* DEM: *$157,000* REP: *$0*
One of 26 retailers that agreed to a $20 million settlement in a federal class action lawsuit brought by garment workers in Saipan alleging sweatshop practices. Agreed to pay $400,000 to finance an independent monitoring program in Saipan as a part of a settlement in 1999. Has operations in and has sourced from countries with widespread, well-documented human and

labor rights abuses and has encouraged sweatshop labor with
its supplier practices. www.dressbarn.com

Dr. Martens Airwair USA
No contributions. Subsidiary of R. Griggs Group Limited (p. 24).
Foreign owned. www.drmartens.com

DSW, Inc.
CONTRIBUTIONS: TOTAL: *$500* DEM: *$0* REP: *$500*
Subsidiary of Retail Ventures, Inc. (p. 24). Brought in federal
investigators after the theft of 108 customers' credit information. The Ohio attorney general later sued, saying the company's failure to contact each customer violated consumer
protection laws. Has helped to raise more than $750,000 for
the March of Dimes, sponsored the 2004 National Urban
League Conference, and contributes funds to community programs aiding needy and abused children. Coinciding with
opening of its Manhattan store, donated $500,000 to the New
York Restoration Projects, which preserves overlooked public
green spaces, especially in underserved neighborhoods.
www.dswshoe.com

Eastbay
No contributions. Subsidiary of Foot Locker, Inc. (p. 12).
www.eastbay.com

Eddie Bauer, Inc.
See p. 173 in Sporting Goods.

Express, LLC
CONTRIBUTIONS: TOTAL: *$4,000* DEM: *$0* REP: *$4,000*
Subsidiary of Limited Brands, Inc. (p. 17).
www.expressfashion.com

Famous Footwear
No contributions. Subsidiary of Brown Shoe Company, Inc.
(p. 6). Outreach supports the March of Dimes.
www.famousfootwear.com

Fashion Bug
No contributions. Subsidiary of Charming Shoppes (p. 8).
www.fashionbug.com

Federated Department Stores

CONTRIBUTIONS: TOTAL: *$26,902* DEM: *$6,278* REP: *$20,612*
Since its $11 billion acquisition of the May Department Stores
Company in 2005, Federated has become the giant of the
department store industry, converting the country's Marshall
Field's stores into Macy's and announcing 6,200 layoffs. Several
recent suits have charged antitrust and price-fixing. Received a
"C" on Co-Op America's retailer scorecard, which alleges that
the company purchases clothing from known sweatshops and

has sourced from countries with well-documented human and labor rights abuses. Foundation supports education, women's issues, arts/culture, HIV/AIDS prevention, and minority and youth education programs. Has a written nondiscrimination policy covering sexual orientation and offers health insurance to employees' domestic partners. www.federated-fds.com

Filene's Basement Corp.
No contributions. Subsidiary of Retail Ventures, Inc. (p. 24). Company's practice is to increasingly discount merchandise for about one month, then give unsold goods to charity. www.filenesbasement.com

Footaction
No contributions. Subsidiary of Foot Locker, Inc. (p. 12). www.footlocker.com

Foot Locker
No contributions. Subsidiary of Foot Locker, Inc. (p. 12). www.footlocker.com

Footlocker.com
No contributions. Subsidiary of Foot Locker, Inc. (p. 12). www.footlocker.com

Foot Locker, Inc.
100% | 0%
CONTRIBUTIONS: TOTAL: *$2,000* DEM: *$2,000* REP: *$0*
Paid $3.5 million to settle an age discrimination suit filed by the EEOC in 1999. Has sourced from countries with widespread, well-documented human and labor rights abuses and encourages sweatshop labor with its supplier practices. Foundation supports volunteerism and disaster relief and donates housewares and other merchandise to disaster victims. Has a written nondiscrimination policy covering sexual orientation but not gender identity. Refuses insurance coverage to employees' domestic partners. www.footlocker.com

Fossil, Inc.
0% | 100%
CONTRIBUTIONS: TOTAL: *$2,000* DEM: *$0* REP: *$2,000*
Pending lawsuit alleging violation of antitrust laws and unfair competition resulting from its proposed licensing agreement with Guess?, Inc. (p. 13), which would give the company control of 60% of the U.S. fashion watch market. www.fossil.com

Fruit of the Loom
0% | 100%
CONTRIBUTIONS: TOTAL: *$15,500* DEM: *$0* REP: *$15,500*
Subsidiary of Berkshire Hathaway (p. 54) since 2002. www.fruit.com

Gap
100% | 0%
CONTRIBUTIONS: TOTAL: *$1,000* DEM: *$1,000* REP: *$0*
Subsidiary of Gap Inc. (p. 13). www.gap.com

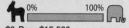

Gap Inc.

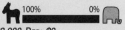

CONTRIBUTIONS: TOTAL: *$357,000* DEM: *$194,345* REP: *$161,553*

The largest specialty retailer in the United States has faced years of (often substantiated) accusations of sweatshop abuses. In 2003, for example, Gap was part of a $20 million settlement over labor abuses—including unpaid overtime and exploitative worker contracts—at a factory in Saipan, just one of the company's many documented union/labor disputes. But lately, Gap seems to have changed its ways and is earning praise from watchdog groups: The company hires independent monitors to check factory conditions and recently began making these reports public; in 2003, it ended relationships with 136 sweatshop vendors. Meanwhile, environmentalists have boycotted Gap for years, protesting its founding family, the Fischers, who are primary stakeholders in the Mendocino Redwood Company, which has been accused of clear-cutting and mismanagement of delicate old-growth forests. Gap supports employee volunteer efforts and company recycling and conservation programs. Has a written nondiscrimination policy covering sexual orientation and gender identity, and offers family benefits including health insurance coverage for employees' domestic partners. www.gap.com

G. H. Bass

No contributions. Subsidiary of Phillips–Van Heusen Corporation (p. 23). www.bassshoes.com

Gordon's Jewelers

No contributions. Subsidiary of Zale Corporation (p. 30). www.gordonsjewelers.com

Guess?, Inc.

CONTRIBUTIONS: TOTAL: *$63,000* DEM: *$11,000* REP: *$52,000*

Agreed to pay a $1 million fine and subsequently moved the bulk of its operations to Mexico following charges by the Department of Labor operating sweatshops in Los Angeles throughout the 1990s. Outreach supports education, environmental protection, and AIDS research and treatment. www.guess.com

Gymboree Corporation, The

CONTRIBUTIONS: TOTAL: *$2,000* DEM: *$2,000* REP: *$0*

One of 26 retailers that agreed to a $20 million settlement in a federal class action lawsuit brought by garment workers in Saipan alleging sweatshop practices. Has sourced from countries with widespread, well-documented human and labor rights abuses. Offers paid volunteer time off for employees. Raised $150,000 for the March of Dimes in 2003. Has been involved with Junior Achievement and Adopt-a-Family. www.gymboree.com

Helzberg Diamonds
No contributions. Subsidiary of Berkshire Hathaway (p. 54).
www.helzberg.com

Henri Bendel
No contributions. Subsidiary of Limited Brands, Inc. (p. 17).
www.henribendel.com

Herberger's
No contributions. Subsidiary of Saks Incorporated (p. 25).
www.herbergers.com

Hugo Boss AG
No contributions. www.hugo-boss.com

Hurley International, LLC
See p. 174 in Sporting Goods.

IZOD
No contributions. Subsidiary of Phillips–Van Heusen Corporation (p. 23). www.izod.com

JanSport, Inc.
See p. 174 in Sporting Goods.

J. C. Penney Company, Inc.

CONTRIBUTIONS: TOTAL: *$187,190* DEM: *$22,326* REP: *$163,965*
One of 26 retailers that agreed to a $20 million settlement in a federal class action lawsuit brought by garment workers in Saipan alleging sweatshop practices. A former employee's 2000 lawsuit (currently held up on appeal) alleges that the company didn't properly announce changes to its managerial severance benefit, the only notice of it being "buried" in the middle of an annual report. Sued in 2005 for more than $140 million by a former employee claiming he was fired because he is HIV-positive—case pending. Has a minority supplier diversity program. Outreach supports health and welfare, education, volunteerism, and diversity. Has a written nondiscrimination policy covering sexual orientation but not gender identity. Offers insurance coverage to employees' domestic partners. www.jcpenney.net

J. Crew Group, Inc.

CONTRIBUTIONS: TOTAL: *$120,000* DEM: *$118,205* REP: *$1,625*
Subsidiary of Texas Pacific Group (p. 168). One of 26 retailers that agreed to a $20 million settlement in a federal class action lawsuit brought by garment workers in Saipan alleging sweatshop practices. A 1997 lawsuit alleged that the company shielded itself from responsibility for labor conditions in its California garment shops by failing to register as an apparel manufacturer in that state. Was investigated and penalized in 1998 by the Department of Labor for wage violations. www.jcrew.com

J. Jill Group, Inc., The

CONTRIBUTIONS: TOTAL: *$4,000* DEM: *$636* REP: *$3,364*

Settled a lawsuit regarding a wardrobing policy requiring employees to buy and wear its clothing as a condition of employment. Outreach supports disenfranchised women and children nationwide through the J. Jill Compassion Fund. Written nondiscrimination policy covers sexual orientation but not gender identity. www.jjill.com

Jockey International, Inc.
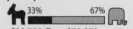
CONTRIBUTIONS: TOTAL: *$21,700* DEM: *$1,314* REP: *$20,386*

Has a written nondiscrimination policy covering sexual orientation but not gender identity. www.jockey.com

Jones Apparel Group, Inc.

CONTRIBUTIONS: TOTAL: *$118,776* DEM: *$39,506* REP: *$79,270*

One of 26 retailers that agreed to a $20 million settlement in a federal class action lawsuit brought by garment workers in Saipan alleging sweatshop practices. Chairman Sidney Kimmel donated $150 million for cancer research and patient care at Johns Hopkins and established cancer research centers in his name at Memorial Sloan-Kettering in New York City and Thomas Jefferson University in Philadelphia. Has a written nondiscrimination policy covering sexual orientation but not gender identity. Offers insurance coverage to employees' domestic partners. www.jny.com

Joseph Abboud

CONTRIBUTIONS: TOTAL: *$1,000* DEM: *$1,000* REP: *$0*

Subsidiary of J. W. Childs Associates, L.P. (p. 86). www.josephabboud.com

Justin Brands
No contributions. Subsidiary of Berkshire Hathaway (p. 54). www.justinboots.com

Kate Spade LLC
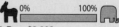
CONTRIBUTIONS: TOTAL: *$445* DEM: *$445* REP: *$0*

Majority owned by Neiman Marcus (p. 21), a subsidiary of Texas Pacific Group (p. 168). Has sourced from countries with widespread, well-documented human and labor rights abuses. Supports community and educational transformation through an organization called Publicolor. www.katespade.com

Kellwood Company
CONTRIBUTIONS: TOTAL: *$2,000* DEM: *$0* REP: *$2,000*

In 2003, Human Rights Watch found labor abuses, including workers being denied bathroom breaks, in a supplier factory in El Salvador. Outreach supports education, health and welfare, and civic causes in areas where the company does business.

Supports Dress for Success, which provides job-seeking, low-income women with apparel and interview coaching. www.kellwood.com

Kenneth Cole Productions, Inc.
CONTRIBUTIONS: TOTAL: *$34,500* DEM: *$34,500* REP: *$0*

A pending lawsuit brought by former corporate employee alleges that her complaints about sexual and racial harassment led to her being passed over for promotion. Pending wage and hour class action lawsuit filed in California by former employees alleges failure to pay overtime wages. Announced its intention not to purchase goods made in Burma, in protest of human rights violations there. Philanthropy supports Rock the Vote, Mentoring USA, and the American Foundation for AIDS Research. Written nondiscrimination policy covers sexual orientation but not gender identity. www.kennethcole.com

Kids Foot Locker
No contributions. Subsidiary of Foot Locker, Inc. (p. 12). www.kidsfootlocker.com

Kohl's Corporation
CONTRIBUTIONS: TOTAL: *$2,000* DEM: *$0* REP: *$2,000*

An advocacy group representing more than 400 black-owned newspapers urged African Americans to boycott Kohl's because the company spends none of its more than $86 million annual advertising budget on ads in African American papers. Has sourced from countries with widespread, well-documented human and labor rights abuses. Outreach supports improving health and educational opportunities for children in communities where Kohl's has a corporate presence. Matches employees' volunteer efforts with corporate grants to children's groups. Has a written nondiscrimination policy covering sexual orientation but not gender identity. Refuses insurance coverage to employees' domestic partners. www.kohls.com

Lady Foot Locker
No contributions. Subsidiary of Foot Locker, Inc. (p. 12). www.ladyfootlocker.com

Lands' End, Inc.
No contributions. Lost several major customers and lucrative accounts amid highly publicized reports of its questionable business practice and alleged labor law violations at supplier factories in El Salvador. Has a written nondiscrimination policy covering sexual orientation and gender identity. Offers insurance coverage to employees' domestic partners. www.landsend.com

Lane Bryant

No contributions. Subsidiary of Charming Shoppes (p. 8). One of 26 retailers that agreed to a $20 million settlement in a federal class action lawsuit brought by garment workers in Saipan alleging sweatshop practices. Has sourced from countries with widespread, well-documented human and labor rights abuses. www.charmingshoppes.com

Levi's

No contributions. Subsidiary of Levi Strauss & Co. (p. 17). Has sourced from countries with widespread, well-documented human and labor rights abuses. Has a written nondiscrimination policy covering sexual orientation and gender identity. Offers insurance coverage to employees' domestic partners. www.levi.com

Levi Strauss & Co.

CONTRIBUTIONS: TOTAL: *$58,050* DEM: *$57,950* REP: *$100*

After years of declining profits, this all-American brand is now an entirely foreign-made product. Between 2002 and 2004, Levi's laid off its remaining several thousand American manufacturing workers and now uses exclusively overseas contractors. Has been criticized in the past for doing business with sweatshop vendors, but has recently won praise for establishing operating guidelines for its manufacturers and conducting audits of its factories on issues such as the exclusion of child labor, maximum work week, and minimum wage. Levi's also ended its business with Burma and China over rights abuses there. Outreach supports labor and living conditions in countries where its products are produced, as well as AIDS/HIV prevention. Levi's was named one of "America's 50 Best Companies for Minorities" by *Fortune* magazine. Has a written nondiscrimination policy that covers sexual orientation and gender identity. Offers insurance coverage to employees' domestic partners. www.levistrauss.com

Levi Strauss Signature

CONTRIBUTIONS: TOTAL: *$250* DEM: *$250* REP: *$0*

Subsidiary of Levi Strauss & Co. (p. 17). Has sourced from countries with widespread, well-documented human and labor rights abuses. Has a written nondiscrimination policy covering sexual orientation and gender identity. Offers insurance coverage to employees' domestic partners. www.levistrausssignature.com

Limited Brands, Inc.

CONTRIBUTIONS: TOTAL: *$348,200* DEM: *$59,006* REP: *$289,174*

Paid $180,000 to settle a lawsuit filed by the EEOC in 2002 against the company's Victoria's Secret subsidiary alleging racial and religious harassment of an African American employee. One of 26 retailers that agreed to a $20 million settlement in a federal class action lawsuit brought by garment workers in Saipan alleging sweatshop practices. Has sourced from countries with widespread, well-documented human and labor rights abuses. Outreach supports women-centered issues, mentoring children, and improving education. Has reduced energy usage by one-third using more efficient lighting and expects to have equipped half of all stores by the end of 2005. In 2003, abandoned use of PVC plastic for its Bath and Body Works products, in favor of the more environmentally friendly and more easily recyclable PET plastic. Has a written nondiscrimination policy covering sexual orientation but not gender identity. Offers health insurance coverage to employees' domestic partners. www.limited.com

Limited, The
25% 75%

CONTRIBUTIONS: TOTAL: *$9,300* DEM: *$2,300* REP: *$7,000*

Subsidiary of Limited Brands, Inc. (p. 17). Paid $200,000 in fines for selling highly flammable clothing in violation of federal law. www.limited.com

Liz Claiborne, Inc.
53% 47%

CONTRIBUTIONS: TOTAL: *$22,250* DEM: *$11,758* REP: *$10,480*

One of 26 retailers that agreed to a $20 million settlement in a federal class action lawsuit brought by garment workers in Saipan alleging sweatshop practices. Has sourced from countries with widespread, well-documented human and labor rights abuses. Among the founding companies of the Fair Labor Association, an industry-wide nonprofit organization whose goal is eliminating global apparel sweatshops. Stopped operations in Burma in 1994 as a protest of that government's human rights violations. Foundation supports nonprofit organizations focused on disadvantaged women and families. Matches employees' charitable gifts. Has a written nondiscrimination policy covering sexual orientation but not gender identity. Offers insurance coverage to employees' domestic partners.

L. L. Bean, Inc.
See p. 175 in Sporting Goods.

Loehmann's Holdings, Inc.
No contributions. Has hosted shopping nights at New York flagship store to benefit charity. www.loehmanns.com

Loews Corporation
See p. 61 in Finance, Insurance, and Real Estate.

London Fog Industries, Inc.
No contributions. Has sourced product from Guatemala, where human and labor rights abuses are well documented and widespread. Discontinued operations in Burma in the late 1990s after public outcry about that government's human rights violations. www.londonfog.com

Lord & Taylor
No contributions. Subsidiary of the May Department Stores Company (p. 20). Has a written nondiscrimination policy covering sexual orientation but not gender identity. Refuses insurance coverage to employees' domestic partners. www.lordandtaylor.com

Luxottica Group, S. p. A.
See p. 114 in Health and Beauty.

LVMH Inc. (U.S.)
50% | 50%

CONTRIBUTIONS: TOTAL: *$500* DEM: *$250* REP: *$250*
Subsidiary of LVMH Moët Hennessy Louis Vuitton SA (p. 88). www.lvmh.com

LVMH Moët Hennessy Louis Vuitton SA
See p. 88 in Food and Beverage.

Macy's
No contributions. Subsidiary of Federated Department Stores (p. 11). Was acquired in 1994. Privately held. Formerly R. H. Macy & Company, the Macy's brand is composed of five regional entities. Agreed to pay $600,000 in damages and costs to the state of New York following a probe by attorney general, Elliot Spitzer, into security policies that included racial profiling in identifying shoplifters. Creative trade efforts include the Rwanda Path to Peace project, which sells baskets made by female survivors of the Rwandan genocide. www.macys.com

Marshall Field's
No contributions. Subsidiary of the May Department Stores Company (p. 20). Settled a discrimination case brought by the National Organization for Women by changing its policy that charged women more for alterations then men. www.fields.com

Marshalls
No contributions. Subsidiary of TJX Companies, Inc. (p. 28). www.marshallsonline.com

Maxwell Shoe Company, Inc.
No contributions. Subsidiary of Jones Apparel Group, Inc. (p. 15). www.maxwellshoe.com

May Department Stores Company, The

CONTRIBUTIONS: TOTAL: *$148,250* DEM: *$33,482* REP: *$113,802*

At time of press, the company was in process of being acquired by Federated Department Stores (p. 11). One of 26 retailers that agreed to a $20 million settlement in a federal class action lawsuit brought by garment workers in Saipan alleging sweatshop practices. Has sourced from countries with widespread, well-documented human and labor rights abuses. One of several retailers ordered to give away $175 million worth of cosmetics as settlement in a price-fixing suit. Settled a lawsuit alleging violations of federal Employee Retirement Security Act for failing to pay retirement and profit-sharing benefits to cosmetics salespeople. Outreach supports elderly services and programs assisting people with AIDS/HIV. Has a written nondiscrimination policy covering sexual orientation but not gender identity. Refuses insurance coverage to employees' domestic partners. www.mayco.com

McRae's

No contributions. Subsidiary of Saks Incorporated (p. 25). www.mcraes.com

Men's Wearhouse, Inc., The

CONTRIBUTIONS: TOTAL: *$58,000* DEM: *$58,000* REP: *$0*

Has sourced from countries with widespread, well-documented human and labor rights abuses. Listed in *Fortune* magazine's "The 100 Best Companies to Work for in America" in 2004. Publicly prominent CEO accepts a compensation package that is significantly lower than retail competitors in order to pay higher compensation to employees. Has a written nondiscrimination policy covering sexual orientation but not gender identity. Offers insurance coverage to employees' domestic partners. www.menswearhouse.com

Mervyns, LLC

No contributions. In 2000, paid $11.3 million to settle a class action lawsuit regarding nonpayment of employee overtime. Paid $2 million settlement, along with five other retailers, to 150 California workers who reportedly worked in "slavelike" conditions. Has sourced from countries with widespread, well-documented human and labor rights abuses. Its 2005 annual "ChildSpree" provided $1 million in clothes for 10,000 underprivileged children returning to school. www.mervyns.com

Michael Kors, LLC

CONTRIBUTIONS: TOTAL: *$7,000* DEM: *$7,000* REP: *$0*

Named in a 2005 class action suit alleging its cosmetics pricing practices violated antitrust laws. Has been targeted by

People for the Ethical Treatment of Animals for using fur in designs. www.michaelkors.com

Movado Group, Inc.

CONTRIBUTIONS: TOTAL: *$14,000* DEM: *$0* REP: *$14,000*

Outreach supports the legacy of jazz music and New York's American Ballet Theater and City Ballet. Offers insurance coverage to employees' domestic partners. www.movadogroupinc.com

Naturalizer

CONTRIBUTIONS: TOTAL: *$2,000* DEM: *$0* REP: *$2,000*

Subsidiary of Brown Shoe Company (p. 6). www.naturalizeronline.com

Nautica Enterprises, Inc.

CONTRIBUTIONS: TOTAL: *$3,000* DEM: *$2,000* REP: *$1,000*

Subsidiary of the VF Corporation (p. 29). Has sourced from countries with widespread, well-documented human and labor rights abuses. Has a written nondiscrimination policy covering sexual orientation but not gender identity. Refuses insurance coverage to employees' domestic partners. www.nautica.com

Neiman Marcus

No contributions. Subsidiary of the Neiman Marcus Group, Inc. (p. 21); parent, Texas Pacific Group (p. 168). Has sourced from countries with widespread, well-documented human and labor rights abuses. Has a written nondiscrimination policy covering sexual orientation but not gender identity. Offers insurance coverage to employees' domestic partners. www.neimanmarcus.com

Neiman Marcus Group, Inc., The

CONTRIBUTIONS: TOTAL: *$750* DEM: *$0* REP: *$750*

Subsidiary of Texas Pacific Group (p. 168). Has a written nondiscrimination policy covering sexual orientation but not gender identity. Offers insurance coverage to employees' domestic partners. www.neimanmarcus.com

New Balance Athletic Shoe, Inc.
See p. 175 in Sporting Goods.

Nike, Inc.
See p. 175 in Sporting Goods.

Nine West Group, Inc.

CONTRIBUTIONS: TOTAL: *$4,000* DEM: *$4,000* REP: *$0*

Subsidiary of Jones Apparel Group, Inc. (p. 15). In 2000, settled claims of price-fixing by paying a $34 million fine, the bulk of which went to charitable organizations assisting victims of assault and domestic violence. Has sourced from countries with widespread, well-documented human and labor rights abuses. Has a written nondiscrimination policy covering sexual orientation but not gender identity. www.ninewest.com

Nordstrom, Inc.
No contributions. Agreed to pay a $7.5 million settlement to investors in a shareholder-filed securities fraud class action suit for concealing its policy requiring employees to work "off the clock." One of 26 retailers that agreed to a $20 million settlement in a federal class action lawsuit brought by garment workers in Saipan alleging sweatshop practices. Has sourced from countries with widespread, well-documented human and labor rights abuses. One of several retailers ordered to give customers $175 million in products as settlement in a cosmetics price-fixing class action suit. Offers a liberal family leave policy, including 60% paid salary. Outreach supports health and human services, community development, education, and cultural enhancement. Has a written nondiscrimination policy covering sexual orientation and gender identity. Offers insurance coverage to employees' domestic partners. www.nordstrom.com

North Face, Inc., The
See p. 176 in Sporting Goods.

O'Neill International Inc.
See p. 176 in Sporting Goods.

Oakley, Inc.
No contributions. Has a written nondiscrimination policy covering sexual orientation but not gender identity. www.oakley.com

Old Navy
100% 0%
CONTRIBUTIONS: TOTAL: *$2,500* DEM: *$2,500* REP: *$0*
Subsidiary of Gap Inc. (p. 13). www.oldnavy.com

OshKosh B'Gosh, Inc.
0% 100%
CONTRIBUTIONS: TOTAL: *$500* DEM: *$0* REP: *$500*
One of 26 retailers that agreed to a $20 million settlement in a federal class action lawsuit brought by garment workers in Saipan alleging sweatshop practices. Has sourced from countries with widespread, well-documented human and labor rights abuses. Has long-standing positive union relations. Outreach supports the education, health, and general well-being of underprivileged children. www.oshkoshbgosh.com

Parisian
No contributions. Subsidiary of Saks Incorporated (p. 25). www.parisian.com

Patagonia
See p. 176 in Sporting Goods.

Payless ShoeSource, Inc.

CONTRIBUTIONS: TOTAL: *$9,500* DEM: *$0* REP: *$9,500*

Connecticut Commission on Human Rights and Opportunities ordered a $20,000 payment in lost wages to an employee found to have been fired because she was Jamaican. In 2000, company was ordered to pay $1.5 million to a female employee who was assaulted while working alone, based on evidence that Payless was aware of previous similar incidents and neither increased security nor cautioned employees. Has sourced from countries with widespread, well-documented human and labor rights abuses. Outreach supports improving the quality of life in the communities where company associates and customers live. www.paylessshoesource.com

Phillips–Van Heusen Corporation
CONTRIBUTIONS: TOTAL: *$1,250* DEM: *$1,250* REP: *$0*

One of 26 retailers that agreed to a $20 million settlement in a federal class action lawsuit brought by garment workers in Saipan alleging sweatshop practices. Has sourced from countries with widespread, well-documented human and labor rights abuses. Among the founding companies of the Fair Labor Association, a nonprofit organization to identify an industry-wide strategy to eliminate global apparel sweatshops. Outreach supports programs to assist the homeless, the elderly, and disadvantaged children. Employees organized free eye exams for poor workers in Bangladesh. Has a written nondiscrimination policy covering sexual orientation but not gender identity. www.pvh.com

Piercing Pagoda
No contributions. Subsidiary of Zale Corporation (p. 30). www.pagoda.com

Polo Ralph Lauren Corporation
CONTRIBUTIONS: TOTAL: *$10,000* DEM: *$10,000* REP: *$0*

One of 26 retailers that agreed to a $20 million settlement in a federal class action lawsuit brought by garment workers in Saipan alleging sweatshop practices. A pending class action suit filed by employees alleges that the company's dress code/wardrobing policy, which forces employees to purchase company products as a condition of employment, costs some employees as much as 40% of their annual salaries. Settled a lawsuit brought by employees in 2002 alleging racial discrimination and unfair labor practices for the company's active promotion of a "blond, blue-eyed" image. Outreach supports medical programs for underserved communities, cancer care, and cancer prevention. Has a written nondiscrimination policy covering sexual orientation but not gender identity. Offers insurance coverage to employees' domestic partners. www.polo.com

Proffitt's
No contributions. Subsidiary of Saks Incorporated (p. 25). www.proffitts.com

PUMA AG Rudolf Dassler Sport
See p. 176 in Sporting Goods.

Recreational Equipment, Inc.
See p. 177 in Sporting Goods.

Red Wing Shoe Company, Inc.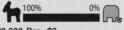
CONTRIBUTIONS: TOTAL: *$1,950* DEM: *$0* REP: *$1,950*
Company is often hit with second- and third-party suits because of workplace injuries suffered by workers wearing Red Wing boots. Red Wing boots are made in America by unionized workers. www.redwingshoe.com

Reebok International Ltd.
See p. 177 in Sporting Goods.

Retail Brand Alliance, Inc.
CONTRIBUTIONS: TOTAL: *$250* DEM: *$0* REP: *$250*
www.retailbrandalliance.com

Retail Ventures, Inc.
CONTRIBUTIONS: TOTAL: *$21,550* DEM: *$1,000* REP: *$20,550*
Outreach focuses on children's health and education, women's health, and diversity staffing and training. www.retailventuresinc.com

R. Griggs Group Limited
No contributions. Foreign owned. www.drmartens.com

Ross Stores, Inc.
CONTRIBUTIONS: TOTAL: *$2,000* DEM: *$2,000* REP: *$0*
In 2000, settled a federal class action lawsuit alleging failure to pay overtime to its store managers. One of many U.S. retailers that agreed to sever ties with Burmese manufacturers, in protest of that country's repressive government. Paid $200,000 in fines for selling highly flammable clothing in violation of federal law. Five hundred of its stores partner with Gifts in Kind International, a foundation distributing retailers' donated goods. Has a written nondiscrimination policy covering sexual orientation but not gender identity. Refuses insurance coverage to employees' domestic partners. www.rossstores.com

Saks Incorporated

9% 91%

CONTRIBUTIONS: TOTAL: *$48,002* DEM: *$4,472* REP: *$43,515*

In a precedent-setting case, fined $21.5 million by the SEC in April 2005 to pay back improper markdown allowances and chargebacks to vendors. Complaint filed in September 2004 alleges illegal wage reductions and labor practices. Placed under federal order to tighten anti–money laundering practices after several alleged instances of illegal pay offs. Community outreach supports breast cancer research, education, preservation of natural habitats, and partners with the United Way. Voluntarily partners with the EPA to reduce emissions, eliminate energy waste, and reduce energy costs resulting in an estimated reduction of 65 million kilowatt hours of energy consumption. Has a written nondiscrimination policy covering sexual orientation but not gender identity. Offers health insurance coverage to employees' domestic partners. www.saksincorporated.com

Saks Off 5th

No contributions. Subsidiary of Saks Incorporated (p. 25). www.saksincorporated.com

Sara Lee Branded Apparel

100% 0%

CONTRIBUTIONS: TOTAL: *$4,500* DEM: *$4,500* REP: *$0*

Subsidiary of Sara Lee Corporation (p. 95). Has sourced from countries with widespread, well-documented human and labor rights abuses. Foundation supports women's issues, housing, and hunger relief. Has a written nondiscrimination policy covering sexual orientation but not gender identity. Offers insurance coverage to employees' domestic partners. www.saralee.com

Sean John Clothing

100% 0%

CONTRIBUTIONS: TOTAL: *$67,500* DEM: *$67,495* REP: *$0*

Subsidiary of Bad Boy Worldwide Entertainment Group (p. 150). Has sourced from countries with widespread, well-documented human and labor rights abuses. Self-monitors vendor practices globally. Has a written nondiscrimination policy. www.seanjohn.com

Sears, Roebuck and Co.

See p. 145 in Major Retailers.

Seiko Corporation of America

No contributions. Foreign owned. www.seikousa.com

Shane Co.

0% 100%

CONTRIBUTIONS: TOTAL: *$4,000* DEM: *$0* REP: *$4,000*

Has no policy to purchase certified diamonds. Company buyers rely solely on the honesty of dealers to guarantee that stones purchased are not conflict diamonds. (See Signet Group

PLC, p. 26, for more information on conflict diamonds.) Has sourced from countries with widespread, well-documented human and labor rights abuses. www.shaneco.com

Shoe Pavilion, Inc.
No contributions. Paid $500,000 in 2004 to settle a federal class action wage and hour lawsuit brought by store managers claiming they were not paid overtime because they were fraudulently recorded as exempt under California wage and labor law. www.shoepavilion.com

Sierra Trading Post
See p. 177 in Sporting Goods.

Signet Group PLC

95%   5%

CONTRIBUTIONS: TOTAL: *$22,000* DEM: *$21,000* REP: *$1,000*

Supports the UN Declaration of Human Rights and the Fundamental Conventions of the International Labor Organization. Is a nonvoting member of the World Diamond Council, which works to end the trade of conflict diamonds, whose sale funds wars in Angola, Sierra Leone, and Liberia. Regularly reviews energy use and environmental impact, seeking methods for making mining procedures more environmentally friendly. Outreach supports the St. Jude Children's Research Hospital, United Way, and the Jeweler's Charity Fund. Has a written nondiscrimination policy covering sexual orientation but not gender identity. www.signetgroupplc.com

Skechers U.S.A., Inc.
100%   0%

CONTRIBUTIONS: TOTAL: *$8,000* DEM: *$8,000* REP: *$0*

Agreed in 2004 to pay up to $1.8 million to settle three lawsuits alleging wage and hour violations including failure to pay overtime. Has been fined for requiring retail workers to meet strict workplace dress codes requiring them to wear company products without compensation. Has sourced from countries with widespread, well-documented human and labor rights abuses. www.skx.com

Spiegel, Inc.

0%   100%

CONTRIBUTIONS: TOTAL: *$1,000* DEM: *$0* REP: *$1,000*

Informed Free Burma Coalition in 2002 that it would cease dealings with Burmese businesses, to protest that country's repressive government. Has sourced from countries with widespread, well-documented human and labor rights abuses. Has a written nondiscrimination policy covering sexual orientation but not gender identity. Offers insurance coverage to employees' domestic partners. www.spiegel.com

Stein Mart, Inc.
41%   59%

CONTRIBUTIONS: TOTAL: *$34,000* DEM: *$14,000* REP: *$20,000*

Outreach focuses on arts, education, and children's needs. www.steinmart.com

Sterling Jewelers, Inc.

CONTRIBUTIONS: TOTAL: *$8,000* DEM: *$8,000* REP: *$0*

Subsidiary of Signet Group PLC (p. 26). Settled allegations that they and another business conspired to evict a discount diamond retailer in proximity, agreeing to pay $45,000 to cover investigation costs. Has sourced from countries with widespread, well-documented human and labor rights abuses. www.sterlingjewelers.com

Steven Madden, Ltd.

No contributions. Founder Steven Madden returned to the company in 2005 after serving more than three years in prison—while still earning $700,000 a year—for failing to provide material-adverse information to shareholders, a violation of federal securities laws. Has sourced from countries with widespread, well-documented human and labor rights abuses. In 1999, designed a shoe for singer Tori Amos, with all the proceeds from its sale going to the Rape, Abuse, and Incest National Network (RAINN). www.stevemadden.com

Stride Rite Corporation, The

No contributions. Paid out $7.2 million settlement in 1993 in a multistate FTC price-fixing lawsuit on behalf of its subsidiary Keds. Has sourced from countries with widespread, well-documented human and labor rights abuses. Listed as one of the 100 best workplaces for working mothers according to *Working Mother* magazine in 2000. www.strideritecorp.com

Swatch Group Ltd., The

No contributions. A 2001 auction of its watches generated $800,000 for donation to a New York foundation providing meals and support for people living with AIDS. Offers insurance coverage to employees' domestic partners. www.swatchgroup.com

TAG Heuer International

No contributions. Subsidiary of LVMH Moët Hennessy Louis Vuitton SA (p. 88). www.tagheuer.com

Talbots, Inc., The

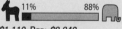

CONTRIBUTIONS: TOTAL: *$10,000* DEM: *$1,110* REP: *$8,840*

One of 26 retailers that agreed to a $20 million settlement in a federal class action lawsuit brought by garment workers in Saipan alleging sweatshop practices. Has sourced from countries with widespread, well-documented human and labor rights abuses. Outreach supports cultural, civic, health, welfare, and educational causes and scholarships for women. www.talbots.com

Target Corporation

See p. 145 in Major Retailers.

TaylorMade–Adidas Golf
See p. 177 in Sporting Goods.

Tiffany & Co.  100%   0%
CONTRIBUTIONS: TOTAL: *$2,000* DEM: *$2,000* REP: *$0*

Has sourced from countries with widespread, well-documented human and labor rights abuses. Has made efforts to ensure that gold and diamonds are mined responsibly in partnership with Oxfam America's "No Dirty Gold" campaign. www.tiffany.com

Timberland Company, The 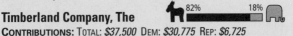 82%   18%
CONTRIBUTIONS: TOTAL: *$37,500* DEM: *$30,775* REP: *$6,725*

Has sourced from countries with widespread, well-documented human and labor rights abuses. Outreach supports community building, environmental stewardship, and global human rights. Has a written nondiscrimination policy covering sexual orientation but not gender identity. Offers insurance coverage to employees' domestic partners. www.timberland.com

T. J. Maxx
No contributions. Subsidiary of TJX Companies, Inc. (p. 28). www.tjmaxx.com

TJX Companies, Inc., The  37%   63%
CONTRIBUTIONS: TOTAL: *$10,700* DEM: *$4,000* REP: *$6,700*

Paid $150,000 in fines for selling highly flammable clothing in violation of federal law. Outreach supports education and domestic violence prevention in communities where the company does business. Has a written nondiscrimination policy covering sexual orientation but not gender identity. Refuses insurance coverage to employees' domestic partners. www.tjx.com

Tommy Hilfiger Corporation 100%   0%
CONTRIBUTIONS: TOTAL: *$15,500* DEM: *$15,500* REP: *$0*

One of 26 retailers that agreed to a $20 million settlement in a federal class action lawsuit brought by garment workers in Saipan alleging sweatshop practices. Agreed to pay $18.1 million to settle a federal investigation into misuse of foreign subsidiaries to avoid taxes. Shareholder class action lawsuit pending for alleged SEC violations. Has sourced from countries with widespread, well-documented human and labor rights abuses. Outreach supports educational opportunities for diverse populations in the United States. www.tommy.com

Tumi, Inc.
No contributions. Subsidiary of Doughty Hanson & Co., a foreign-held company. www.tumi.com

Urban Outfitters, Inc.
CONTRIBUTIONS: TOTAL: *$6,500* DEM: *$250* REP: *$6,250*
www.urbanoutfittersinc.com

Value City Department Stores, Inc.
CONTRIBUTIONS: TOTAL: *$1,000* DEM: *$0* REP: *$1,000*
Subsidiary of Retail Ventures, Inc. (p. 24). Fined $28,000 for violating Ohio asbestos removal rules allegedly putting employees and customers in danger of exposure. Donated funds to build Value City Arena in the Jay Schottenstein Center at Ohio State University. Gave $30,000 to Twin Towers Orphans Fund. www.valuecity.com

Van Heusen
No contributions. Subsidiary of Phillips–Van Heusen Corporation (p. 23). Was cited in a report issued by the U.S. Labor Education in the Americas Project as having shifted production from a unionized factory in Guatemala to poverty-wage sweatshops, a move that appears to violate a White House–initiated Apparel Industry Partnership (AIP) agreement. Has sourced from countries with widespread, well-documented human and labor rights abuses. www.pvh.com

VF Corporation
CONTRIBUTIONS: TOTAL: *$11,750* DEM: *$10,750* REP: *$1,000*
Has a written nondiscrimination policy covering sexual orientation but not gender identity. Refuses insurance coverage to employees' domestic partners. www.vfc.com

Victoria's Secret
CONTRIBUTIONS: TOTAL: *$3,900* DEM: *$716* REP: *$3,184*
Subsidiary of Limited Brands, Inc. (p. 17). Agreed to pay $179,300 to settle a race and religion discrimination lawsuit brought by the EEOC on behalf of a former African American employee. Settled allegations that security vulnerabilities in the company's website had exposed its customers' personal ordering information to interception in violation of its posted privacy policy. www.victoriassecret.com

Warnaco Group, Inc., The
No contributions. One of 26 retailers that agreed to a $20 million settlement in a federal class action lawsuit brought by garment workers in Saipan alleging sweatshop practices. Settlement of a 2004 suit alleging false financial reporting required former Warnaco executives and the company auditor PricewaterhouseCoopers to pay fines and relinquish bonuses. Has sourced from countries with widespread, well-documented human and labor rights abuses. Has a written nondiscrimination policy covering sexual orientation but not gender identity. www.warnaco.com

Wet Seal, Inc., The

CONTRIBUTIONS: TOTAL: *$3,200* **DEM:** *$3,080* **REP:** *$108*

Paid $1.28 million to settle a wage hour lawsuit brought by store managers alleging they were denied overtime wages and wrongly classified as exempt in violation of California law. Currently under investigation by the SEC for potential violations of securities laws. Pending shareholder class action for alleged violations of the Securities Exchange Act. www.wetsealinc.com

White House/Black Market
CONTRIBUTIONS: TOTAL: *$3,951* **DEM:** *$0* **REP:** *$3,951*

Subsidiary of Chico's FAS (p. 8). www.whiteandblack.com

Williamson-Dickie Manufacturing Company
No contributions. www.dickies.com

Wilson Sporting Goods Co.
See p. 178 in Sporting Goods.

Wilsons The Leather Experts Inc.
CONTRIBUTIONS: TOTAL: *$3,500* **DEM:** *$0* **REP:** *$3,500*
www.wilsonsleather.com

Wolverine World Wide, Inc.
CONTRIBUTIONS: TOTAL: *$500* **DEM:** *$0* **REP:** *$500*

Outreach supports health and human services, arts, education, research, and disaster relief organizations. www.wolverineworldwide.com

Woolrich, Inc.
CONTRIBUTIONS: TOTAL: *$1,000* **DEM:** *$0* **REP:** *$1,000*

One of 26 retailers that agreed to a $20 million settlement in a federal class action lawsuit brought by garment workers in Saipan alleging sweatshop practices. Settled an FTC lawsuit for failing to disclose the origin of textile products in its Internet catalog. Has sourced from countries with widespread, well-documented human and labor rights abuses. www.woolrich.com

Younkers
No contributions. Subsidiary of Saks Incorporated (p. 25). www.younkers.com

Zale Corporation
CONTRIBUTIONS: TOTAL: *$2,500* **DEM:** *$278* **REP:** *$2,210*

Has sourced from countries with widespread, well-documented human and labor rights abuses. Founding member of the Council for Responsible Jewelry Practices (CRJP), committed to stopping the trade in conflict diamonds—

diamonds mined in certain African combat zones. Outreach supports children's health and well-being. Has a written non-discrimination policy covering sexual orientation but not gender identity. www.zalecorp.com

Zales Jewelers
No contributions. Subsidiary of Zale Corporation (p. 30). www.zales.com

Computers and Electronics

If the computer and electronics sector has so far dodged the kind of criticism hovering around the oil, media, food, and pharmaceutical industries, it's only because its controversies have been less dramatic.

That may be changing. As the public grows more familiar with issues of consumer privacy, online security, the outsourcing of electronics manufacturing jobs, e-pollution, and intellectual property law, corporations will be forced to address them more directly. As this happens, the computer and electronics lobbies will find their efforts increasingly scrutinized.

Within the industry, China has emerged as a focus for lobbying efforts. A growing number of U.S. and multinational computer and electronics companies are both selling products and setting up factories there—and then selling their products back to the United States—bringing them to the larger push for free trade arrangements. The industry has also spent millions lobbying in favor of the Central America Free Trade Agreement (CAFTA), which would open up new markets, and for legislation that would improve cybersecurity. In general, the tech industry has been generally bipartisan in its contributions. The 2004 election saw over $28 million pass from the computer industry along to candidates.

Environmental concerns have dogged manufacturers in recent years. Notably, the industry fought regulation of harmful chemicals used in a variety of electronics products. One prominent battle has been fought over PBDEs, a chemical additive intended to reduce flammability in computers and other electronics. Scientists have found PBDE levels to be growing rapidly in humans here in the United States—which is the world's largest producer and consumer of PBDEs—and falling in countries where it was banned. As pressure mounted, Apple, Dell, Sony, and Xerox eventually volunteered to eliminate deca-BDE, a common PBDE mixture, from their products. The government, however, has lagged in its response.

Although some of the bigger companies have yet to address fully a variety of persistent labor, pollution, and health care concerns, a trend toward greater responsibility seems to have legs lately. Apple made headlines when it joined a list of companies pulling their business out of Burma in the 1990s, for instance, and more recently it committed to using a more expensive but environmentally responsible paper for its promotional and educational materials. Microsoft, in turn, has given generously to a number of educational programs around the world.

While the government itself tends to follow rather than lead on matters of corporate responsibility, the Energy Star program of the Environmental Protection Agency (EPA) has made impressive achievements. By encouraging consumers to buy energy-efficient electronics and other appliances, the program cut greenhouse gas emissions and saved enough energy in 2004 to power 24 million homes. More significantly, this program netted a savings of $10 billion—suggesting financial incentive might well lead the way to improvements in the industry in years to come.

Top Ten Republican Contributors

Microsoft Corporation	$960,870
Dell Computer Corporation	360,529
Cisco Systems, Inc.	276,165
Intel Corporation	264,705
Motorola, Inc.	233,877
Hewlett-Packard Company	120,691
Activision, Inc.	112,250
Eastman Kodak Company	104,485
Gateway, Inc.	97,940
Best Buy Company, Inc.	54,434

Top Ten Democratic Contributors

Microsoft Corporation	$692,074
Gateway, Inc.	167,937
Cisco Systems, Inc.	162,835
Adobe Systems, Inc.	138,250
Motorola, Inc.	75,994
Google, Inc.	71,500
Intel Corporation	68,544
Hewlett-Packard Company	61,109
Dell Computer Corporation	47,359
GameStop Corp.	36,600

Activision, Inc. 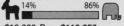 14% 86%

CONTRIBUTIONS: TOTAL: *$131,250* DEM: *$19,000* REP: *$112,250*

Pending investigation by the Securities and Exchange Commission (SEC) and several class action suits for alleged securities violations and accounting irregularities.
www.activision.com

Adobe Systems, Inc.  99% 1%

CONTRIBUTIONS: TOTAL: *$139,500* DEM: *$138,250* REP: *$1,250*

A pending sex discrimination suit alleges company allowed a harmful environment and did nothing to hamper a sexist, male-dominated culture at its London offices. Pending cross-suit over patent infringement on its embedded fonts. Donates funds, software and training, and employee volunteers to groups and schools in areas where Adobe has facilities. Partners with Project HIRED, a nonprofit that places individuals with disabilities in regular employment. Was among DiversityInc.com's top five best companies for diversity and *Fortune* magazine's top 100 best places to work. Has a written nondiscrimination policy covering sexual orientation but not gender identity. Offers insurance coverage to employees' domestic partners. www.adobe.com

Advanced Micro Devices, Inc.

0%   100%

CONTRIBUTIONS: TOTAL: *$1,000* DEM: *$0* REP: *$1,000*

Settled a class action suit alleging violations of federal securities laws, fraudulent misrepresentation, and artificial inflation of common stock. Has been involved in several major legal battles with competitors for patent infringement and antitrust issues. Has sourced from countries with widespread, well-documented human and labor rights abuses. Voluntary participant in EPA's Climate Leaders program with the goal of a 40% reduction in greenhouse gas emissions by 2007. Has a written nondiscrimination policy covering sexual orientation not gender identity. Offers insurance coverage to employees' domestic partners. www.amd.com

Agfa-Gevaert N.V.

No contributions. Foreign owned. Voluntarily supports chemical industry's "Responsible Care" initiative. Offers family benefits including health insurance coverage for employees' domestic partners at its Teterboro, NJ, manufacturing facility. www.agfa.com

Apple Computer, Inc.

100%   0%

CONTRIBUTIONS: TOTAL: *$1,000* DEM: *$1,000* REP: *$0*

After years of complaints from environmental groups, Apple recently began a free recycling program from its stores. According to the Computer Take Back campaign, Apple is behind its competitors Dell and Hewlett-Packard in creating responsible disposal options for its equipment. Has operations in and sources from countries with widespread well-documented human and labor rights abuses. In 2004, the company went after several Mac enthusiast websites for divulging trade secrets about future Apple products. Apple's claim that the sites were not "legitimate press" (and therefore did not enjoy the same free speech guarantees) convinced the judge to rule in its favor, setting what critics consider to be a dangerous precedent. Outreach supports genomic research, environmental causes and research and development in multiple discipline areas. Has a written nondiscrimination policy that covers sexual orientation and gender identity. Offers health insurance coverage to employees' domestic partners. www.apple.com

Atari, Inc.

No contributions. Subsidiary of Infogrames Entertainment, S.A. (p. 41). Foreign owned. Operates in and sources from countries with widespread, well-documented human and labor rights abuses. www.atari.com

Best Buy Company, Inc.

4%   96%

CONTRIBUTIONS: TOTAL: *$56,434* DEM: *$2,000* REP: *$54,434*

A pending suit brought by the state of Wisconsin alleges violations of consumer protection laws and misleading and fraudulent advertising practices. Several lawsuits filed in 2004 alleged deceptive business practices, including false advertising. Was cleared of SEC violations alleged in material fraud class action. Foundation donated 2.9 million to schools in the United States in 2004 to integrate interactive technology into classrooms. Also has a $3 million grant program for schools within 25 miles of one of its retail stores. Has a written nondiscrimination policy including sexual orientation and gender identity. Offers insurance coverage to employees' domestic partners. www.bestbuy.com

Brookstone, Inc.
No contributions. www.brookstone.com

Brother Industries, Ltd.
No contributions. Foreign owned. Has operated in and sourced from countries with widespread, well-documented human and labor rights abuses. Established "Green Procurement Standard" to ensure suppliers' products meet company-established standards of environmental impact, recyclables, and low chemical hazard. Has reduced carbon dioxide output by 30% since 1990; has begun generating solar power at Mizuho factory. Brother USA distributes prepaid shipping labels for return and recycling of used cartridges. www.brother.com

Canon, Inc.

CONTRIBUTIONS: TOTAL: *$2,000* DEM: *$0* REP: *$2,000*
Foreign owned. A pending suit alleges patent infringement and improper use of patented technology in its flat-screen televisions. Has operated in and sourced from countries with widespread, well-documented human and labor rights abuses. Established a "Green Procurement" program that establishes material declaration guidelines and includes inspection of suppliers' manufacturing facilities. First company worldwide to recycle toner cartridges. Is in the process of shifting from truck to rail and ship transportation of products in an effort to reduce carbon dioxide emissions. Outreach supports the World Wildlife Fund (WWF) in conservation efforts. Has donated digital cameras and printers to the National Center for Missing & Exploited Children. www.canon.com

Canon U.S.A., Inc.

CONTRIBUTIONS: TOTAL: *$2,000* DEM: *$0* REP: *$2,000*
Subsidiary of Canon, Inc. (p. 37). A pending suit brought by former executives alleges racial discrimination and wrongful termination. Environmental programs and community involvement include three-year, $78,000 grants to graduate students exploring issues crucial to national parks' ecosystems, funding for the Yellowstone Park Foundation, and partnerships with the EPA. Has a written nondiscrimination policy covering sexual

orientation not gender identity. Offers insurance coverage to employees' domestic partners. www.usa.canon.com

Circuit City Stores, Inc.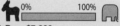

CONTRIBUTIONS: TOTAL: *$29,000* DEM: *$2,494* REP: *$26,013*

Settled a suit for an undisclosed amount brought by the Equal Employment Opportunity Commission (EEOC) for discrimination and violation of the Americans with Disabilities Act. Foundation supports community giving in the areas of children and families and improving economic opportunity. In fiscal year 2002, the foundation dispersed $2.3 million to charity. Has a written nondiscrimination policy covering sexual orientation but not gender identity. Offers insurance coverage to employees' domestic partners. www.circuitcity.com

Cisco-Linksys, LLC

CONTRIBUTIONS: TOTAL: *$7,000* DEM: *$0* REP: *$7,000*

Subsidiary of Cisco Systems, Inc. (p. 38). www.linksys.com

Cisco Systems, Inc.

CONTRIBUTIONS: TOTAL: *$439,000* DEM: *$162,835* REP: *$276,165*

A pending class action brought about by shareholders alleges securities violations, misrepresentation, and material omission of fact. Has operated in and sourced from countries with widespread, well-documented human and labor rights abuses. Foundation supports community capacity building and sustainable practice. Was ranked 12th of 50 companies with the best reputations for employing and accommodating the disabled in a 2004 survey by *disABLED* magazine. Also listed as one of the 100 best places for working mothers. Has a written nondiscrimination policy covering sexual orientation and gender identity. Offers insurance coverage to employees' domestic partners. www.cisco.com

CompUSA Inc.

No contributions. Agreed to pay $150,000 to settle allegations by the SEC that members of its executive staff traded on inside information regarding the merger with CompUSA Inc. Has a written nondiscrimination policy covering sexual orientation but not gender identity. www.compusa.com

Dell Computer Corporation

CONTRIBUTIONS: TOTAL: *$407,888* DEM: *$47,359* REP: *$360,529*

The world's largest supplier of direct-sale personal computers is also a major government contractor whose lobbying dollars support Republican Party committees three to one over Democratic ones. A pending class action lawsuit alleges violations of the Consumer Protection Act, negligence, and breach of contract in connection with consumer-purchased service agreements and shipping charges. Agreed to pay $800,000 to settle allegations of security violations brought by the FTC. Dell's environmental scores are better than Apple's and some other computer manufacturers'—but still makes a "C" grade from the Computer Take Back campaign. Under pressure from human rights groups, Dell has stopped using prison workers (many of whom make under $1/hour) to recycle hardware. Dell's human rights record is marred by a report issued by the Catholic Agency for Overseas Development in 2004 accusing Dell of committing labor abuses in factories in Mexico, China, and Thailand. Foundation supports nonprofit education, health, and literacy programs for youth and infants near Dell facilities. Has a written nondiscrimination policy that covers sexual orientation and gender identity. Offers insurance coverage to employees' domestic partners. www.dell.com

D-Link Corporation
No contributions. Has operated in and sourced from countries with widespread, well-documented human and labor rights abuses. www.dlink.com.tw

Duracell
No contributions. Subsidiary of the Gillette Company (p. 110); parent, Procter & Gamble (p. 116). Has operated in and sourced from countries with widespread, well-documented human and labor rights abuses. www.duracell.com

Eastman Kodak Company
25% | 75%

CONTRIBUTIONS: TOTAL: *$138,500* DEM: *$34,015* REP: *$104,485*
A pending 2004 class action lawsuit alleges Kodak offered payments to avoid discrimination lawsuits brought by African Americans due to unfair pay, lack of advancement, and a hostile work environment. Pending $75 million lawsuit brought by families whose children grew up near the Rochester facility and developed rare brain and nervous system cancers. In 1999, paid $775,000 for state environmental violations dating from 1993 to 1999. Was fined $175,000 by the EPA for leaking hazardous waste in 2001. Recognized by the EPA in 2003 and 2004 for reducing greenhouse gases and planning cleanup of contaminated groundwater, bedrock, and soil at 1,900-acre Kodak Park campus. Outreach sponsored six Rochester-area Habit for Humanity houses. Donated $10 million worldwide in 2004, including Tsunami relief, the National Association for the Advancement of Colored People (NAACP), and scholarships for Rochester area students. Has a written nondiscrimination policy covering sexual orientation and gender identity. Offers insurance coverage to employees' domestic partners. www.kodak.com

Electronics Boutique Holdings Corp.

1% 99%

CONTRIBUTIONS: TOTAL: *$18,142* DEM: *$250* REP: *$17,892*

In the process of being acquired by rival GameStop Corp. (p. 41) in a move alleged to purposefully fend off Wal-Mart and expand overseas. www.ebgames.com

Energizer Holdings, Inc.

45% 55%

CONTRIBUTIONS: TOTAL: *$11,000* DEM: *$5,000* REP: *$6,000*

Lost a lawsuit filed by its rival Duracell (p. 39) for making false claims in its advertising regarding the longevity of its batteries. Has a written nondiscrimination policy covering sexual orientation but not gender identity. www.energizer.com

Epson America, Inc.

No contributions. Subsidiary of Seiko Epson Corporation (p. 47). Foreign owned. www.epson.com

Eveready Battery Company, Inc.

No contributions. Subsidiary of Energizer Holdings, Inc. (p. 40). Has a written nondiscrimination policy covering sexual orientation. www.energizer.com

Fry's Electronics, Inc.

No contributions. Currently pending two lawsuits alleging unfair business practices and violations of the Unfair Competition Law. Sponsors professional car racing. www.frys.com

Fuji Photo Film Co., Ltd.

No contributions. Foreign owned. www.fujifilm.co.jp

Fuji Photo Film U.S.A., Inc.

No contributions. Subsidiary of Fuji Photo Film Co., Ltd. (p. 40). Environmental activities include recycling of single-use camera components and pursuing certification in the International Standard for Environmental Management Systems. Outreach and philanthropic activities include an annual volunteer day, scholarships, and product donations. home.fujifilm.com

Fujitsu Computer Products of America, Inc.

No contributions. Subsidiary of Fujitsu Limited (p. 40). Foreign owned. Has a written nondiscrimination policy covering sexual orientation but not gender identity. Offers insurance coverage to employees' domestic partners. www.fcpa.fujitsu.com

Fujitsu Limited

No contributions. Foreign owned. Has operated in and sourced from countries with widespread, well-documented human and labor rights abuses. In 2005, started three-year reforestation plan in Southeast Asia, aimed at reviving endemic species and promoting economic self-sufficiency through ecotourism. Policies target "green" suppliers, reducing chemical emissions, and

achieving zero-waste emissions for Japanese plants.
www.fujitsu.com

GameStop Corp.

99% 1%

CONTRIBUTIONS: TOTAL: *$37,000* DEM: *$36,600* REP: *$400*

Settled a 2003 class action lawsuit for an undisclosed sum
alleging its stores sold used or returned video game software
as new merchandise. Has a written nondiscrimination policy
covering sexual orientation but not gender identity.
www.gamestop.com

Gateway, Inc.

63% 37%

CONTRIBUTIONS: TOTAL: *$266,413* DEM: *$167,937* REP: *$97,940*

Has sourced from countries with widespread, well-documented
human and labor rights abuses. Foundation provides equipment and support to underserved schools. Has a written nondiscrimination policy covering sexual orientation but not gender
identity. Offers insurance coverage to employees' domestic
partners. www.gateway.com

Gillette Co., The

See p. 110 in Health and Beauty.

Good Guys

No contributions. Subsidiary of CompUSA (p. 38).

Google, Inc.

100% 0%

CONTRIBUTIONS: TOTAL: *$71,500* DEM: *$71,500* REP: *$0*

Settled with the SEC over failure to register employee's stock
options worth over $80 million. Has a written nondiscrimina-
tion policy covering sexual orientation but not gender identity.
Offers insurance coverage to employees' domestic partners.
www.google.com

Hewlett-Packard Company

34% 66%

CONTRIBUTIONS: TOTAL: *$181,800* DEM: *$61,109* REP: *$120,691*

A major supplier to the U.S. military, HP paid a $7 million fine to
settle U.S. government claims alleging they were sold defec-
tive products. Company gets average grades from environmental groups but has made recent efforts to improve. HP also
designs many products to be more easily recycled and often
uses recycled parts in construction. In 2002, HP supported a
California bill to make manufacturers responsible for electronic waste. Encourages diversification in education through
a minority scholarship program. Focuses 33% of charitable
giving outside the U.S. Has a written nondiscrimination policy
that covers sexual orientation and gender identity. Offers
insurance coverage to employees' domestic partners.
www.hp.com

Infogrames Entertainment, S.A.

No contributions. Foreign owned. www.infogrames.com

Intel Corporation

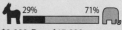

21%   79%

CONTRIBUTIONS: TOTAL: *$333,589* DEM: *$68,544* REP: *$264,705*

A pending $55 million antitrust lawsuit alleges violations of the Sherman Antitrust Act and anticompetitive and abusive monopolistic practice, following on the heels of European regulators' evidence raids on Intel offices across Europe. A pending securities violation class action alleges false and misleading financial statements. Has sourced from countries with widespread, well-documented human and labor rights abuses. Invested $4.4 billion in 2003 for research and development, initiating major advances in microprocessors and microcomputers. Has a written nondiscrimination policy covering sexual orientation and gender identity. Offers insurance coverage to employees' domestic partners. www.intel.com

International Business Machines Corporation (IBM)

29%   71%

CONTRIBUTIONS: TOTAL: *$21,000* DEM: *$6,000* REP: *$15,000*

A pending suit brought by 130,000 current and former employees claims that the company's cash-balance pension plan, introduced in 1999, lowered benefits for older workers by $1.4 billion. In the same action, IBM agreed to a partial settlement of $300 million for improperly converting plans for pre-1999 employees. In 1998, it was ordered to pay $300,000 to an employee discharged in violation of the Americans with Disabilities Act and $800,000 to an employee discharged in a breach of contract. More than 200 employees have filed suits claiming exposure to toxic chemicals. Endicott, NY, manufacturing facility was designated a Superfund toxic waste site in 2004. Has reduced its carbon emissions by 65% from 1990 levels. Has an internal mandate to incorporate accessibility into product development. Outreach program offers free technology for use by retirees who volunteer at schools and nonprofits. In 2005, received an award from the EEOC for recruiting women, underrepresented minorities, and people with disabilities. Has a written nondiscrimination policy covering sexual orientation and gender identity. Offers insurance coverage to employees' domestic partners. www.ibm.com

Intuit, Inc.

35%   65%

CONTRIBUTIONS: TOTAL: *$73,000* DEM: *$25,474* REP: *$47,526*

A pending lawsuit alleges TurboTax employs spyware depositing cookies in users' accounts (allowing marketers to track customers' online movements), in violation of user privacy. A pending class action seeks restitution for alleged false and deceptive advertising and unlawful business practices. Intuit matches employee charitable gifts and offers paid time off to volunteer. Eligible disadvantaged individuals have free access to tax preparation software (more than seven million returns filed free since 1998). Intuit Foundation funds financial literacy programs and donates software. Has a written nondiscrimination policy covering sexual orientation and gender identity. Offers insurance coverage to employees' domestic partners. www.intuit.com

Kenwood Corporation

No contributions. Foreign owned. Pending investigation by the U.S. International Trade Commission for alleged patent infringement. Was cited by the European Union for unfair business practices and slapped with antidumping duties. Has a written nondiscrimination policy covering sexual orientation but not gender identity. www.kenwood.com

LaCie Group S.A.

No contributions. Foreign owned. www.lacie.com

LeapFrog Enterprises, Inc.

0% ▬▬▬▬▬▬▬▬ 100%

CONTRIBUTIONS: TOTAL: *$1,500* DEM: *$0* REP: *$1,500*

The president and two saleswomen resigned in 2004 after investigations into a $1 million no-bid deal with the Baltimore school district. Several pending class action lawsuits filed in 2005 allege that company officials misrepresented earnings and sold millions of their own shares at inflated stock prices. Donated 20,000 LeapTrack systems to 50 school districts nationwide, allowing teachers to assess students' needs and individualize instruction. www.leapfrog.com

Lexmark International, Inc.

No contributions. Lost a 2003 lawsuit brought by a former employee who was fired after "blowing the whistle" on inflated inventory reports. "Pre-bate" discount cartridge return program (touted as environmentally beneficial) called a ploy to reclaim empty cartridges, preventing competitors from refilling them more cheaply. A related lawsuit brought by Lexmark against Static Control Components (SCC) for circumventing Lexmark's safeguards against such refills was decided on appeal in defendant SCC's favor. Supports employee volunteerism by allowing paid time off for charity work and matching gifts up to $5,000 per employee. Donated materials for five Habitat for Humanity homes. Has a written nondiscrimination policy covering sexual orientation and gender identity. Offers insurance coverage to employees' domestic partners. www.lexmark.com

Matsushita Electric Industrial Co., Ltd.

No contributions. Foreign owned. A pending suit brought by three former employees in 2003 alleges age discrimination and substantially lower pension benefits than promised under a voluntary resignation program. Multiple age and gender discrimination suits brought against the company in the United States were thrown out of higher courts because of U.S-

Japanese bilateral agreements negotiated that allow Japanese companies to discriminate on the basis of citizenship. Cracked down in 2005 on employees receiving gifts from suppliers, going so far as to set up a hotline for suppliers to call with information on breaches of this policy. www.matsushita.co.jp

Mattel, Inc.
See p. 131 in Home and Garden.

Microsoft Corporation
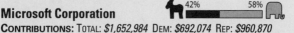
42% 58%

CONTRIBUTIONS: TOTAL: *$1,652,984* DEM: *$692,074* REP: *$960,870*

Despite the more than $3 billion it has had to pay out over the last few years for antitrust violations, Microsoft continues to face suits from its competitors citing unfair business practices. Microsoft has fought hard, both in the courtrooms and the halls of Congress: In 2000, while it was fighting a massive antitrust suit, Microsoft doubled its lobbying dollars and tripled its campaign contributions, roughly two-thirds of which went to Republicans. In the 2004 elections, it favored Republicans by the same ratio. Like other tech companies, Microsoft is making major efforts to join the China market, but news reports have shown that the company's firewall software helps China to keep a tight lid on online political dissent. Donated $47 million in cash and $363 million in software to nonprofit organizations throughout the world. Has a written nondiscrimination policy covering sexual orientation and gender identity. Offers insurance coverage to employees' domestic partners. www.microsoft.com

Motorola, Inc.
25% 75%

CONTRIBUTIONS: TOTAL: *$309,871* DEM: *$75,994* REP: *$233,877*

Cited by Human Rights Watch (HRW) in 2001 for marketing two-way radios to the Chinese police. After being cited in 1995 by HRW for involvement in antipersonnel mine production, Motorola instituted policies to prevent the sale of its technology to known mine manufacturers and investigate export practices. Sponsors "Donate a Phone," which provides used cell phones to abuse victims. Has reduced hazardous waste and water and energy use by 10% per year since 1998 and was lauded by the EPA in 2003 for exceeding required cleanup levels. Has a written nondiscrimination policy covering sexual orientation and gender identity. Offers insurance coverage to employees' domestic partners. www.motorola.com

NETGEAR, Inc.
No contributions. Two pending class action lawsuits allege the company misrepresented the data transfer speed of its wireless products. www.netgear.com

Nikon Americas, Inc.
No contributions. Subsidiary of Nikon Corporation (p. 45). The Nikon Fellowship is awarded annually to a prominent cell biologist and sponsors a summer research program.
www.nikon.com

Nikon Corporation
No contributions. Foreign owned. Agreed to pay $1.2 million in damages to settle a patent violation suit in 2003. Several pending patent infringement and antitrust suits. Implementing 1992 comprehensive environmental plan whose goals include reducing carbon dioxide emissions and use of hazardous chemicals, and improving waste reduction and recycling.
www.nikon.com

Nintendo Co., Ltd.
No contributions. Foreign owned. Fined $146 million by the European Union in 2001 for price-fixing and limiting cross-border sales from 1991 to 1998. www.nintendo.com

Nintendo of America, Inc.
No contributions. Subsidiary of Nintendo Co., Ltd. (p. 45). Donated 500 GameCube DVD-equipped entertainment centers to an organization that supports seriously ill, hospitalized children. Also supports Habitat for Humanity. www.nintendo.com

Olympus America, Inc.

CONTRIBUTIONS: TOTAL: *$250* DEM: *$0* REP: *$250*
Subsidiary of Olympus Corporation (p. 45). Has been implicated in several lawsuits involving the design of medical endoscopes and other digital scoping equipment amid allegations that the design inhibits proper sterilization. The company manufactures self-designated "ecoproducts" aiming to reduce the use of harmful chemicals, promote recycling, and reduce energy consumption. Has a written nondiscrimination policy covering sexual orientation but not gender identity. Offers insurance coverage to employees' domestic partners.
www.olympusamerica.com

Olympus Corporation
CONTRIBUTIONS: TOTAL: *$250* DEM: *$0* REP: *$250*
Lost an infringement case in Japanese courts after refusing payment for an employee's invention. Donates endoscopes to hospitals in developing nations. Has comprehensive environmental policy aimed at reducing carbon dioxide emissions, creating recyclable packaging, and exercising "green" procurement. www.olympus.com

PC Connection, Inc.
No contributions. Written nondiscrimination policy does not include sexual orientation or gender identity.
www.pcconnection.com

Petters Group Worldwide, LLC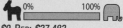
CONTRIBUTIONS: TOTAL: *$67,624* DEM: *$18,000* REP: *$49,624*

Privately held. In May 2005, as a part of the purchase of Polaroid Corporation (p. 46) the chairman and CEO (both of whom were only employed for three years) were given a combined payout of $21.3 million, while roughly 6,000 retirees were given $47. The John T. Petters Foundation promotes diversity in higher education and provides scholarships to students studying international business. Offers insurance coverage to employees' domestic partners. www.pettersgroup.com

Polaroid Corporation
CONTRIBUTIONS: TOTAL: *$37,482* DEM: *$0* REP: *$37,482*

Subsidiary of Petters Group Worldwide, LLC (p. 46). Suit pending for loss of pay and benefits by 180 employees who were on disability when Bank One purchased Polaroid out of bankruptcy. Polaroid Fund donated more than $900,000 in 2003 to groups promoting English as a second language, job training, and life skills. Environmental program seeks to reduce solid waste and carbon dioxide emissions, and increase use of recycled and remanufactured goods. Received EPA honors in 1999 for leadership in energy efficiency. Has a written nondiscrimination policy covering sexual orientation but not gender identity. Offers insurance coverage to employees' domestic partners. www.polaroid.com

Radio Shack Corporation
CONTRIBUTIONS: TOTAL: *$25,850* DEM: *$6,165* REP: *$19,685*

In 2003, class action status was granted to a lawsuit filed by employees alleging violation of federal law and intentional avoidance to pay overtime wages. In partnership with the National Center for Missing & Exploited Children, posts information in its retail stores on missing children within 30 minutes of notification. Also supports educational programs providing children with tools to avoid abduction, violence, and abuse. Has a written nondiscrimination policy covering sexual orientation but not gender identity. Refuses insurance coverage to employees' domestic partners. www.radioshack.com

Samsung Electronics America, Inc.
No contributions. Subsidiary of Samsung Group (p. 46). Foreign owned. Has a series of class action lawsuits pending in state and federal courts alleging unfair business practice and microchip price-fixing. Has several pending class action lawsuits over the health risks caused by cell phone use. www.samsung.com

Samsung Group
No contributions. The vice chairman of Samsung Electronics was sentenced in 2004 to prison for political funding violations during the 2002 presidential race. Pending investigation into

Samsung chairman's allegedly illegal campaign contributions made before the 1997 South Korean presidential election. Subsidiary Samsung SDI was investigated in 2004 for 238 alleged labor law violations, including tracking employees' movements in an effort to prevent their organizing a union. In 1998, Human Rights Watch reported that women applicants at Samsung's Tijuana, Mexico, plant were questioned about their sexual activity, contraceptive use, and pregnancy status, in violation of Mexican labor law. Operates a Japanese assembly plant constructed specifically for employees who use wheelchairs. Supports community programs promoting literacy, economic self-sufficiency, and child care for low-income families. Donates computers to elementary schools. Develops environmentally friendly products and sponsors "Adopt-a-River" and "Adopt-a-Mountain" cleanup programs. www.samsung.com

SEGA Corporation

No contributions. In a 2004 settlement of an EEOC lawsuit, SEGA and Spherion, its employment agency, paid a total of $600,000 to 18 employees alleging racial discrimination and retaliation. Investigated in 1999 by the Fair Trade Commission for allegations of price-fixing. Several pending patent infringement suits. www.sega.co.jp

Seiko Epson Corporation

No contributions. Foreign owned. Was investigated by the ITC for alleged illegal imports of products infringing on patents. Joined the UN's Global Compact, whose principles include human rights, environmentally friendly policies, and fair labor practices. Outreach includes environmental education in Japan and China, tree-planting programs in Indonesia, and support for the arts. Provides longer child care and nursing leaves than the law requires. Has a written nondiscrimination policy that mentions eliminating the wage gap between men and women. www.epson.co.jp

Sharper Image Corporation

97% | 3%

CONTRIBUTIONS: TOTAL: *$31,500* DEM: *$30,400* REP: *$1,100*

Paid the Consumers Union $525,000 in attorneys' fees in 2005 after losing a case alleging *Consumer Reports* lied in a review of its Ionic Breeze product. One of several businesses targeted in recent years by lawsuits alleging gift certificate violations, including expiration dates and nonuse fees. Has a written nondiscrimination policy including sexual orientation but not gender identity. www.sharperimage.com

Sony Corporation

73% | 27%

CONTRIBUTIONS: TOTAL: *$18,500* DEM: *$13,597* REP: *$4,853*

This Tokyo-based company owns the fifth largest media group in the United States and is often cited as an example of worrisome media consolidation. In 2005, Sony paid $10 million in fines for paying radio stations to put Sony-BMG performers, such as Britney Spears, on the air. Sony is also being boycotted for doing business with Burma, where human rights violations, censorship and political imprisonment are common. Has been praised for its in-house recycling and conservation efforts. Over half its 2004 outreach funds went to education; it also has several music and arts education foundations. www.sony.net

Sony Corporation of America, Inc.

25% 75%

CONTRIBUTIONS: TOTAL: *$1,500* DEM: *$372* REP: *$1,128*

Subsidiary of Sony Corporation (p. 47). Supports Teach for America, Phoenix House (a substance abuse program), literacy, and humanitarian and disaster aid. Offers employees two paid volunteer days per year. Has a written nondiscrimination policy covering sexual orientation but not gender identity. Offers insurance coverage to employees' domestic partners. www.sony.com

Spectrum Brands, Inc.

0% 100%

CONTRIBUTIONS: TOTAL: *$1,000* DEM: *$0* REP: *$1,000*

Formerly Rayovac Corporation. Pending class action suit alleging violations of the Securities Exchange Act, misrepresentation, and fraudulent overstatement of company potential. A pending civil action filed by the SEC arose out of a former holding company's fraudulent scheme to manipulate stock price by exploiting the fear of bioterrorism following September 11, 2001, and alleges that the company is simply a front for a team of convicted felons. Spectrum Brands' principals—two of whom have previous convictions for money laundering and racketeering—are also under criminal indictment in the Eastern District of New York, according to SEC filings. Donated DEET-based mosquito repellants for distribution to low-income seniors, families with young children, and others in California who are particularly susceptible to the mosquito-borne West Nile virus. Has a written nondiscrimination policy covering sexual orientation but not gender identity. www.spectrumbrands.com

Texas Instruments, Inc.

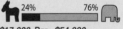
24% 76%

CONTRIBUTIONS: TOTAL: *$71,000* DEM: *$17,000* REP: *$54,000*

Was assessed a minimal $18,900 fine for what the Occupational Safety and Health Administration (OSHA) termed as "serious" violations following the death of a subcontract worker at its North Dallas manufacturing facility. Has received many awards and citations as a forward-thinking employer and corporate citizen, including recognition for environmentally beneficial process changes in semiconductor manufacturing. Outreach supports education, arts, culture, and health and human services—primarily in Dallas metro area. Has a written nondiscrimination policy covering sexual orientation but not gender identity. Offers insurance coverage to employees' domestic partners. www.ti.com

Tivo Inc.
See p. 154 in Media and Entertainment.

Toshiba America, Inc.
No contributions. Subsidiary of Toshiba Corporation (p. 49). Foreign owned. Has maintained a low profile in the United States in response to the 1987 boycott following Cold War sales of electronics to the former Soviet Union. Dramatically expanded marketing and promotions in Israel following accusations it was participating in an "Arab boycott." Was fined $18,300 for violating federal election laws and making illegal campaign contributions in 1995. Outreach supports science and mathematics education programs, projects, and activities for kindergarten through 12th grade in the United States. www.toshiba.com

Toshiba Corporation
No contributions. Foreign owned. Paid $30.13 million to California public agencies in settlement of a lawsuit alleging violation of the state False Claim Act for knowingly selling defective products. Involved in several racketeering, infringement, extortion, and pay-off suits in Japan. www.toshiba.co.jp

Xerox Corporation
34% ■ 66%

CONTRIBUTIONS: TOTAL: *$44,000* DEM: *$15,015* REP: *$28,985*

In a 2002 settlement, Xerox agreed to pay a $10 million fine to the SEC for accounting irregularities. Paid $239 million to 17,000 retired employees in 2003 settling allegations that it miscalculated pension benefits. Offers employees a one-year paid leave program to work for a community organization of their own choosing; nine employees participated in 2004. Outreach supports environmental protections, education, diversity, and community activities. Has a written nondiscrimination policy covering sexual orientation and gender identity. Offers insurance coverage to employees' domestic partners. www.xerox.com

Yahoo! Inc.
See p. 188 in Telecommunications and Internet.

Finance, Insurance, and Real Estate

With the accounting scandals at Enron, WorldCom, and Arthur Andersen came a barrage of criticism of the companies in this sector. In the wake of those scandals, loopholes allowing widespread fraud and corruption have indeed begun to close. Still, some of the most damaging practices—predatory lending, loans to questionable governments, lobbying in the real estate industry for imminent domain actions—persist.

Although the number of companies represented in this sector is small compared to other sectors in this book, they constitute the largest source of campaign contributions to federal candidates. These companies gave heavily to Republicans in 2003–2004—support, in part, for the Republican-backed bankruptcy bill, whose passage in 2005 made it harder for consumers to wipe away debt. Leading the fight was MBNA, recently purchased by Bank of America, the largest single contributor to the Republican party. The industry as a whole spent millions on lobbying over a period of several years, and the legislation was finally passed when a handful of MBNA-funded Democrats got on board.

Nearly every firm in this sector has a company PAC. Employees tend to give to their company PACs, more so than in any other sector; the top five recipients of contributions are Republicans. President George W. Bush took more money in 2003–2004 from these industries ($33,854,515) than the combined total of the next five recipients.

But the sector's relentless focus on profit doesn't always spell trouble, as evidenced by an ironic new development. As the Bush administration presses on with its skepticism over global warming, the insurance industry—standing to lose billions from an increase in storms and other disasters—has quietly acknowledged the science supporting climate change. As bad policy starts to make bad financial sense, it just might be the GOP bedfellows who end up blowing the whistle.

Top Ten Republican Contributors

General Electric Company	$1,013,039
Bank of America Corporation	751,488
Blue Cross and Blue Shield Association	738,458
Wachovia Corporation	676,533
MetLife, Inc.	542,201
CIGNA Corporation	538,999
WellPoint, Inc.	534,378
Citigroup Inc.	525,464
Capital One Financial Corporation	406,233
J. P. Morgan Chase & Co.	400,283

Top Ten Democratic Contributors

General Electric Company	$562,011
Bank of America Corporation	506,582
MetLife, Inc.	445,289
J. P. Morgan Chase & Co.	369,612
Blue Cross and Blue Shield Association	336,655
Citigroup Inc.	305,688
Washington Mutual, Inc.	264,269
Apollo Advisors LP	217,784
Capital One Financial Corporation	196,516
American International Group, Inc. (AIG)	174,769

AEA Investors

100%   0%

CONTRIBUTIONS: TOTAL: *$50,500* DEM: *$50,500* REP: *$0*

Owns interest in diverse companies ranging from beauty products to industrial tile. Was sued for issuing merger proxy statements that were materially misleading and failure to disclose full financial liability of transaction to shareholders. www.aeainv.com

Aetna, Inc.

36%   64%

CONTRIBUTIONS: TOTAL: *$361,500* DEM: *$129,223* REP: *$232,277*

Settled a $470 million class action lawsuit filed by 700,000 physicians and medical societies in federal court alleging violation of the federal Racketeer Influenced and Corrupt Organization Act (RICO). Was ordered to pay $1.2 million to an employee terminated for refusing to sign a noncompetition agreement, a violation of California employment law. In 2003, began requesting racial and ethnic information from some of its health plan members, in order to research the racial gap in care between whites and minorities, raising concerns about racial profiling and patient privacy. Foundation has disbursed over $270 million in grants since 1980. Has a written nondiscrimination policy covering sexual orientation and gender identity. Offers family benefits including health insurance coverage for employees' domestic partners. www.aetna.com

Allstate Corporation, The   28%   72%

CONTRIBUTIONS: TOTAL: *$186,500* DEM: *$53,008* REP: *$133,493*

Eliminated retirement benefits for its agents and was sued for alleged nonfiduciary duty claims and violations of the Employee Retirement Income Security Act (ERISA). Paid $150,000 fine as one of 29 firms targeted for alleged late reporting by the National Association of Securities Dealers. Foundation supports programs focused on tolerance, inclusion and diversity, community safety, and economic empowerment. Has a written nondiscrimination policy covering sexual orientation but not gender identity. Offers health insurance coverage to employees' domestic partners. www.allstate.com

American Automobile Association (AAA)

No contributions. Most AAA members join this nonprofit group for its towing and emergency roadside service; few realize their annual fees support a major political lobby that uses its vast membership (25% of U.S. households) to campaign against gas price hikes, air bags, antisprawl measures, and public transportation and for new road construction and lax emissions standards. The AAA does most of its lobbying through the American Highway Users Alliance, whose other members include GM, Ford, and Goodyear. The company's community action programs include supporting employee volunteerism, environmental stewardship, driver safety education, and used battery recycling. AAA offers insurance coverage for employees' domestic partners. www.aaa.com

American Express Company   41%   59%

CONTRIBUTIONS: TOTAL: *$382,750* DEM: *$155,865* REP: *$226,885*

American Express's campaign contributions favor Republicans by a small margin, but the company gives regularly to candidates on both sides of the fence. Through its PAC, American Express has lobbied for reduced postal rates and against a patient's bill of rights (which would increase the company's employee benefits costs), among other issues. The company has also been criticized for continuing to do business with Burma, despite widespread documented human rights violations there. American Express's charitable contributions benefit major performing arts organizations, preservation of cultural and architectural heritage, and education in economic independence. Has a written nondiscrimination policy covering sexual orientation and gender identity. Offers health insurance coverage to employees' domestic partners. www.americanexpress.com

American International Group, Inc. (AIG)   45%   55%

CONTRIBUTIONS: TOTAL: *$388,160* DEM: *$174,769* REP: *$213,391*

Fired its CFO for financial irregularities just before a 2005 investigation forced the resignation of the CEO and the chair of the board Hank Greenberg, a major Republican donor and Bush family friend. In 2004, two company executives pled guilty to charges in an alleged price-fixing scheme. Paid a $126 million settlement to federal regulators over allegations of financial misrepresentation. Supports youth charities in New York state. Has a written nondiscrimination policy covering sexual orientation but not gender identity. Offers health insurance coverage to employees' domestic partners. www.aig.com

Apollo Advisors LP

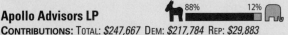 88% | 12%

CONTRIBUTIONS: TOTAL: *$247,667* DEM: *$217,784* REP: *$29,883*

Private equity firm implicated in a lawsuit alleging fraudulent concealment of involvement with Credit Lyonnais in the purchase of Executive Life Insurance Co. www.apollo-re.com

Assurant Health

 18% | 82%

CONTRIBUTIONS: TOTAL: *$414,999* DEM: *$74,347* REP: *$335,684*

Spun off by Fortis SA/NV in 2004 to become a separate, publicly traded company. Outreach supports the arts, AIDS education, and hunger relief in communities where company has a presence. www.assuranthealth.com

Bank of America Corporation

 40% | 60%

CONTRIBUTIONS: TOTAL: *$1,258,070* DEM: *$506,582* REP: *$751,488*

Bank of America has paid hundreds of millions of dollars in fines over the last few years, following charges by both the Securities and Exchange Commission (SEC) and New York attorney general Elliot Spitzer that the banking giant engaged in illegal mutual fund trading and other violations that cost long-term investors millions. Bank of America also paid $69 million for its role in the Enron scandal and faces accusations of tax evasion. Though Bank of America tends to support candidates on both sides of the fence, it recently merged with MBNA, the fifth largest contributor to both Bush campaigns. Among the company's lobbying interests are bankruptcy reform and offshore tax havens. On the bright side, Bank of America topped Rainforest Action Network's ranking of environmentally responsible finance firms. It also contributed $1 billion in 2000 in low-interest loans for low-income and minority borrowers. Bank of America's written nondiscrimination policy covers sexual orientation but not gender identity; it offers insurance coverage to employees' domestic partners. www.bankofamerica.com

Berkshire Hathaway

 30% | 70%

CONTRIBUTIONS: TOTAL: *$107,250* DEM: *$32,140* REP: *$75,110*

Berkshire Hathaway's chairman, Warren Buffett, the "Oracle of Omaha," was a major contributor to John Kerry's 2004 presidential bid and has publicly criticized many of President Bush's economic policies, including tax cuts, the country's growing trade deficit, and its limits on estate tax, as well as international matters such as the proliferation of nuclear and biological weapons. Buffett, a critic of inherited wealth, is one of the world's largest philanthropists (along with his former wife, Susan) and famously pledged to bequeath most of his $42 billion fortune to the Warren Buffett Foundation, which supports population control, education, and health care. Berkshire Hathaway has been implicated in a recent insurance scandal through one of its largest holdings, General Re, whose executives pled guilty to charges of orchestrating a phony reinsurance deal with insurance giant AIG. Berkshire Hathaway's nondiscrimination policy covers sexual orientation but not gender identity. The company refuses insurance coverage to employees' domestic partners. www.berkshirehathaway.com

Blue Cross and Blue Shield Association

31%   69%

CONTRIBUTIONS: TOTAL: *$1,075,113* DEM: *$336,655* REP: *$738,458*

An umbrella association that licenses chapters in 40 states, many of which have merged with other insurers, Blue Cross/Blue Shield spent $5.6 million on lobbying in 2004 and employs Michael Hightower, a major Bush campaign contributor, as one of its lobbyists. In general, the HMO's campaign contributions favor Republicans. Following its recent merger with WellPoint, Blue Cross/Blue Shield faces suits by doctors claiming they did not receive timely payment and that reimbursement rates are set too low. Member organizations have been sued by insureds who charge that Blue Cross/Blue Shield made coverage decisions without regard for medical standards or doctors' recommendations. www.bcbs.com

Capital One Financial Corporation

33%   67%

CONTRIBUTIONS: TOTAL: *$602,750* DEM: *$196,517* REP: *$406,234*

Was sued by former employees in 2003 for alleged age discrimination, settling out of court without admission. Provides grants, loans and equity investments to local nonprofit organizations for neighborhood redevelopment through its support of the Local Initiatives Support Corporation (LISC). Has a written nondiscrimination policy covering sexual orientation and gender identity. Offers insurance coverage to employees' domestic partners. www.capitalone.com

Cendant Corporation

See p. 192 in Travel and Leisure.

Century 21 Real Estate LLC

No contributions. Subsidiary of Cendant Corp. (p. 192). A pending class action brought by former franchisees alleges consumer fraud and breach of contract. Settled a racial discrimination, human rights, and negligence case in 2000. Paid a $450,000 settlement for allegations of federal housing discrimination and racial bias. www.century21.com

CIGNA Corporation

13%   87%

CONTRIBUTIONS: TOTAL: *$621,306* DEM: *$82,307* REP: *$538,999*

Currently facing class action litigation claiming CIGNA paid kickbacks to brokers and inflated premiums. Settled an $11.5 million lawsuit filed by physicians claiming payments were diminished in 2005. Settled a lawsuit in 2005 filed by employees whose 401(k) accounts lost money because the company's stock dropped and the plan restricted the sale of company stock. Ordered to pay $4.4 million in punitive and compensatory damages in 2002 for "malicious prosecution" of an insured individual the company knew it was obligated to cover. Outreach supports health education, community causes, and youth education. Has a written nondiscrimination policy covering sexual orientation. Offers health insurance coverage to employees' domestic partners. www.cigna.com

Citigroup Inc.

37%   63%

CONTRIBUTIONS: TOTAL: *$831,162* DEM: *$305,688* REP: *$525,464*

In 2004 and 2005, Citigroup—one of the world's largest financial institutions—paid more than $4 billion in settlement fees over its alleged role in the WorldCom and Enron scandals. A pending 2005 lawsuit alleges gender discrimination against female employees at SmithBarney. In 2004, Rainforest Action Network dropped its four-year campaign against Citigroup after the banking giant signed the Equator Principles, a voluntary set of guidelines for responsible overseas investment. In 2002, Citigroup paid a $215 million settlement after the Federal Trade Commission (FTC) charged it with engaging in predatory and abusive lending practices. Citigroup's foundation supports financial education, microenterprise, sustainable forestry, and renewable energy programs. Has a written nondiscrimination policy covering sexual orientation and gender identity. Offers insurance coverage to employees' domestic partners. www.citigroup.com

Coldwell Banker Real Estate Corporation

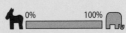
0%   100%

CONTRIBUTIONS: TOTAL: *$500* DEM: *$0* REP: *$500*

Subsidiary of Cendant Corp. (p. 192). Agreed to pay a $250,000 settlement in allegations of violations by the Department of Housing and Urban Development (HUD) for offering incentives and perks to agents who used Coldwell Banker's affiliated title company. Paid $296,000 to settle claims of violations of federal real estate law brought by the state of Minnesota and HUD for failure to disclose referral relationships and fees and imposing referral quotas on its sales agents. Supports Habitat for Humanity. www.coldwellbanker.com

Costco Wholesale Corporation
See p. 142 in Major Retailers.

Countrywide Financial Corporation
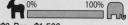
39%   61%

CONTRIBUTIONS: TOTAL: *$197,500* DEM: *$76,965* REP: *$120,535*

Paid $30 million to 400 employees as settlement for alleged failure to pay overtime wages. Philanthropy targets community development projects with interest in education and expansion of affordable housing and social services. Has a written nondiscrimination policy covering sexual orientation but not gender identity. Offers insurance coverage to employees' domestic partners. www.countrywide.com

Coventry Health Care, Inc.

0%   100%

CONTRIBUTIONS: TOTAL: *$1,500* DEM: *$0* REP: *$1,500*

Settled a lawsuit filed by shareholders, accusing the company of withholding information related to the purchase of First Health. Was named (along with other large heath insurance companies) in lawsuits filed by doctors accusing the company of conspiring to defraud physicians in violation of the federal civil RICO Act. Has a written nondiscrimination policy covering sexual orientation but not gender identity. Does not offer health insurance coverage to employees' domestic partners. www.cvty.com

Discover Financial Services, Inc.
64%   36%

CONTRIBUTIONS: TOTAL: *$11,000* DEM: *$7,000* REP: *$4,000*

Subsidiary of Morgan Stanley. At the center of the security lapse that left more than 200,000 people's credit card data and personal information vulnerable for fraud. Pending suit brought by a San Diego–based consumer advocacy group alleging that the practice of raising interest rates for late payment constitutes an unlawful business practice and is a violation of state law. www.discoverfinancial.com

Ditech.com
No contributions. Subsidiary of General Motors Acceptance Corporation (p. 58). Pending Securities Exchange Act violations, subprime lending practice, and class action suits. Offered and was refused settlement in alleged gouging class action lawsuit. Sponsors professional car racing and a foundation benefiting abused children in Orange County, CA. www.ditech.com

Farmers Group, Inc.
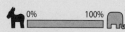
0%   100%

CONTRIBUTIONS: TOTAL: *$4,000* DEM: *$0* REP: *$4,000*

Subsidiary of Zurich Financial Services (p. 67). Paid a $117.5 million settlement in 2003 concerning allegations of unfair pricing practices. Also involved in several suits concerning its alleged policy to use knock-off parts for repairs. Supports programs that improve safety, enhance educational opportunity, and increase civic participation. www.farmers.com

GE Consumer Finance

CONTRIBUTIONS: TOTAL: *$3,000* DEM: *$1,000* REP: *$2,000*

Subsidiary of General Electric Company (p. 58). Paid a $5.5 million settlement in a class action suit alleging unfair and deceptive business practices. Philanthropy focuses on children, education, and economic development. www.geconsumerfinance.com

GEICO General Insurance Co.

CONTRIBUTIONS: TOTAL: *$1,950* DEM: *$140* REP: *$1,810*

Subsidiary of Berkshire Hathaway (p. 54). At the center of two federal cases currently on appeal that may require insurers to issue adverse action notices whenever credit information is used in underwriting. Sponsors neighborhood and educational programs that encourage active citizenship and environmental stewardship. Has an employee matching and volunteer program. Allows domestic partners to have joint car insurance policies. Has a written nondiscrimination policy that includes sexual orientation but not gender identity. www.geico.com

General Electric (GE) Company

CONTRIBUTIONS: TOTAL: *$1,575,080* DEM: *$562,011* REP: *$1,013,039*

Until recently GE was the world's largest corporation, with products ranging from dishwashers, insurance, NBC TV shows, nuclear power, and military airplanes. It's also one of the most notorious: GE got out of the nuclear weapons business a decade ago, but that hasn't saved it from an onslaught of convictions of environmental pollution and fraud, as well as accusations of human rights and labor abuses. The company has been accused of knowingly exposing thousands of people to nuclear radiation from its power plants and releasing enough PCBs to seriously contaminate the Housatonic River, and it was blamed for the creation of some 80 Superfund sites. More recently, GE was sued for failing to warn employees of exposure to hazardous materials and improperly disposing of hazardous waste. It has been praised for its diversity initiatives. Its written nondiscrimination policy covers sexual orientation but not gender identity. Offers insurance coverage to employees' domestic partners. www.ge.com

General Motors Acceptance Corporation

CONTRIBUTIONS: TOTAL: *$2,000* DEM: *$2,000* REP: *$0*

Subsidiary of General Motors Corporation (p. 215). Paid $32.4 million to settle a class action suit alleging discrimination in lending to African American customers. Has a pending suit brought by the Ohio state attorney general alleging consumer deception for rolling back the odometers of motor vehicles in the state of Ohio. Supports medical research, arts and education, diversification, financial literacy, and environmental programs independent of parent. www.gmacfs.com

Golden Rule Insurance Company

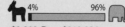
4% 96%

CONTRIBUTIONS: TOTAL: *$219,850* DEM: *$9,016* REP: *$210,684*

Is the subject of several investigations into its practices brought by the state of Illinois. Paid $660,000 to resolve a multistate investigation into its practices and misconduct, including $385,000 for failing to cooperate with state examiners with the Ohio Department of Insurance. Was cited in 1997 for its direct influence brokering in connection with the Medicare Bill and relationships with political consultant Joseph Gaylord and former speaker of the house Newt Gingrich. Its PAC and executives gave a combined $150,000 to GOPAC, $42,500 to friends of Newt Gingrich, and $600,000 in GOP soft money. Offers health insurance coverage to employees' domestic partners. www.goldenrule.com

Group Health Incorporated

50% 50%

CONTRIBUTIONS: TOTAL: *$43,880* DEM: *$21,979* REP: *$21,901*

Was determined by a jury in 2002 to have engaged in "deceptive acts and practices against the public at large" by refusing to honor valid claims. Was fined $30,000 for violating New York state's Prompt Pay law. Outreach supports health education and children's issues. Has a written employee nondiscrimination policy for sexual orientation. www.ghi.com

Guardian Life Insurance Company of America, The

74% 26%

CONTRIBUTIONS: TOTAL: *$17,000* DEM: *$12,506* REP: *$4,494*

Outreach supports education and entrepreneurship initiatives for girls and affordable housing in communities where company has a presence. Does not offer health insurance coverage to employees' domestic partners. www.guardianlife.com

Hartford Financial Services Group, Inc., The

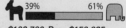
39% 61%

CONTRIBUTIONS: TOTAL: *$262,595* DEM: *$102,760* REP: *$159,835*

In 2005, the Ninth U.S. Circuit Court of Appeals ruled that The Hartford customers should be given notice when an insurer charges them a higher rate based on their credit record. Outreach focuses on educational grants. Has a written nondiscrimination policy covering sexual orientation. Offers health insurance coverage to employees' domestic partners. www.thehartford.com

Health Net, Inc.

CONTRIBUTIONS: TOTAL: *$125,500* DEM: *$54,196* REP: *$71,304*

Settled a class action suit filed by doctors in federal court alleging price rigging by their software. Health Net California was fined $250,000 in 2005 for nonpayment or mishandling of claims by the state's Department of Managed Health Care. Was assessed a $100,000 fine for the same violations in 2001. Has a written nondiscrimination policy covering sexual orientation. Offers domestic partner coverage on healthcare plans. www.healthnet.com

HealthPartners, Inc.

CONTRIBUTIONS: TOTAL: *$2,950* DEM: *$100* REP: *$2,850*

Paid a $15,000 fine and agreed to modify its mental health policies to allow for treatment of children with behavioral problems after the families of two teenage children who were denied services sued. The state of Minnesota sought reforms of extravagant spending by and compensation of board members. Outreach supports health education in communities where the company has a presence. Has a written nondiscrimination policy covering sexual orientation. Offers health insurance coverage to employees' domestic partners. www.healthpartners.com

Highmark Inc.

CONTRIBUTIONS: TOTAL: *$37,600* DEM: *$5,726* REP: *$31,875*

HealthGuard of Lancaster subsidiary fined for illegally pricing health insurance policies. In 2000, the American Medical Association asked the Department of Justice to investigate alleged restraints on competition. Foundation supports cancer health awareness, as well as senior citizen and youth health in communities where the company has a presence. Has a nondiscrimination policy covering sexual orientation. www.highmark.com

Humana Inc.

CONTRIBUTIONS: TOTAL: *$152,499* DEM: *$35,518* REP: *$115,476*

History of legal suits and imposed fines regarding violations of federal and state laws. Named with other HMOs in pending class action lawsuit for allegedly conspiring to defraud physicians in violation of the federal civil RICO Act. Agreed to pay more than $1 million in back wages to 2,510 employees for violations of the Fair Labor Standards Act. Foundation supports domestic and international health issues, education, and cultural development in communities where the company has a presence. Has a written nondiscrimination policy covering sexual orientation. Plans to include gender identity in nondiscrimination policy, and offer health insurance coverage to employees' domestic partners in 2005. www.humana.com

J. P. Morgan Chase & Co.

48%   52%

CONTRIBUTIONS: TOTAL: *$769,895* DEM: *$369,612* REP: *$400,283*

Paid $2 billion to settle the WorldCom class action lawsuit alleging the bank had knowledge of the accounting fraud. Agreed to pay a $2.2 billion settlement for its alleged participation in the accounting scandal that led to Enron's collapse. Paid $2.7 million to settle allegations that it broke rules limiting the sale of stock after initial public offerings. Supports community development, contributing over $140 million to various nonprofits. Provided more than $3 billion in loans and investments in low- and moderate-income communities. Has a written nondiscrimination policy covering sexual orientation and gender identity. Offers insurance coverage to employees' domestic partners. www.jpmorganchase.com

Kaiser Foundation Health Plan, Inc.

No contributions. Subsidiary of Kaiser Permanente (p. 61). Fined by state of California for privacy law violations because it maintained a website with patients' health information that could be accessed by the general public. www.kff.org

Kaiser Permanente

100%   0%

CONTRIBUTIONS: TOTAL: *$1,000* DEM: *$1,000* REP: *$0*

After years of conflict, California's largest HMO has recently won praise for its relationships with labor groups: In 2005, a spokesperson for the Service Employees International Union (SEIU) described Kaiser's new labor contract as "the best private-sector health care system contract in the United States." In 2003, the HMO agreed to publish its treatment guidelines online as part of a settlement with consumer groups that had accused Kaiser of letting cost cutting determine the course of patients' treatment. Outreach supports health education, particularly in areas of breast cancer, asthma, and obesity. Has a written nondiscrimination policy that covers sexual orientation and gender identity. Offers health insurance coverage to employees' domestic partners. www.kaiserpermanente.org

Loews Corporation

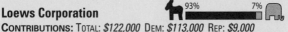

93%   7%

CONTRIBUTIONS: TOTAL: *$122,000* DEM: *$113,000* REP: *$9,000*

Diversified holding company with subsidiaries ranging from off-shore drilling to Bulova timepieces. Targeted with 11 other companies in a well-publicized slave reparation class action suit for pre-1865 gains. Named in antitrust class action suit alleging price-fixing by tobacco firms. Agreed to pay a $7.5 billion settlement for class action punitive damage claims. Has a written nondiscrimination policy covering sexual orientation but not gender identity. Offers insurance coverage to employees' domestic partners. www.loews.com

MasterCard Incorporated

No contributions. Pending suit alleging antitrust violations, fraud, and monopolistic dominance after a court determination that MasterCard was a monopoly. Supports organizations serving youth, emphasizing education and access to technology. Has a written nondiscrimination policy covering sexual orientation but not gender identity. Offers insurance coverage to employees' domestic partners. www.mastercard.com

MBNA Corporation

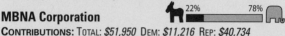 22% 78%

CONTRIBUTIONS: TOTAL: *$51,950* DEM: *$11,216* REP: *$40,734*

The world's largest credit card issuer is also the top all-time career donor to President Bush. MBNA was a major mover behind the passage of the 2005 bankruptcy reforms, which make it much harder for individuals to file for Chapter 11 and offer far less protection from creditors. In 2005, the Human Rights campaign gave MBNA the lowest rating among financial institutions for its record on gay, lesbian and transgender rights charging that the company supports anti-gay groups. The EEOC filed a lawsuit in 2004 alleging MBNA failed to prevent racial and ethnic verbal abuse of its South Asian and African American employees. Still MBNA is often included on *Working Mother* magazine's list of the 100 best workplaces for education initiatives. Has donated $34 million in scholarships for its education initiative as of June 2004. Has a written nondiscrimination policy covering sexual orientation but not gender identity. Offers health insurance coverage to employees' domestic partners. www.mbna.com

Medica Inc.

No contributions. Pending suit brought by Minnesota State attorney general alleges that the insurer paid improper bonuses to executives and failed to address service and quality issues. Outreach supports community health care initiatives. Has a written employment nondiscrimination policy that includes sexual orientation. www.medica.com

Mercury General Corporation

0% 100%

CONTRIBUTIONS: TOTAL: *$79,500* DEM: *$0* REP: *$79,500*

Was publicly investigated over eight substantial political contributions made to then–California governor Gray Davis, alleged to have influenced Davis's signing a bill favorable to the company. Involved in several similar investigations involving political contributions and "buying favor" on a smaller scale. www.mercuryinsurance.com

MetLife, Inc.

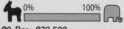 45% 55%

CONTRIBUTIONS: TOTAL: *$987,490* DEM: *$445,289* REP: *$542,201*

Paid $1.5 million in fines for questionable mutual fund practices. Settled a gender discrimination lawsuit in 2003. Currently under investigation by the SEC for its reinsurance practices.

Foundation supports educational, health and welfare, civic, and cultural organizations. Social investment program supports community revitalization and economic development. Has a written nondiscrimination policy covering sexual orientation and gender identity. Offers insurance coverage to employees' domestic partners. www.metlife.com

Oxford Health Plans, LLC

37%   63%

CONTRIBUTIONS: TOTAL: *$33,650* DEM: *$12,286* REP: *$21,276*

Subsidiary of UnitedHealth Group Incorporated (p. 64). Agreed to pay $250,000 to settle a SEC investigation into revenue statements. Named in class action lawsuits filed in state courts by doctors alleging that Oxford violates states' prompt-payment laws. Outreach supports health education and initiatives in communities where company has a presence. Has a written nondiscrimination policy covering sexual orientation. Does not offer health insurance coverage to employees' domestic partners. www.oxhp.com

PacifiCare Health Systems, Inc.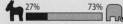

27%   73%

CONTRIBUTIONS: TOTAL: *$293,000* DEM: *$78,507* REP: *$207,453*

Acquisition by UnitedHealth Group Incorporated (p. 64) scheduled for 2006. Paid fines and settled state lawsuits alleging payment violations and negligence regarding patients' rights. Named with other insurance companies in a pending class action lawsuit filed by doctors and states in federal court alleging violation of the federal RICO Act. Foundation supports domestic health issues, education, and cultural development in communities where the company has a presence. Has a written nondiscrimination policy covering sexual orientation and gender identity. Offers health insurance coverage to employees' domestic partners. www.pacificare.com

Progressive Corporation, The

99%   1%

CONTRIBUTIONS: TOTAL: *$58,600* DEM: *$58,043* REP: *$557*

Currently under investigation by the Connecticut attorney general for possible violations of antitrust laws. Has four pending class action suits alleging breach of contract and fraud for purchasing after-market replacement parts for vehicle repairs. Has a notable gain-sharing program; employees collectively earned $169 million from 1992 to 2002. All employees are eligible for awards based on predetermined targeted goals. Has a written nondiscrimination policy covering sexual orientation but not gender identity. Offers health insurance coverage to employees' domestic partners. www.progressive.com

Prudential Financial, Inc.

36%   64%

CONTRIBUTIONS: TOTAL: *$358,329* DEM: *$127,744* REP: *$230,505*

Fined $2 million and censured by the National Association of Securities Dealers and ordered to pay another $9.5 million to customers for questionable sales practices. Implicated in California insurance scheme scandals alleging bid rigging and payouts. Foundation supports public education, skill development, and initiatives that promote community well-being. Social investment program supports neighborhood and community revitalization. Has a written nondiscrimination policy that covers sexual orientation and gender identity. Offers insurance coverage to employees' domestic partners. www.prudential.com

Safeco Corporation

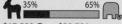
18%   82%

CONTRIBUTIONS: TOTAL: *$48,220* DEM: *$8,862* REP: *$39,358*

Implicated in California's insurance scheme scandal involving bid rigging and kickbacks. Outreach supports community enrichment, diversification and artistic endeavors. Received achievement award in 2003 from the Points of Light Foundation for its volunteer program. Company has matching charitable gift program. Has a written nondiscrimination policy covering sexual orientation and gender identity. Offers insurance coverage to employees' domestic partners. www.safeco.com

State Farm Insurance Companies

35%   65%

CONTRIBUTIONS: TOTAL: *$44,050* DEM: *$15,266* REP: *$28,784*

More than 15 affiliated privately held companies. Settled a class action suit agreeing to pay $135 million to 2,600 employees who alleged they were denied overtime. Agreed to $40 million settlement involving vehicles it sold but failed to identify as totaled. Outreach focuses on education, safety, diversification, and community building. Has a nondiscrimination policy covering sexual orientation but not gender identity. Refuses insurance coverage to employees' domestic partners. www.statefarm.com

UnitedHealth Group Incorporated

12%   88%

CONTRIBUTIONS: TOTAL: *$314,485* DEM: *$39,294* REP: *$274,953*

Named with other leading insurance companies in a pending class action lawsuit filed by doctors and states in federal court alleging violation of the RICO Act. Fined by several states for failure to adhere to state patients' rights laws. Outreach supports health education and initiatives in communities where the company has a presence. Has a written nondiscrimination policy covering sexual orientation. Offers health insurance coverage to employees' domestic partners. www.unitedhealthgroup.com

United Services Automobile Association (USAA)

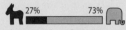

CONTRIBUTIONS: TOTAL: *$510,000* DEM: *$140,000* REP: *$370,000*

Involved in several notable discrimination suits involving alleged civil rights and federal tort law violations as well as libel and slander. Was sued for unlawfully firing an employee after violating the National Labor Relations Act with unlawful interrogation. Foundation supports education in financial management, safety concerns and significant life events. Has received repeated recognition as a family-friendly employer. Has a written nondiscrimination policy covering sexual orientation but not gender identity. Refuses insurance coverage for employees' domestic partners. www.usaa.com

U.S. Bancorp

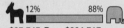

CONTRIBUTIONS: TOTAL: *$232,462* DEM: *$27,745* REP: *$204,717*

Paid $2.5 million to settle allegations of negligence when a former broker bilked 38 mostly elderly and disabled clients of $1.4 million. Foundation and community development loan program supports affordable housing, economic revitalization, education, and artistic and cultural enrichment. Has employee volunteer program. Gave employees generous one-time stock option grant following Firstar–U.S. Bancorp merger. Has a written nondiscrimination policy covering sexual orientation but not gender identity. Offers insurance coverage to employees' domestic partners. www.usbancorp.com

Visa International

No contributions. Implicated in security breach and identity theft scandals. Has been cited worldwide for infringement of competition laws in the financial services market. Outreach supports village banking initiatives and small enterprise development. Developed a system of "virtuous circle" designed to help world economies grow, support themselves, and prosper. Has a written nondiscrimination policy covering sexual orientation but not gender identity. Offers insurance coverage to employees' domestic partners. www.visa.com

Visa U.S.A. Inc.

No contributions. Subsidiary of Visa International (p. 65). www.usa.visa.com

Wachovia Corporation

CONTRIBUTIONS: TOTAL: *$823,100* DEM: *$144,629* REP: *$676,533*

Claims on its website to "support progressive legislation" despite its obvious support of Republican candidates and PACs. Evergreen Investments subsidiary is under SEC investigation for alleged market timing violations. Supports educational improvement and neighborhood strengthening. Has an employee volunteer program, two corporate PACs, two government relations groups, and an issues management group.

Has a written nondiscrimination policy covering sexual orientation but not gender identity. Offers insurance coverage to employees' domestic partners. www.wachovia.com

Washington Mutual, Inc.

CONTRIBUTIONS: TOTAL: *$552,700* DEM: *$264,270* REP: *$288,430*

Faces several class action suits alleging improper marketing and sales practices. An April 2003 lawsuit alleges improper charges and excessive penalties for mortgage customers. Washington Mutual is one of the country's leading sub-prime lenders—meaning that it offers loans at high interest rates to customers with bad credit—and has been criticized for targeting African-Americans with these loans. The bank's campaign contributions favor Republicans. Has a generous employee volunteer program and makes substantial cash grants for affordable housing initiatives. Has a written nondiscrimination policy covering sexual orientation and gender identity and offers insurance coverage to employees' domestic partners. www.wamu.com

WellPoint, Inc.

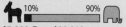

CONTRIBUTIONS: TOTAL: *$669,900* DEM: *$135,522* REP: *$534,378*

WellPoint is the nation's largest health insurer, providing health insurance under the Blue Cross and Blue Shield names in 13 states and under the entities HealthLink and UniCare. Named with other leading insurance companies in a class action lawsuit filed by doctors and states in federal court alleging violation of the RICO Act. Settled a suit with physicians for $200 million in 2005. The state of California conducted hearings on whether a 2005 rate increase was used to finance a merger with other insurance companies to become the largest HMO in the nation. Blue Shield of California customers and brokers are suing for a refund of $4 billion in raised premiums associated with the purchase by Anthem, which then changed its name to WellPoint. Outreach supports health care initiatives and public policy in communities where the company has a presence. Has a written nondiscrimination policy covering sexual orientation. Offers health insurance coverage to employees' domestic partners. www.wellpoint.com

Wells Fargo & Company

CONTRIBUTIONS: TOTAL: *$77,000* DEM: *$7,660* REP: *$69,340*

Wells Fargo has been criticized by groups like the Association of Community Organizations for Reform Now (ACORN) for its "predatory lending" practices, which use deceptive marketing to sell high-interest loans to low-income borrowers, and for its investments in check-cashing and payday-lending businesses, which charge high fees to people without bank accounts. In response, the bank recently issued a new set of safeguards to give low-income borrowers access to better loans. In 2005, the National Resources Defense Council and other environmental groups launched a campaign to urge Wells Fargo to sign on to a set of environmental standards adopted by Bank of America, Citigroup, and others. Wells Fargo consistently earns praise as a progressive, family-friendly employer. Has a written nondiscrimination policy that covers sexual orientation and gender identity. Offers insurance coverage to employees' domestic partners. www.wellsfargo.com

Zurich Financial Services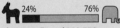

CONTRIBUTIONS: TOTAL: *$270,369* DEM: *$63,819* REP: *$206,550*

Foreign owned. Recently restructured employee pension; forced employees to accept an autonomous plan with a defined contribution approach, phasing out several early-retirement benefits. Two former employees pled guilty to violating the New York State antitrust law in relation to New York attorney general Elliot Spitzer's probe. www.zurich.com

Food and Beverage

In 2001, the U.S. military saw fit to drop 2.4 million Pop-Tarts on Afghanistan along with its more explosive fare. It's a subtler bombardment we get here from the food and beverage industry, but history may reveal it to be no less consequential in the coming years.

From genetic modification to mad cow to trans fat to obesity to carcinogenic pesticides, the industry has been dogged by public criticism and lawsuits recently. Some companies have begun to respond—slowly and ineffectively, critics argue—but even more startling is the extensive influence peddling in Washington that remains largely hidden.

Each year, multinational corporations spend billions of dollars lobbying the government to dilute dietary regulations and health warnings. Although a comprehensive study in the *Journal of the American Medical Association* established a clear link between soft drinks and diabetes, for example, the U.S. Department of Agriculture (USDA) has been reluctant to acknowledge the connection. Recent studies show a strong correlation between the consumption of red meat and heart disease, and refined white flour and its contribution to blood sugar disorders. Critics have complained that members of such toothless regulating agencies often have financial ties to the industries they are meant to regulate.

Companies in this sector primarily contribute to Republicans, which was the case even during the Clinton years. The contributions have not gone unnoticed. A major victory for industry groups such as the International Dairy Foods Association was the passage of the nearly $250 billion Farm Bill in 2002. In the 2000 and 2002 elections, the sector gave over $110 million mostly to Republican candidates. Critics call the bill welfare for corporate agribusiness, led by companies such as Chevron Corporation (see p. 212 in Vehicles, Parts, and Gas) and the 14 members of Congress who drafted it.

The food industry, not surprisingly, is dominated by corporate giants with wildly mixed records. The Coca-Cola Company (p. 76), for instance, can earn a spot on *Fortune* magazine's 2004 list of the "50 Best Companies for Minorities," while managers at its bottling plants in Colombia stand accused of hiring paramilitary death squads to assassinate trade unionists.

The environmental record of a company can vary even more. McDonald's Corporation (see p. 165 in Restaurants), for example, has implemented a proactive meat-purchasing policy that restricts use of growth hormones and antibiotics. On the other hand, it creates enormous demand for livestock, which in turn leads to deforestation, soil erosion, water scarcity, and loss of biodiversity. Poultry and meat processing accounts for millions of gallons of wastewater entering treatment plants weekly. In Delmarva, Maryland, 12 local slaughterhouses process approximately 12,200,000 chickens weekly, creating 12,240,000 gallons of polluted water. With legislation and enforcement trailing demand, violations have become the only way to monitor the industry excess. The resulting fines don't compensate for the environmental impact and destruction, so local communities end up paying the tab.

Some of the most prominent consumer actions have been directed at multinationals in the food sector, from the decades-long Nestlé S.A. (p. 90) boycott to an innovative hedge fund designed to "short" the share price of the Coca-Cola Company. And there have been successes, one of the more dramatic being the recent capitulation of Taco Bell's parent company, Yum! Brands, Inc. (see p. 169 in Restaurants), after consumer pressure over labor abuses. As more Americans begin paying attention to what they put in their mouths—even with little attention paid by the government itself—the companies responsible may take notice as it translates to bottom-line profitability.

Top Ten Republican Contributors

Altria Group Inc.	$913,613
Anheuser-Busch Companies, Inc.	723,533
Smithfield Foods, Inc.	340,295
PepsiCo, Inc.	271,819
Dean Foods Company	241,841
Cargill, Incorporated	215,189
Brown-Forman Corporation	201,299
ConAgra Foods, Inc.	199,266
J. W. Childs Associates, L.P.	192,000
Safeway Inc.	187,461

Top Ten Democratic Contributors

Anheuser-Busch Companies, Inc.	$423,907
Altria Group Inc.	408,865
Brown-Forman Corporation	255,935
PepsiCo, Inc.	121,891
Dean Foods Company	94,153
Tyson Foods, Inc.	92,658
Vestar Capital Partners	88,323
E. & J. Gallo Winery	85,960
Newman's Own, Inc.	76,790
Safeway Inc.	72,286

7-Eleven, Inc.
CONTRIBUTIONS: TOTAL: *$4,750* DEM: *$4,000* REP: *$750*
Agreed to stop advertising cigarettes (which constitute 30% of its sales) near products that appeal to minors and pay a $375,000 settlement. While the company appears to spend relatively little on lobbying and political campaigns, its environmental record is marred by its relationship with CITGO Petroleum Corporation (see p. 212). Has a written nondiscrimination policy covering sexual orientation but not gender identity. Offers insurance coverage to employees' domestic partners. www.7-eleven.com

Acme Markets, Inc.
No contributions. Subsidiary of Albertsons, Inc. (p. 72). A six-month probe by the U.S. Occupational Safety and Health Administration (OSHA) proposed $232,000 in fines for 37 alleged workplace safety violations, including possible exposure to hazardous chemicals. www.acmemarkets.com

Ahold USA, Inc.
CONTRIBUTIONS: TOTAL: *$10,950* DEM: *$907* REP: *$10,039*
Subsidiary of Royal Ahold N.V. (p. 94). A pending investigation with the U.S. attorney's office in New York alleges major accounting fraud, irregularities, and conspiracy at its U.S.

Foodservice subsidiary. Outreach supports causes in communities where the company has a presence. No information on benefit structure. www.aholdusa.com

Albertsons, Inc.

24%   76%

CONTRIBUTIONS: TOTAL: *$142,459* DEM: *$34,003* REP: *$108,456*

Dogged by disputes over labor and workplace conditions, including a long and expensive strike at its southern California stores. Has two lawsuits pending alleging violation of California antitrust law following an alliance with Safeway Inc. (p. 95) and the Kroger Co./Ralphs Grocery Company (p. 93) that required all three companies to lock out union employees if a strike was called. Allows its pharmacists to refuse, on ethical grounds, to fill prescriptions for the morning-after pill. Donated 23 million pounds of food to hunger relief efforts in 2003, and has contributed $3.1 million toward muscular dystrophy research. Does not distribute irradiated food or sell milk from cows treated with bovine growth hormone. Does not have a written nondiscrimination policy covering sexual orientation or gender identity. Only some subsidiaries offer health insurance coverage to employees' domestic partners. www.albertsons.com

Allied Domecq PLC

22%   78%

CONTRIBUTIONS: TOTAL: *$61,040* DEM: *$13,527* REP: *$47,513*

Purchased by Pernod Ricard (p. 92) in 2005, this conglomerate is a member of the Distilled Spirits Council, a trade group representing 90% of liquor sales, that lobbies against restrictions on alcohol sales, trade tariffs, and taxation and contributes primarily to Republican campaigns. Also contributes to the Century Council, a liquor industry–funded nonprofit dedicated to fighting drunk driving and underage drinking. www.allieddomecq.com

Allied Domecq Wines, USA

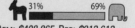
100%   0%

CONTRIBUTIONS: TOTAL: *$540* DEM: *$540* REP: *$0*

Subsidiary of Allied Domecq PLC (p. 72); parent, Pernod Ricard (p. 92). www.allieddomecqwines.com

Altria Group Inc.

31%   69%

CONTRIBUTIONS: TOTAL: *$1,322,478* DEM: *$408,865* REP: *$913,613*

It's easy to see why tobacco giant Philip Morris might seek a name change: the company spent most of the 1990s under a deluge of cigarette-related lawsuits, racking up billions of dollars in settlement charges and fines. Broke with others in the industry in its support of Food and Drug Administration (FDA) regulation of tobacco products. The measure ultimately failed, however, with antiregulation voters in Congress receiving five times the contributions received by proregulation voters. Spends more on campaign donations than any other tobacco producer. Contributes millions of dollars to arts, hunger, AIDS, and domestic violence prevention programs. www.altria.com

Anheuser-Busch Companies, Inc.

37% 63%

CONTRIBUTIONS: TOTAL: *$1,147,440* DEM: *$423,907* REP: *$723,533*

Employs the former chief fund-raiser for the 2004 Bush-Cheney campaign as one of its lobbyists. In 2003, the company spent $1 million on a bill to classify malt-based "alcopop" drinks, which are popular with teenagers, as beer, allowing for sales in convenience stores. Charitable giving supports many community causes and includes an extensive program to prevent alcohol abuse. Its Partners in Economic Progress program promotes diversification in its supplier practices. Has a written nondiscrimination policy covering sexual orientation but not gender identity. Offers insurance coverage to employees' domestic partners. www.anheuser-busch.com

Bacardi Limited

14% 86%

CONTRIBUTIONS: TOTAL: *$28,363* DEM: *$4,004* REP: *$24,359*

The Environmental Protection Agency (EPA) found violations of the federal Clean Water Act for wastewater discharge from a company distillery in Puerto Rico. Indicted on charges of allegedly making an illegal $20,000 campaign contribution to the PAC founded by Republican Tom DeLay. The DeLay-Bacardi connection is cited in a footnote to the extortion, bribery, and abuse of power complaint that was filed against DeLay with the House Ethics Committee in June 2004. The connection becomes even more suspect with the revelation of "the Bacardi bill," that would give Bacardi the rights to the Havana Club label in the United States—at the expense of CubaExport (a subsidiary of the Cuban government) and its French partner Pernod Ricard (p. 92). Named, with other alcohol producers, in several suits for encouraging alcohol consumption by minors through advertising and entertainment tie-ins. Outreach includes the Century Council, an industry-funded nonprofit dedicated to fighting drunk driving and underage drinking. www.bacardi.com

Bacardi U.S.A., Inc.

16% 84%

CONTRIBUTIONS: TOTAL: *$25,363* DEM: *$4,004* REP: *$21,359*

Subsidiary of Bacardi Limited (p. 73). Privately held. Named in various lawsuits filed by watchdog groups and consumer attorneys claiming alcohol producers market to minors, specifically mentioning Mike's Hard Lemonade and Captain Morgan's Rum. www.bacardi.com

BI-LO, LLC

No contributions. Subsidiary of Ahold USA, Inc. (p. 71); parent, Royal Ahold N.V. (p. 94). Pending acquisition by Lone Star

Funds. Outreach supports education, hunger relief, and children's services in communities in which the company has a presence. www.bi-lo.com

Birds Eye Foods, Inc.

CONTRIBUTIONS: TOTAL: *$3,000* DEM: *$73* REP: *$2,927*
Subsidiary of Vestar Capital Partners (p. 100). The Birds Eye brand is represented in the U.K. by Unilever (p. 118). Foundation supports education, health, and youth services in communities where the company has a presence.
www.birdseyefoods.com

Boston Beer Company, Inc., The

CONTRIBUTIONS: TOTAL: *$4,250* DEM: *$4,250* REP: *$0*
The company's most notable brand is its Samuel Adams line of beers. www.bostonbeer.com

Brown-Forman Beverages
CONTRIBUTIONS: TOTAL: *$2,000* DEM: *$2,000* REP: *$0*
Subsidiary of Brown-Forman Corporation (p. 74). The Early Times distillery was cited in a 2002 EPA study as having higher-than-allowed emissions of 38 air and water pollutants. Member of the Distilled Spirits Council organized to combat alcohol abuse and encourage social responsibility.
www.brown-forman.com

Brown-Forman Corporation

CONTRIBUTIONS: TOTAL: *$457,234* DEM: *$255,935* REP: *$201,299*
In 1990, 105 employees, dismissed in 1986, sued for damages and job recovery, citing age discrimination. Company distilleries claim to follow strict environmental procedures, though they continue to be cited for excessive emissions. Founding member of the Century Council, an industry-funded nonprofit dedicated to fighting drunk driving and underage drinking. Its Fetzer Vineyards subsidiary is certified organic.
www.brown-forman.com

Bruno's Supermarkets, Inc.
No contributions. Subsidiary of Ahold USA, Inc. (p. 71); parent, Royal Ahold N.V. (p. 94). Pending acquisition by Lone Star Funds. Outreach supports education and children's services in communities where the company has a presence.
www.brunos.com

Bumble Bee Seafoods, L.L.C.

CONTRIBUTIONS: TOTAL: *$19,750* DEM: *$10,750* REP: *$9,000*
Since adopting the "dolphin-safe" label in 1990, the company appears to have followed the rules for responsible tuna fishing (thanks, in part, to the failure of a 2003 Bush administration attempt to relax the law). In 2004, after FDA and EPA warnings of

dangerous mercury levels in tuna, Californians passed Proposition 65 requiring tuna companies to label their products accordingly. All three major tuna companies refused to comply, and their lawsuit with the state of California is still pending. Outreach includes hunger and tsunami relief efforts. www.bumblebee.com

Cadbury Schweppes Americas Beverages
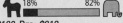
CONTRIBUTIONS: TOTAL: *$1,000* DEM: *$182* REP: *$813*
Subsidiary of Cadbury Schweppes plc (p. 75). Partners with the American Diabetes Association to fight diabetes and obesity. www.cadburyschweppes.com

Cadbury Schweppes plc
CONTRIBUTIONS: TOTAL: *$1,000* DEM: *$182* REP: *$813*
Foreign owned. Implemented a strict code of conduct for operations including human and labor rights initiatives after several lawsuits. Suffered losses during extended labor strikes by Nigerian workers in 2004. Fined for violations of sanctions for exports to Sudan. Foundation supports projects in areas where the company has a corporate presence. Founded Africa Aid to support education, capacity building, and sustainable environmental practices and to assist children orphaned by HIV/AIDS. Has a written nondiscrimination policy covering sexual orientation but not gender identity. Does not offer insurance coverage to employees' domestic partners. www.cadburyschweppes.com

Campbell Soup Company

CONTRIBUTIONS: TOTAL: *$22,800* DEM: *$3,704* REP: *$18,936*
Paid a substantial fine to settle a federal Clean Air Act violation in 2004. Foundation supports educational, cultural, and residential projects that promote sustainable development in areas of corporate presence. Has a written nondiscrimination policy covering sexual orientation and plans to add gender identity. Offers insurance coverage to employees' domestic partners. www.campbellsoup.com

Capricorn Management, G.P.
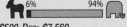
CONTRIBUTIONS: TOTAL: *$8,060* DEM: *$500* REP: *$7,560*
Current managing general partner was the head of the finance committee on Enron's board of directors. www.capricornholdings.com

Cargill, Incorporated
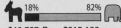
CONTRIBUTIONS: TOTAL: *$261,934* DEM: *$46,737* REP: *$215,189*
Largest privately held firm in the United States. The International Labor Rights Fund sued Cargill, Incorporated, and other multinationals in 2005 alleging industry complicity in trafficking, torture, and forced labor of children working in cocoa harvesting/

processing. Sued with other large poultry producers for violations of the Comprehensive Environmental Response Compensation and Liability Act, state and federal nuisance laws, and Oklahoma Environmental Quality and Agriculture rules. Paid $24 million in a class action settlement for fixing the price of corn-based sweeteners. Paid $7.7 million in a suit for misrepresenting animal feed. Recalled 8,500 tons of poultry in a 2004 *Listeria* scare. Outreach supports higher education, housing, food, and environmental stewardship. Has a written nondiscrimination policy covering sexual orientation and gender identity. Offers health insurance coverage to employees' domestic partners. www.cargill.com

Cargill Meat Solutions, Inc.

CONTRIBUTIONS: TOTAL: *$3,000* DEM: *$136* REP: *$2,864*

Subsidiary of Cargill, Incorporated (p. 75). Recalled 45,000 pounds of ground beef due to possible *Escherichia coli (E. coli)* contamination in April 2004. Has a written nondiscrimination policy covering sexual orientation and gender identity. Offers health insurance coverage to employees' domestic partners. www.excelmeats.com

Caribou Coffee Company Inc.

CONTRIBUTIONS: TOTAL: *$42,200* DEM: *$42,000* REP: *$200*

A class action lawsuit filed in 2005 by former Caribou managers alleges wage and overtime violations. Outreach supports environmental stewardship, medical, and educational programs in coffee-producing communities. Has a nondiscrimination policy that covers sexual orientation. Offers benefits for employees' domestic partners. www.cariboucoffee.com

Chocoladefabriken Lindt & Sprüngli AG
No contributions. Foreign owned. Was fined $57,750 by OSHA for "exposing workers to serious injury" following two accidents at its chocolate factory in New Hampshire. www.lindt.com

Clif Bar Inc.
No contributions. Company claims to use fair-trade and organic ingredients as well as environmentally sound production processes. Provides mind–body enrichment opportunities to employees and encourages volunteerism. Outreach supports environmental stewardship. www.clifbar.com

Coca-Cola Company, The

CONTRIBUTIONS: TOTAL: *$179,750* DEM: *$64,807* REP: *$114,943*

Named one of the "Worst Corporations of 2004" by *Multinational Monitor*, the company's record is filled with social and environmental abuses, especially in South America, where the company was accused of using paramilitary groups to kill union activists. Has also faced accusations of major environmental offenses at its plants in India, and was cited by Human

Rights Watch as encouraging child labor in El Salvador. Has made some efforts toward expanding AIDS treatment to workers at its African bottling plants. Ranked 26th on *Fortune* magazine's list of the "50 Best Companies for Minorities" in 2004. Has a written nondiscrimination policy covering sexual orientation but not gender identity. Offers health insurance coverage to employees' domestic partners. www.cocacola.com

ConAgra Foods, Inc.

CONTRIBUTIONS: TOTAL: *$231,500* DEM: *$31,081* REP: *$199,267*

Settled two fraud suits in 2005, one for $14 million. Sued for negligence by former workers with "popcorn worker's lung," a severe obstructive lung disease due to chronic exposure to diacetyl, a chemical used in making artificial butter flavoring. Pleaded guilty and paid a criminal fine for violating the Clean Water Act in Minnesota. A pending lawsuit brought by the state of Rhode Island seeks restitution for the public health effects of lead paint sold in the state. Outreach supports hunger cessation and food safety programs. Does not have a written nondiscrimination policy covering sexual orientation or gender identity. Refuses insurance coverage to employees' domestic partners. www.conagrafoods.com

Constellation Brands, Inc.

CONTRIBUTIONS: TOTAL: *$158,472* DEM: *$64,591* REP: *$93,881*

Settled a suit (for an undisclosed sum) alleging violations of the Americans with Disabilities Act in 2002. www.cbrands.com

CoolBrands International Inc.

CONTRIBUTIONS: TOTAL: *$4,000* DEM: *$0* REP: *$4,000*

Subsidiary of Capricorn Management, G.P. (p. 75). www.coolbrandsinternational.com

Costco Wholesale Corporation
See p. 142 in Major Retailers.

Cott Corporation
No contributions. A bitter contract dispute with a longtime can supplier in 2002 led to an out-of-court settlement for an undisclosed sum. Outreach supports educational programs. Its CEO donated his entire salary to a scholarship fund for the children of Cott Corporation employees. www.cott.com

Cumberland Packing Corp.
CONTRIBUTIONS: TOTAL: *$1,450* DEM: *$1,450* REP: *$0*

Sells saccharin (Sweet-N-Low), which has a long history of controversy since the 1970s when it was banned after being found to cause cancer in lab rats. The experiments were later found to be flawed. Other products, artificial butter flavorings, are suspected of being the cause of popcorn worker's lung (see ConAgra Foods, Inc., p. 77). Philanthropy sponsors the Brooklyn Museum. www.cpack.com

D'Agostino Supermarkets, Inc.

CONTRIBUTIONS: TOTAL: *$4,000* DEM: *$2,192* REP: *$1,802*

Privately held. One of four supermarket chains in New York City sued by the Legal Action Center for allegedly discriminating against homeless people by refusing to redeem bottles and cans for them. www.dagnyc.com

Dannon Company, Inc., The

No contributions. Subsidiary of foreign-owned Groupe Danone (p. 83). The FDA cited the company's Actimel product for violation of regulations and issues of compliance for potential false claims and health statements. The Federal Trade Commission (FTC) also came after the Dannon Company, Inc., for falsely implying that some flavors in its Pure Indulgence frozen yogurt line were low in fat and calories, resulting in a $150,000 penalty. www.dannon.com

Davide Campari-Milano S.p.A.

CONTRIBUTIONS: TOTAL: *$4,000* DEM: *$0* REP: *$4,000*

Foreign owned. Italian distributor for Brown-Forman Corporation's (p. 74) spirit portfolio. www.campari.com

Dean Foods Company

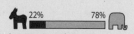

CONTRIBUTIONS: TOTAL: *$336,002* DEM: *$94,153* REP: *$241,841*

Exposed for country-of-origin labeling violations on its Birds Eye Foods, Inc., brand (p. 74). Fined $4 million in 1996 for repeated violation of the federal Clean Water Act. The company's White Wave Foods (p. 100) subsidiary uses wind energy in the production of soy foods. Community outreach supports health/nutrition, education, and environmental stewardship and conservation. Has a written nondiscrimination policy covering sexual orientation but not gender identity. Refuses health insurance coverage to employees' domestic partners. www.deanfoods.com

Delhaize America, Inc.

CONTRIBUTIONS: TOTAL: *$49,900* DEM: *$10,768* REP: *$39,129*

Subsidiary of Delhaize Group (p. 78). www.delhaizeamerica.com

Delhaize Group

CONTRIBUTIONS: TOTAL: *$49,900* DEM: *$10,768* REP: *$39,129*

Its Kash n' Karry Food Stores, Inc. (p. 86), subsidiary settled a 2003 class action sex discrimination case for $3.1 million. Its Food Lion, LLC (p. 81), subsidiary has a history of litigation over alleged food safety, overtime pay violations, and antiunion activities. Outreach supports hunger cessation, health care, and education. www.delhaizegroup.com

Del Monte Foods Company

 3% 97%

CONTRIBUTIONS: TOTAL: *$5,500* DEM: *$146* REP: *$5,349*

The company's recent record is marred by numerous pending lawsuits (along with other banana producers) over price-fixing; many charges of human rights violations have been made as well. A 2001 lawsuit filed by Earthrights International alleges that the company used violence and detention to deter organizers at its Guatemalan and Kenyan farms. As parent of StarKist, Del Monte Foods Company was named in a suit filed by the state of California against producers and retailers to require mercury warning labels on canned tuna. Outreach includes hunger relief, health care, and youth mentoring programs. Has a written nondiscrimination policy covering sexual orientation but not gender identity. www.delmonte.com

Diageo Chateau & Estate Wines Company, The

 97% 3%

CONTRIBUTIONS: TOTAL: *$27,500* DEM: *$26,642* REP: *$858*

Subsidiary of Diageo PLC (p. 79). www.aboutwines.com

Diageo North America

41% 59%

CONTRIBUTIONS: TOTAL: *$79,505* DEM: *$32,531* REP: *$46,974*

Subsidiary of Diageo PLC (p. 79). Diageo North America and other alcohol producers and distributors were sued by the Colombian government and several regional authorities for alleged unfair competition, racketeering, kickbacks, and money laundering. www.diageo.com

Diageo PLC

 55% 45%

CONTRIBUTIONS: TOTAL: *$107,005* DEM: *$59,173* REP: *$47,832*

Foreign owned. Settled a class action suit alleging its advertising campaigns were targeting juvenile consumers. Was sued for more than $1 billion for compensatory damages for the alleged 60-year violation of the Smirnoff trademark. Foundation supports (with more than $34 million annually) responsible drinking, microenterprise development, access to clean, safe drinking water, and disaster relief. www.diageo.co.uk

Dial Corporation

See p. 109 in Health and Beauty.

Diedrich Coffee, Inc.

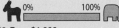 0% 100%

CONTRIBUTIONS: TOTAL: *$4,000* DEM: *$0* REP: *$4,000*

www.diedrich.com

Dillon Companies, Inc.

No contributions. Subsidiary of the Kroger Co. (p. 88). www.dillons.com

Dole Food Company, Inc.

5% 95%

CONTRIBUTIONS: TOTAL: *$73,000* DEM: *$4,000* REP: *$69,000*

Paid $1 million to settle a class action suit brought by employees who were not given proper notification of a plant closing in California. In 2002, Human Rights Watch reported that the company's Ecuadorian suppliers and subsidiaries employed children as young as nine, exposing them to pesticides and sexual harassment. Involved in ongoing litigation from workers exposed to the pesticide DBCP on banana and pineapple plantations in the 1970s. Uses organic farming methods for some banana production, but the CEO of Dow Chemical sits on its board of directors. Outreach supports environmental stewardship and social, educational, and cultural programs. Has a written nondiscrimination policy covering sexual orientation but not gender identity. Offers insurance coverage to employees' domestic partners. www.dole.com

Dreyer's Grand Ice Cream Holdings, Inc.

1% 99%

CONTRIBUTIONS: TOTAL: *$41,200* DEM: *$361* REP: *$40,839*

Outreach supports educational and family causes in communities where the company has a presence. www.dreyersinc.com

Dunkin' Brands, Inc.

0% 100%

CONTRIBUTIONS: TOTAL: *$5,000* DEM: *$0* REP: *$5,000*

Subsidiary of Allied Domecq PLC (p. 72). www.dunkinbrands.com

E. & J. Gallo Winery

85% 15%

CONTRIBUTIONS: TOTAL: *$101,381* DEM: *$85,960* REP: *$15,421*

The United Farm Workers union called a boycott of all products in 2005 following a failed contract negotiation for workers who have no benefits, live in primitive conditions, and receive no vacation time. Outreach supports education and causes in its local community. www.gallo.com

Energy Brands Inc.

No contributions. Privately held. www.energybrands.com

Ferolito, Vultaggio & Sons

0% 100%

CONTRIBUTIONS: TOTAL: *$1,000* DEM: *$0* REP: *$1,000*

Garnered national press for the legal battle it fought to use and brand the name *Crazy Horse* for its malt liquor despite protests from Native American groups and the namesake's estate. Pending a class action suit based on health claims made by the company for Rx Herbal Teas and some of its popular Arizona brand teas. The Center for Science in the Public Interest contends that barely detectable levels of herbal ingredients in the company's "herbal teas" constitute fraud. No information on outreach or benefit structure. www.arizonabev.com

Florida's Natural Growers
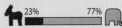
CONTRIBUTIONS: TOTAL: *$18,800* DEM: *$1,000* REP: *$17,800*
Privately held. www.floridanatural.com

Food 4 Less of Southern California, Inc.
No contributions. Subsidiary of the Kroger Co. (p. 88).
www.food4less1.com

Food Lion, LLC

CONTRIBUTIONS: TOTAL: *$46,400* DEM: *$10,672* REP: *$35,728*
Subsidiary of Delhaize America, Inc. (p. 78); parent, Delhaize
Group (p. 78). An extensive list of litigation in the 1990s sur-
rounds poor food-handling practices, questionable labor practices, and securities violations. In 1993, paid $16.3 million to
settle labor claims. Does not have a written nondiscrimination
policy covering sexual orientation or gender identity. Offers
insurance coverage to employees' domestic partners.
www.foodlion.com

Fortune Brands, Inc.
CONTRIBUTIONS: TOTAL: *$29,750* DEM: *$6,998* REP: *$22,752*
Accused with other alcohol producers in several class action
suits of encouraging and profiting from underage alcohol use.
Outreach supports education and social causes in communities where the company has a presence. Does not have a written nondiscrimination policy covering sexual orientation or
gender identity. Refuses insurance coverage to employees'
domestic partners. www.fortunebrands.com

Fred Meyer Stores, Inc.
No contributions. Subsidiary of the Kroger Co. (p. 88).
www.fredmeyerstores.com

Frito-Lay, Inc.
No contributions. Subsidiary of PepsiCo, Inc. (p. 92). Paid OSHA
$57,000 in fines following the drowning death of an employee
who slipped and fell into a vat of vegetable oil. Has a written
nondiscrimination policy covering sexual orientation and gender identity. Offers insurance coverage to employees' domestic
partners. www.fritolay.com

Fry's Food & Drug Stores
No contributions. Subsidiary of the Kroger Co. (p. 88). Settled
violations of the federal Racketeer Influence and Corrupt
Organizations Act (RICO) lawsuit for $5.1 million.
www.frysfood.com

General Mills, Inc.

CONTRIBUTIONS: TOTAL: *$193,522* DEM: *$44,506* REP: *$148,976*
The Physician's Committee for Responsible Medicine submitted
a petition in August 2005 to the FDA against dairy producers,

including General Mills, Inc., and the Dannon Company, Inc. (p. 78), for making unqualified health claims that dairy consumption promotes weight and fat loss. Many of its products contain genetically modified ingredients, and the company recently spent almost $90,000 to defeat an Oregon measure that would have required that such foods be labeled. Is also fighting a proposal by Senator Tom Harkin (D-Iowa) for federal oversight over the way companies market unhealthy food to children. As a member of the Grocery Manufacturers of America, a powerful lobbying group, General Mills, Inc., spends millions to influence governmental diet recommendations and other food issues. Has provided more than five million free books inside cereal boxes, and donates to nonprofit organizations focused on education and increasing literacy. Has a written nondiscrimination policy that covers sexual orientation and gender identity. Offers insurance coverage to employees' domestic partners. www.GeneralMills.com

Ghirardelli Chocolate Company
No contributions. Subsidiary of Chocoladefabriken Lindt & Sprüngli AG (p. 76). www.ghirardelli.com

Godiva Chocolatier, Inc.
No contributions. Subsidiary of Campbell Soup Company (p. 75). www.godiva.com

Gorton's of Gloucester
14% — 86%

CONTRIBUTIONS: TOTAL: *$1,500* DEM: *$211* REP: *$1,289*
Privately held. Has a written nondiscrimination policy covering sexual orientation but not gender identity. www.gortons.com

Goya Foods, Inc.
0% — 100%

CONTRIBUTIONS: TOTAL: *$32,800* DEM: *$0* REP: *$32,800*
Was issued a warning by the FDA for false and misleading labeling. Found guilty of 40 unfair labor practices and ordered to reinstate four workers and begin negotiations with the union after the workers had been fired for seeking better working conditions. Outreach supports Hispanic culture, community building, and leadership. www.goya.com

Great Atlantic & Pacific Tea Company, Inc., The
0% — 100%

CONTRIBUTIONS: TOTAL: *$1,000* DEM: *$0* REP: *$1,000*
Named with other New York grocers in several class action lawsuits for violations of the Fair Labor Standards Act, settling one for $3.1 million. One of four supermarket chains in New York City sued by the Legal Action Center for allegedly discriminating against homeless people by refusing to redeem bottles and cans. Outreach supports education and community building. www.aptea.com

Green Mountain Coffee Roasters, Inc.

CONTRIBUTIONS: TOTAL: *$18,500* DEM: *$18,500* REP: *$0*

Purchases up to 50% of its coffee from fair-trade-identified farms and cooperatives. Grants 100 stock options to all full-time employees after their first year of employment. Offers training in financial literacy. Was commended for the design and efficiency of its "green" roasting facility in Vermont. Was the 1994 recipient of the Deane C. Davis Award for community participation, employee recognition, and environmental concern and action. www.GreenMountainCoffee.com

Groupe Danone

No contributions. The Physician's Committee for Responsible Medicine submitted a petition in August 2005 to the FDA against dairy producers, specifically its subsidiary the Dannon Company, Inc. (p. 78), for making unqualified health claims that dairy consumption promotes weight and fat loss. Outreach supports environmental stewardship and educational programs. www.danonegroup.com

Hain Celestial Group

CONTRIBUTIONS: TOTAL: *$2,000* DEM: *$2,000* REP: *$0*

Withdrew a pledge to abandon genetically modified organisms in 2001. Makes products with ingredients that are grown without artificial pesticides, fertilizers, or chemicals. Has an extremely strict supplier verification program. Has a written nondiscrimination policy covering sexual orientation but not gender identity. Offers insurance coverage to employees' domestic partners. www.hain-celestial.com

Hannaford Bros. Co.

CONTRIBUTIONS: TOTAL: *$500* DEM: *$0* REP: *$500*

Subsidiary of Delhaize America, Inc. (p. 78); parent, Delhaize Group (p. 78). Outreach includes environmental stewardship, health care, and educational programs in communities where the company has a presence. Has a written nondiscrimination policy covering sexual orientation but not gender identity. Offers insurance coverage to employees' domestic partners. www.hannaford.com

Hansen Natural Corporation

No contributions. Outreach supports breast cancer research. www.hansens.com

H. E. Butt Grocery Company

CONTRIBUTIONS: TOTAL: *$13,750* DEM: *$7,750* REP: *$6,000*

Entered into several discrimination and harassment settlements in the 1990s. Paid $1 million each in settlement to two families whose children were sexually molested in separate incidences by an employee in the grocery store. Outreach supports education and hunger cessation in communities where the company has a presence. Has a written nondiscrimination policy covering sexual orientation but not gender identity. Refuses insurance coverage to employees' domestic partners. www.heb.com

Heineken N.V.

 24% | 76%

CONTRIBUTIONS: TOTAL: *$43,250* DEM: *$10,269* REP: *$32,981*

Named with other alcohol producers in several suits for encouraging alcohol consumption by minors through advertising and entertainment tie-ins. Outreach supports HIV/AIDS education. www.heinekeninternational.com

Heineken USA Inc.

 24% | 76%

CONTRIBUTIONS: TOTAL: *$43,250* DEM: *$10,269* REP: *$32,981*

Subsidiary of Heineken N.V. (p. 84). Outreach supports HIV/AIDS education. Has a written nondiscrimination policy covering sexual orientation but not gender identity. Offers insurance coverage to employees' domestic partners. www.heineken.com

Hershey Foods Corporation

4% | 96%

CONTRIBUTIONS: TOTAL: *$37,750* DEM: *$1,415* REP: *$36,295*

Boycotted in 2003 for alleged racial discrimination in hiring practices and "gross indifference" to the needs and economic troubles of local minorities. Sued by the American Environmental Safety Institute for allowing high levels of lead and cadmium in its products, though the California attorney general later reported that such levels are naturally occurring. Paid an $85,000 settlement to the FTC for violations of the Children's Online Privacy Protection Act for soliciting personal information from children over the Internet without parental permission. Provides subsidized child care in-house, flextime, telecommuting, job-share options, and extensive family leave. Has a written nondiscrimination policy covering sexual orientation but not gender identity. www.hersheys.com

H. J. Heinz Company

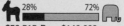 28% | 72%

CONTRIBUTIONS: TOTAL: *$207,538* DEM: *$58,515* REP: *$149,023*

Paid a $13,100 fine to the EPA for a chemical-related violation following failure to disclose a release of anhydrous ammonia. Spilled 1,500 gallons of corrosive sodium hydroxide—its second major hazardous materials spill in less than six months. Fined $200,000 following an OSHA violation that resulted in the death of an employee at a Canadian production facility. Faces controversies over its marketing of breast milk substitutes, baby food, snack foods aimed at children, and infant formula. Outreach supports research into methods to treat childhood anemia. Has a written nondiscrimination policy covering sexual orientation but not gender identity. Refuses insurance coverage to employees' domestic partners. www.heinz.com

Horizon Organic Holding Corporation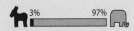
CONTRIBUTIONS: TOTAL: *$1,000* DEM: *$86* REP: *$914*
Subsidiary of Dean Foods Company (p. 78).
www.horizonorganic.com

Hormel Foods Corporation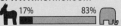
CONTRIBUTIONS: TOTAL: *$5,500* DEM: *$170* REP: *$5,314*
Subsidiary Jennie-O was sued in 2004 for failing to pay workers for full meal breaks and time spent changing into safety gear. Subsidiary Mountain Prairie Farms was fined $116,000 for safety and environmental violations on its Colorado hog farm. Has a written nondiscrimination policy covering sexual orientation but not gender identity. Refuses insurance coverage to employees' domestic partners. www.hormel.com

Hy-Vee, Inc.
CONTRIBUTIONS: TOTAL: *$18,250* DEM: *$3,027* REP: *$15,207*
Privately held. www.hy-vee.com

IGA, Inc.
CONTRIBUTIONS: TOTAL: *$12,275* DEM: *$960* REP: *$11,285*
Privately held. www.igainc.com

Ilitch Holdings, Inc.
See p. 164 in Restaurants.

InBev
No contributions. Foreign owned. Foundation supports science, education, and the arts. www.inbev.com

InBev USA
No contributions. Subsidiary of InBev (p. 85). Foreign owned. www.inbev.com

International Multifoods Corporation
CONTRIBUTIONS: TOTAL: *$1,500* DEM: *$128* REP: *$1,361*
Subsidiary of the J. M. Smucker Company (p. 86). Has a written nondiscrimination policy covering sexual orientation but not gender identity. www.multifoods.com

Interstate Bakeries Corporation
CONTRIBUTIONS: TOTAL: *$3,050* DEM: *$15* REP: *$3,035*
Shareholders filed a class action lawsuit against management for manipulating financial records and misleading investors, settling for $18 million in 2005. Has a written nondiscrimination policy covering sexual orientation but not gender identity.

Refuses insurance coverage to employees' domestic partners.
www.interstatebakeriescorp.com

Jamba Juice Company

CONTRIBUTIONS: TOTAL: *$1,500* DEM: *$1,500* REP: *$0*

Fined $18,560 by the state of California OSHA for employee safety violations and failure to report serious injury. Outreach supports environmental stewardship, physical fitness, and nutrition education efforts. Offers insurance coverage to employees' domestic partners. www.jambajuice.com

Jewel-Osco
No contributions. Subsidiary of Albertsons, Inc. (p. 72).
www.jewelosco.com

Jim Beam Brands Worldwide, Inc.

CONTRIBUTIONS: TOTAL: *$29,750* DEM: *$6,998* REP: *$22,752*

Subsidiary of Fortune Brands, Inc. (p. 81). Named with other alcohol producers in several suits for encouraging alcohol consumption by minors. Under pressure from unions and public backlash, rescinded a policy restricting bottling line workers in Kentucky to only four breaks per shift.
www.jimbeambrandsworldwide.com

J. M. Smucker Company, The

CONTRIBUTIONS: TOTAL: *$72,000* DEM: *$978* REP: *$70,931*

Report released in 2005 found that the company's jams advertised as "100% fruit" were often less than 50% fruit. OSHA opened a safety investigation when replacement workers called in to work through a strike caused a 4,000-gallon tank to topple in 2002. Selected by *Fortune* magazine as a top company to work for in America in 2003. Outreach supports education. Has a written nondiscrimination policy covering sexual orientation but not gender identity. www.smucker.com

Jones Soda Co.
No contributions. www.jonessoda.com

J. W. Childs Associates, L.P.

CONTRIBUTIONS: TOTAL: *$193,000* DEM: *$1,000* REP: *$192,000*
www.jwchilds.com

Kash n' Karry Food Stores, Inc.

CONTRIBUTIONS: TOTAL: *$3,000* DEM: *$96* REP: *$2,901*

Subsidiary of Delhaize America, Inc. (p. 78); parent, Delhaize Group (p. 78). Settled a class action sex discrimination suit for $3.1 million in 2003. Accused of violating child labor laws by the U.S. Department of Labor, fined $46,000 in civil penalties, and barred from any further violations. Also cited for 19 violations of mislabeling foreign-grown produce as local and selling adulterated beef. Outreach includes early education in communities where the company has a presence. No information on benefit structure. www.kashnkarry.com

Kellogg Company

CONTRIBUTIONS: TOTAL: *$126,606* DEM: *$43,614* REP: *$82,992*

Snack food ads geared toward children prompted calls for restrictions and closer monitoring of the industry. Created, with three other food companies, the Alliance for American Advertising, a lobbying group that disputes any linkage between advertising and childhood obesity. Cited for enclosing toys containing mercury batteries in cereal boxes. Fined $20,110 by the EPA for a hazardous chemical release and failure to report the release of 820 pounds of anhydrous ammonia from a faulty rooftop refrigeration system. Fined $40,000 by the EPA when its Mrs. Smith's Frozen Foods subsidiary released 2,600 pounds of ammonia over a two-day period from a faulty safety valve. Supports the Alliance for Youth founded by General Colin Powell to strengthen the character and competence of America's youth. Has a written nondiscrimination policy covering sexual orientation but not gender identity. Offers insurance coverage to employees' domestic partners only in some subsidiaries. www.kelloggcompany.com

Kellogg Snacks Division

No contributions. Subsidiary of Kellogg Company (p. 87). Has a written nondiscrimination policy covering sexual orientation but not gender identity. Offers insurance coverage to employees' domestic partners only in some subsidiaries. www.keebler.com

Kendall-Jackson Wine Estates, Ltd.

CONTRIBUTIONS: TOTAL: *$10,500* DEM: *$6,000* REP: *$4,500*

Privately held. Cleared and uprooted 600 acres of old-growth oak trees in California, prompting local officials to put a land stewardship proposition on the ballot. Offers insurance coverage to employees' domestic partners. www.kj.com

Kraft Foods Inc.

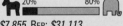

CONTRIBUTIONS: TOTAL: *$38,968* DEM: *$7,855* REP: *$31,113*

Controlled (85%) by the Altria Group Inc. (p. 72), though spun off as a subsidiary in 2001. Helped create a lobbying group, the Alliance for American Advertising, primarily to dispute any link between advertising targeted toward youth and childhood obesity. Outreach supports projects focused on world hunger and healthy lifestyles. Has a written nondiscrimination policy covering sexual orientation and gender identity. Offers insurance coverage to employees' domestic partners. www.kraft.com

Kroger Co., The

CONTRIBUTIONS: TOTAL: *$21,000* DEM: *$2,102* REP: *$18,895*

Has two lawsuits pending that allege violation of California antitrust law following an alliance with Albertsons, Inc., and Safeway Inc. that required all three companies to lock out union employees if a strike were called. Paid $30.6 million to six employees who alleged sexual harassment in 2002. Donated approximately $42 million in food and products to America's Second Harvest, an organization working to alleviate hunger in the United States. Has a written nondiscrimination policy covering sexual orientation but not gender identity. Refuses insurance coverage to employees' domestic partners. www.kroger.com

Lindt & Sprüngli (USA) Inc.

No contributions. Subsidiary of Chocoladefabriken Lindt & Sprüngli AG (p. 76). Was fined by OSHA in 1997 for extensive serious safety violations at its chocolate factory in New Hampshire. www.lindtusa.com

LVMH Moët Hennessy Louis Vuitton SA

CONTRIBUTIONS: TOTAL: *$31,750* DEM: *$31,500* REP: *$250*

Foreign owned. Has a pending trade union dispute over retail job futures in France. Has sourced products from countries with widespread, well-documented human and labor rights abuses. www.lvmh.com

Mars, Incorporated

No contributions. In late 2004, a Mexican subsidiary was forced to halt the sale of its products because they contained a dangerously high level of lead. A subsidiary in Thailand (manufacturers of Pedigree and Whiskas cat and dog foods) prompted apologies following the discovery of molds in its products alleged to be responsible for renal and kidney failure in pets. To avoid legislation that would have forced chocolate companies to label their products with "slave-free" labels, the industry agreed to a voluntary protocol to end abusive and forced child labor on cocoa farms by 2005. www.mars.com

McDonald's Corporation

See p. 165 in Restaurants.

Meijer, Inc.

CONTRIBUTIONS: TOTAL: *$22,875* DEM: *$2,134* REP: *$20,729*

Escaped paying a fine imposed by the Indiana Election Commission for admitting it had given too much cash to three legislative candidates, who later returned the money. Settled a sexual harassment lawsuit for $600,000 when a jury determined that management was negligent in having ignored the victim's multiple complaints. Forced to allow employees to wear union insignia while on the job after the company violated the National Labor Relations Act by taking disciplinary action on employees who wore union pins. Outreach supports education. Does not have a written nondiscrimination policy covering sexual orientation or gender identity. Refuses insurance coverage to employees' domestic partners. www.meijer.com

Miller Brewing Company
CONTRIBUTIONS: TOTAL: *$93,500* DEM: *$41,515* REP: *$51,985*

Named with other alcohol producers in several suits for encouraging alcohol consumption by minors. Several informal boycotts were called by interest groups due to racially discriminatory advertising or language printed on its products. Has too many union disputes with distributors and laborers to list. Outreach supports HIV/AIDS education and alcohol education in communities where the company has a presence. Has a written nondiscrimination policy covering sexual orientation and gender identity. Offers insurance coverage to employees' domestic partners. www.millerbrewing.com

Molson Coors Brewing Company
CONTRIBUTIONS: TOTAL: *$133,700* DEM: *$28,977* REP: *$104,723*

Before its merger with Molson, Coors Brewing Company had numerous civil rights violations and citations for unfair labor practices. Funds voter advertising, recently giving at least $100,000 to influence a California vote allowing for personal data collection and supporting a referendum in Michigan banning affirmative action. Has donated money to conservative watchdog groups that target universities over the use of race in admissions policies. Boycotts were called in 2002 citing unfair treatment of workers after Coors Brewing Company locked them out when the union rejected a contract deal. Has been the target of boycotts called by affirmative action advocates. Agreed to a $71,000 fine for violations stemming from an explosion at a Virginia plant that killed two workers. Has a written nondiscrimination policy covering sexual orientation and gender identity. Offers insurance coverage to employees' domestic partners. www.molsoncoors.com

Mrs. Fields' Original Cookies, Inc.
CONTRIBUTIONS: TOTAL: *$560* DEM: *$0* REP: *$560*

Subsidiary of Capricorn Management, G.P. (p. 75). Paid a $100,000 settlement to the FTC for violations of the Children's Online Privacy Protection Act for soliciting personal information from children over the Internet without parental permission. www.mrsfields.com

Murphy-Brown LLC

CONTRIBUTIONS: TOTAL: *$5,700* DEM: *$1,090* REP: *$4,610*

Subsidiary of Smithfield Foods, Inc. (p. 96). Received International Certification Service ISO 14001 environmental management status in 2001, though environmental complaints in the vicinity of its Raleigh, North Carolina, processing plant have not diminished. Cited for releasing nitrogen-rich wastewater into local rivers. Devotes research money to documenting and reducing antibiotic use in pork, as well as eliminating use of human-grade antibiotics. www.smithfieldfoods.com

Naked Juice Company

No contributions. Subsidiary of North Castle Partners, a private equity firm. Privately held. Formerly Ultimate Juice Company. www.nakedjuice.com

National Grape Cooperative Association, Inc.

CONTRIBUTIONS: TOTAL: *$4,700* DEM: *$0* REP: *$4,700*

Terminated the memberships of grape suppliers in an alleged price-fixing scheme to reduce supply and fraudulently increase prices. Was honored by the EPA in 2002 for implementing an environmental pesticide and integrated pest management program toward advancing pollution prevention. www.nationalgrape.com

Nestlé S.A.

CONTRIBUTIONS: TOTAL: *$70,850* DEM: *$22,410* REP: *$47,419*

The International Labor Rights Fund sued Nestlé S.A. and other multinationals in 2005 alleging industry complicity in trafficking, torture, and forced labor of children working in cocoa harvesting/processing. A pending suit in Puerto Rico alleges Nestlé S.A. sought fraudulently to monopolize the ice cream market on the island, leaving a local supplier with millions of dollars in losses. Gained notoriety in the late 1970s for its aggressive marketing of infant formula in developing countries, inspiring an international boycott that, after a brief respite in the 1990s, remains to this day. The U.S. division produces and sells unlabeled foods containing genetically modified ingredients, including infant formulas. Outreach supports nutrition education, hunger cessation, HIV/AIDS education, and agricultural assistance. www.nestle.com

Nestlé USA, Inc.

CONTRIBUTIONS: TOTAL: *$70,850* DEM: *$22,410* REP: *$47,419*

Subsidiary of Nestlé S.A. (p. 90). Was fined $32,500 for three serious offenses and one repeat offense by OSHA for inadequate training of employees after an employee fell to his death. Refuses insurance coverage to employees' domestic partners. www.nestleusa.com

Newman's Own, Inc.

100%   0%

CONTRIBUTIONS: TOTAL: *$77,000* DEM: *$76,790* REP: *$210*

Privately held. All after-tax profits and royalties go to charity, supporting causes such as the Hole in the Wall Gang camps for ill children, UNICEF, and Habitat for Humanity. www.newmansown.com

Nippon Suisan Kaisha, Ltd.

14%   86%

CONTRIBUTIONS: TOTAL: *$1,500* DEM: *$211* REP: *$1,289*

Foreign owned. Outreach supports environmental education. www.nissui.co.jp

NutraSweet Company, The

No contributions. Subsidiary of J. W. Childs Associates, L.P. (p. 86). Named in a $350 million class action suit alleging the company suppressed research that had found serious detrimental health effects associated with aspartame (the generic name for NutraSweet). www.nutrasweet.com

Ocean Spray Cranberries, Inc.

55%   45%

CONTRIBUTIONS: TOTAL: *$16,500* DEM: *$8,993* REP: *$7,508*

A pending class action suit alleges six counts of antitrust violations and using market dominance and monopolistic tactics to cripple its competitors. Uses methane gas from a nearby landfill to power its manufacturing operation in Wisconsin. www.oceanspray.com

Odwalla, Inc.

No contributions. Subsidiary of the Coca-Cola Company (p. 76). Supports community projects with a small grant program. www.odwalla.com

Pathmark Stores, Inc.

10%   90%

CONTRIBUTIONS: TOTAL: *$2,000* DEM: *$192* REP: *$1,802*

Outreach supports children's causes, coat drives, and hunger relief. Has a written nondiscrimination policy covering sexual orientation but not gender identity. Refuses insurance coverage to employees' domestic partners. www.pathmark.com

Peapod, LLC

No contributions. Subsidiary of Ahold USA, Inc. (p. 71); parent, Royal Ahold N.V. (p. 94). www.peapod.com

Pepperidge Farm, Inc.

0%   100%

CONTRIBUTIONS: TOTAL: *$800* DEM: *$4* REP: *$796*

Subsidiary of the Campbell Soup Company (p. 75). Largest corporate supporter of the United Way. Also supports Habitat for Humanity. www.pepperidgefarm.com

PepsiCo, Inc.

CONTRIBUTIONS: TOTAL: *$393,726* DEM: *$121,891* REP: *$271,819*

Has come under fire in India for major environmental problems caused by its bottling plants. Opposed deposit legislation endorsed by environmental groups. Asked its suppliers to discontinue the use of genetically modified seed, but gave $127,000 to defeat an Oregon measure that would require the labeling of genetically modified foods. Received top scores from the Human Rights Campaign 2004 Corporate Equality Index for its progay, -lesbian, -bisexual, and -transgender policies. Has a written nondiscrimination policy that covers sexual orientation and gender identity. Offers insurance coverage to employees' domestic partners. www.pepsico.com

Perdue Farms, Inc.

CONTRIBUTIONS: TOTAL: *$17,312* DEM: *$10,576* REP: *$6,735*

Recently agreed to $20 million in back pay to settle a class action lawsuit brought by employees and to change a company policy requiring workers to don protective clothing off the clock. Has a long history of environmental violations, labor union clashes over the treatment of workers, wage and hour disputes, and worker safety/injuries. Has been accused of animal cruelty from activists and in governmental investigations. Outreach includes partnership with America's Second Harvest, United Way, March of Dimes, and Relay for Life. Has a partnership with the Poultry Welfare Program and an on-site program to help ensure humane treatment. www.perdue.com

Pernod Ricard

CONTRIBUTIONS: TOTAL: *$70,540* DEM: *$20,002* REP: *$50,538*

Foreign owned. www.pernod-ricard.com/fr

Pernod Ricard USA

CONTRIBUTIONS: TOTAL: *$9,500* DEM: *$6,475* REP: *$3,025*

Subsidiary of Pernod Ricard (p. 92). Pernod Ricard USA and other producers and distributors were sued by the Colombian government and several regional authorities for alleged unfair competition, racketeering, kickbacks, and money laundering. www.pernod-ricardusa.com

Pinnacle Foods Group Inc.

No contributions. Subsidiary of J. W. Childs Associates, L.P. (p. 86). Settled with the Center for Science in the Public Interest over false labeling on its Aunt Jemima products. www.pinnaclefoodscorp.com

Procter & Gamble

See p. 116 in Health and Beauty.

Publix Super Markets, Inc.

CONTRIBUTIONS: TOTAL: *$21,000* DEM: *$2,288* REP: *$18,703*

Settled a suit charging noncompliance with the Americans with Disabilities Act by paying $260,000 in August 2005. Outreach supports Special Olympics, children's issues, and hunger relief. Has a written nondiscrimination policy covering sexual orientation but not gender identity. Refuses insurance coverage to employees' domestic partners. www.publix.com

QTG (Quaker Foods/ Tropicana/Gatorade)

CONTRIBUTIONS: TOTAL: *$3,500* DEM: *$3,500* REP: *$0*

Subsidiary of PepsiCo, Inc. (p. 92). Has a written nondiscrimination policy covering sexual orientation and gender identity. Offers insurance coverage to employees' domestic partners. www.pepsi-qtg.com

Quality Food Centers, Inc.

No contributions. Subsidiary of Fred Meyer Stores, Inc. (p. 81); parent, the Kroger Co. (p. 88). A pending lawsuit charges failure to warn customers who had purchased meat recalled due to potential contamination with deadly bovine spongiform encephalopathy, or mad cow disease. A pending class action suit alleges that the grocery chain failed to properly label farmed salmon as containing artificial coloring. www.qfconline.com

R.A.B. Holdings, Inc.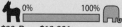

CONTRIBUTIONS: TOTAL: *$9,500* DEM: *$1,500* REP: *$8,000*

Sued by 10 deaf employees for alleged discrimination and civil rights violations for allowing safety hazards and shutting them out of contract negotiations because the company failed to provide sign language interpreters. Agreed to a $1 million fine after pleading no contest to antitrust violations in its matzo marketing. www.rabfoodgroup.com

Raley's Inc.

CONTRIBUTIONS: TOTAL: *$19,000* DEM: *$96* REP: *$18,901*

Sued for violating contract terms in a lawsuit bought by the United Wholesaler & Retailers union on behalf of its member employees. Outreach supports hunger relief efforts in communities where the company has a presence. www.raleys.com

Ralphs Grocery Company

No contributions. Subsidiary of the Kroger Co. (p. 88). One of three companies sued in a class action suit for failure to pay overtime to 2,000 union janitors and responsible for part of a $22.4 million settlement. Sued by unions and the Industry International Pension Fund for failing to make contractual contributions to the fund. www.ralphs.com

Randall's Food & Drugs, LP

CONTRIBUTIONS: TOTAL: *$4,000* DEM: *$0* REP: *$4,000*

Subsidiary of Safeway Inc. (p. 95). A Dallas store was found to have sold adulterated "beef" (containing 25% other meat products) in violation of state law, as exposed on NBC's *Dateline*. Received a "good corporate citizen" award by the Sanitation District of Los Angeles County for consistent compliance with all of its wastewater discharge requirements. Has a written nondiscrimination policy covering sexual orientation but not gender identity. Refuses insurance coverage to employees' domestic partners. www.randalls.com

Reckitt Benckiser Inc.

See p. 135 in Home and Garden.

Red Bull GmbH

No contributions. The Swedish government opened an investigation into the safety of Red Bull energy drink after three people died allegedly due to the consumption of Red Bull combined with alcohol or to excessive consumption after exercise. Outreach supports a yearly music academy, and break dancing and stunt competitions. www.redbull.com

Robert Mondavi Corporation, The

CONTRIBUTIONS: TOTAL: *$12,972* DEM: *$6,473* REP: *$6,499*

Subsidiary of Constellation Brands, Inc. (p. 77). Paid $120,000 in fines and agreed to spend $30,000 to educate the wine industry on illegal gratuities following an independent counsel investigation of its relationship with former agriculture secretary Mike Espy. Has sustainable farming, biodiversity, and environmental conservation programs. Outreach sponsors events to benefit local cultural organizations and research into wine cultivation and refinement. www.robertmondavi.com

Royal Ahold N.V.

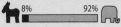

CONTRIBUTIONS: TOTAL: *$10,950* DEM: *$907* REP: *$10,039*

Foreign owned. Awaiting trial in a class action lawsuit filed by U.S. shareholders alleging the company overstated its earnings over three years by $1.2 billion. Settled an SEC complaint against its U.S. Foodservice subsidiary alleging fraud and insider trading surrounding a scheme to overstate earnings, consenting to permanent injunctions and payment of $332,000 in fines. Outreach supports environmental stewardship and social issues in areas where the company has a presence. No information on benefit structure or legal, environmental, or labor issues. www.ahold.com

Russell Stover Candies Inc.

CONTRIBUTIONS: TOTAL: *$64,500* DEM: *$0* REP: *$64,500*

Privately held. No information on outreach, benefit structure, environmental impact, or legal or labor issues. www.russellstover.com

SABMiller plc

CONTRIBUTIONS: TOTAL: *$93,500* DEM: *$41,515* REP: *$51,985*

Foreign owned. Its purchase by South African Breweries in 2002 produced SABMiller plc. See Miller Brewing Company (p. 89) for its U.S. contribution record. Former parent Altria Group Inc. (p. 72) still owns nearly 34% of SABMiller. A pending class action suit alleges that the brewer violates California law by promoting and facilitating underage drinking with reckless disregard for human life and public well-being. Outreach supports public health initiatives, education, and environmental stewardship. www.sabmiller.com

Safeway Inc.

CONTRIBUTIONS: TOTAL: *$259,750* DEM: *$72,286* REP: *$187,461*

Faces two pending lawsuits alleging violation of California antitrust law following an alliance with Albertsons, Inc., and the Kroger Co./Ralphs Grocery Company that required all three companies to lock out union employees if a strike were called. One of three companies sued in a class action suit for failure to pay overtime to 2,000 union janitors and responsible for part of a $22.4 million settlement. Donated nearly $100 million in 2003 to support hunger relief, education, and medical research. Has a written nondiscrimination policy covering sexual orientation but not gender identity. Refuses insurance coverage to employees' domestic partners. www.safeway.com

S&C Holdco 3, Inc.

CONTRIBUTIONS: TOTAL: *$29,750* DEM: *$17,000* REP: *$12,750*

Privately held.

Sara Lee Bakery Group

CONTRIBUTIONS: TOTAL: *$250* DEM: *$1* REP: *$249*

Subsidiary of Sara Lee Corporation (p. 95). The EPA fined its Earthgrains division $5.25 million for "the largest-ever corporate-wide violations" of ozone protection regulations. Foundation supports women's issues, housing, and hunger relief. Has a written nondiscrimination policy covering sexual orientation but not gender identity. Offers insurance coverage to employees' domestic partners. www.saraleebakery.com

Sara Lee Corporation

CONTRIBUTIONS: TOTAL: *$5,650* DEM: *$4,624* REP: *$1,026*

Paid $310,000 in fines and agreed to upgrade its wastewater treatment system for allegedly exceeding effluent release levels more than 1,500 times in a one-year period at a poultry-processing facility in Michigan. Foundation supports women's issues, housing, and hunger relief. Has a written nondiscrimination policy covering sexual orientation but not gender identity. Offers insurance coverage to employees' domestic partners. www.saralee.com

Sara Lee Foods  14% 86%
CONTRIBUTIONS: TOTAL: *$900* DEM: *$122* REP: *$778*
Subsidiary of Sara Lee Corporation (p. 95). Paid $3.5 million to settle 139 racial discrimination suits filed by employees of its Hygrade plant in Philadelphia. Paid a $200,000 fine and pleaded guilty to two misdemeanors in 2001 for causing 21 deaths and 100 injuries due to *Listeria*-contaminated Ball Park hot dogs in 1998. Has a written nondiscrimination policy covering sexual orientation but not gender identity. Offers insurance coverage to employees' domestic partners. www.saralee.com

Schwan Food Company, The  15% 85%
CONTRIBUTIONS: TOTAL: *$75,950* DEM: *$11,696* REP: *$64,255*
Called a nationwide recall of multiple frozen food products in 2005 after finding that they might be contaminated with small shards of glass. Outreach supports the United Way. www.schwans.com

Seed Restaurant Group, Inc.
No contributions.

Skyy Spirits, LLC  0% 100%
CONTRIBUTIONS: TOTAL: *$4,000* DEM: *$0* REP: *$4,000*
Subsidiary of Davide Campari-Milano, S.p.A. (p. 78). Agreed to revise an ad featuring a woman in see-through clothing in violation of the advertising code. Named with other alcohol producers in several suits for encouraging alcohol consumption by minors through advertising and entertainment tie-ins. www.skyy.com

Smithfield Foods, Inc.  6% 94%
CONTRIBUTIONS: TOTAL: *$363,200* DEM: *$22,898* REP: *$340,302*
Paid a $12.6 million fine in 1997 for discharge of wastewater and pollutants. Cited by Human Rights Watch in a 2005 report for widespread safety problems and failure to train workers properly. Paid $24,000 in fines in 2005 after inspections found 50 safety violations. Settled with the state of North Carolina for $65 million and agreed to upgrade its wastewater treatment facility. Was exposed for union-busting tactics, including forced termination and systematic suppression, in testimony before a Senate committee, bringing about a ruling of 400-plus pages for massive violations of federal law and conspiracy to instigate violence. Outreach supports education. Devoted $15 mil-

lion for research into better and safer methods of hog waste disposal. Has a written nondiscrimination policy covering sexual orientation but not gender identity. Refuses insurance coverage to employees' domestic partners.
www.smithfieldfoods.com

Smith's Food & Drug Centers, Inc.
No contributions. Subsidiary of Fred Meyer Stores, Inc. (p. 81); parent, the Kroger Co. (p. 88). A pending suit alleges failure to accommodate an employee with asthma under the American with Disabilities Act. www.smithsfoodanddrug.com

Smoothie King Franchises, Inc.
No contributions. www.smoothieking.com

Snapple Beverage Corporation
No contributions. Subsidiary of Cadbury Schweppes plc (p. 75). Has been criticized for encouraging high-sugar drink consumption and childhood obesity in elementary and middle schools. www.snapple.com

South Beach Beverage Company
No contributions. Subsidiary of PepsiCo, Inc. (p. 92). Paid a $219,000 penalty to settle charges of false advertising for claims on packaging that consumption would stop illness, enhance memory, or reduce stress. Has a written nondiscrimination policy covering sexual orientation and gender identity. Offers insurance coverage to employees' domestic partners.
www.sobebev.com

Specialty Foods Group, Inc.
No contributions. Foreign owned. www.sfgtrust.com

Spectrum Organic Products
No contributions. At time of press, was in the process of being acquired by Hain Celestial Group (p. 83). Joined in the boycott of the Canadian Fishing/Seafood Industry against the killing of baby seals. Uses only small-scale organic farmers with sustainable practices and active biodiversity of crops.
www.spectrumnaturals.com

Starbucks Corporation
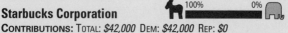

CONTRIBUTIONS: TOTAL: *$42,000* DEM: *$42,000* REP: *$0*

A pending class action suit brought by former managers nationwide alleges wage and overtime violations. Paid an $18 million settlement in a similar 2001 wage and overtime violation suit brought by California managers. Was listed as number one on *Fortune* magazine's "100 Best Companies to Work For" in 2005. Donated $4.7 million to charitable causes, including CARE international. Purchases and promotes fair-trade coffee and sustainable practice. Has a written nondiscrimination policy covering sexual orientation but not gender identity. Offers insurance coverage to employees' domestic partners. www.starbucks.com

Stater Bros. Holdings Inc.

6% 94%

CONTRIBUTIONS: TOTAL: *$15,050* **DEM:** *$869* **REP:** *$14,154*

Settled two lawsuits for $3.2 million in 2003 for violating overtime laws. Does not have a written nondiscrimination policy covering sexual orientation. No information on a policy covering gender identity or insurance coverage to employees' domestic partners. www.staterbros.com

Stop & Shop Supermarket Company, The

No contributions. Subsidiary of Ahold USA, Inc. (p. 71); parent, Royal Ahold N.V. (p. 94). Settled a lawsuit over deceptive "buy one, get one free" practices for $79,000 in donations to food banks in 2005. Was sued in 2002 over $18 million in overtime pay withheld from managers. Paid a $25,000 fine to the U.S. Department of Labor for violation of child labor laws. Outreach supports children's services and education in communities where the company has a presence. Has a written nondiscrimination policy covering sexual orientation but not gender identity. www.stopandshop.com

Sunny Delight Beverages Co.

No contributions. Privately held portfolio company of J. W. Childs Associates, L.P. (p. 86). Formerly held by Procter & Gamble (p. 116). www.sunnyd.com

SUPERVALU Inc.

8% 92%

CONTRIBUTIONS: TOTAL: *$2,450* **DEM:** *$192* **REP:** *$2,252*

Locked out union employees and hired replacement workers in a four-week strike in St. Louis in 2003. Has a written nondiscrimination policy covering sexual orientation but not gender identity. Refuses insurance coverage to employees' domestic partners. www.supervalu.com

Swift & Company

20% 80%

CONTRIBUTIONS: TOTAL: *$10,000* **DEM:** *$2,000* **REP:** *$8,000*

Subsidiary of S&C Holdco 3, Inc. (p. 95). Currently facing a lawsuit filed by Idaho county commissioners charging subsidiary Swift Beef with violating immigration and federal racketeering laws. No information on outreach, benefit structure, or environmental issues. www.swiftbrands.com

Tate & Lyle PLC

No contributions. Foreign owned. In 2004, the company agreed to pay $100 million to settle a U.S. lawsuit regarding allegations of price-fixing high-fructose corn syrup. Outreach supports education, environment, health, and the arts in communities throughout the world. No information on benefit structure, or environmental or labor issues. www.tate-lyle.co.uk

Thai Union Frozen Products PCL

59% 41%

CONTRIBUTIONS: TOTAL: *$7,250* DEM: *$4,250* REP: *$3,000*

Outreach supports educational institutions, needy children, and the underprivileged. No information on benefit structure or legal, environmental, or labor issues. www.thaiuniongroup.com

Tops Markets, LLC

5% 95%

CONTRIBUTIONS: TOTAL: *$2,900* DEM: *$134* REP: *$2,761*

Subsidiary of Ahold USA, Inc. (p. 71); parent, Royal Ahold N.V. (p. 94). www.topsmarkets.com

Trader Joe's Company, Inc.

No contributions. Paid $225,000 to settle allegations that it misled customers in its advertising brochures. Named with other producers and retailers in a lawsuit filed by the state of California seeking to require canned tuna to bear mercury warning labels in accordance with state law. Outreach supports activities in communities where stores are located. Offers insurance coverage to employees' domestic partners. www.traderjoes.com

Trinchero Family Estates

60% 40%

CONTRIBUTIONS: TOTAL: *$12,958* DEM: *$7,813* REP: *$5,145* www.tfewines.com

Tri-Union Seafoods, LLC

60% 40%

CONTRIBUTIONS: TOTAL: *$7,250* DEM: *$4,250* REP: *$3,000*

Subsidiary of Thai Union Frozen Products PCL (p. 99). Named with other producers and retailers in a lawsuit filed by the state of California that seeks to require canned tuna to bear mercury warning labels in accordance with California Proposition 65 regarding toxins. www.chickenofthesea.com

Tyson Foods, Inc.

34% 66%

CONTRIBUTIONS: TOTAL: *$276,113* DEM: *$92,658* REP: *$183,455*

Paid a $2.2 million fine in 2005 for perks received by former chairman Don Tyson. Facing a federal class action suit for allegedly smuggling illegal workers into the United States. Pleaded guilty and paid a $7.5 million fine for felony violations of the Clean Water Act in 2003. Paid $6 million in fines following an investigation of influence brokering and illegal gratuities in connection with former agriculture secretary Mike Espy. Outreach supports hunger relief, education, environmental protections, and family and community initiatives. Has a written nondiscrimination policy covering sexual orientation but not gender identity. Refuses insurance coverage to employees' domestic partners. www.tysonfoodsinc.com

Tyson Fresh Meats, Inc.

6% 94%

CONTRIBUTIONS: TOTAL: *$6,050* DEM: *$339* REP: *$5,711*

Subsidiary of Tyson Foods, Inc. (p. 101). Paid $3.1 million as settlement for labor and overtime violations in 2005. Outreach supports hunger relief, education, and environmental stewardship. Has a written nondiscrimination policy covering sexual orientation but not gender identity. Refuses insurance coverage to employees' domestic partners. www.tysonfoodsinc.com

Unilever; Unilever North America

See p. 118 in Health and Beauty.

Vestar Capital Partners

87% 13%

CONTRIBUTIONS: TOTAL: *$101,250* DEM: *$88,323* REP: *$12,927*

Privately held firm specializing in leveraged buyouts. www.vestarcapital.com

Wal-Mart Stores, Inc.

See p. 146 in Major Retailers.

Welch Foods Inc., A Cooperative

0% 100%

CONTRIBUTIONS: TOTAL: *$3,500* DEM: *$0* REP: *$3,500*

Subsidiary of National Grape Cooperative Association, Inc. (p. 90). Settled with the EPA for violations of the federal hazardous chemical inventory reporting laws by paying a $15,659 fine and funding a $58,632 environmental project in 2004. Was charged with violations of discharging wastewater in 2001. www.welchs.com

White Wave Foods

100% 0%

CONTRIBUTIONS: TOTAL: *$5,000* DEM: *$5,000* REP: *$0*

Subsidiary of Dean Foods Company (p. 78). Fought against the merger of parent Dean Foods Company and Suiza Foods Corp, the nation's two largest dairy producers. Uses wind energy in the production of its soy products. www.whitewave.com

Whole Foods Market, Inc.

No contributions. No employees are represented by labor unions in a sector where the industry average is 50% to 70%. Listed in *Fortune* magazine's "100 Best Companies to Work For" eight years in a row. Outreach supports local community building and environmental education. Has a written nondiscrimination policy covering sexual orientation but not gender identity. Offers insurance coverage to employees' domestic partners. www.wholefoodsmarket.com

Wild Oats Markets, Inc.

No contributions. Outreach supports environmental causes and work in local communities. Listed as one of the "100 Best

Corporate Citizens" by *Business Ethics* magazine. Has a written nondiscrimination policy covering sexual orientation but not gender identity. Offers insurance coverage to employees' domestic partners. www.wildoats.com

Wine Group, Inc., The   29%   71%
CONTRIBUTIONS: TOTAL: *$29,428* DEM: *$8,565* REP: *$20,863*

Winn-Dixie Stores, Inc.   17%   83%
CONTRIBUTIONS: TOTAL: *$44,021* DEM: *$7,284* REP: *$36,737*
Paid $800,000 to settle an age discrimination suit filed by two workers in 2004. Outreach supports disaster relief, Special Olympics, and hunger relief. Has a written nondiscrimination policy covering sexual orientation but not gender identity. Refuses insurance coverage to employees' domestic partners. www.winn-dixie.com

Yum! Brands, Inc.
See p. 169 in Restaurants.

Health and Beauty

Maybe Representative Rahm Emanuel (D-Illinois) put it most succinctly: "There's a pharmaceutical lobbyist and a half for every member of Congress." It's no wonder politicians were condemned by consumer groups for passing the 2004 Prescription Drug Bill with its high cost to taxpayers.

The health and beauty sector has achieved a number of lobbying successes in Washington. The biggest was the Medicare Bill, passed during President George W. Bush's first term and loaded with perks for the sector. The pharmaceutical industry gave $21.7 million to Republicans and $7.6 million to Democrats in the corresponding election cycle; the insurance sector gave $25.9 million to Republicans and $11.7 million to Democrats. These contributions proved to be a good indicator of how members of Congress would behave. House Republicans who voted for the bill received more than three times as much money from pharmaceutical firms and lobbies as those who didn't. House Democrats who voted for it got more than twice the health insurance contributions than those who didn't.

This was par for the course. And as the pharmaceutical industry reels from its latest scandals—Merck appears to have withheld from regulators information about potentially fatal side effects of its drug Vioxx; criticism is mounting over the blocking of generic AIDS medications in Africa—lobbyists work all the harder to shore up government support.

For its part, the beauty industry has been accused of producing the very chemicals and byproducts the health industry should be working against. The cosmetics industry—self-regulated and beyond the purview of the Food and Drug Administration (FDA)—continues to use carcinogenic ingredients such as nitrosamines, as well as harmful dioxins released in chlorine bleaching.

Enormous multinational corporations often have mixed records, making responsible shopping all the trickier: While Unilever owns the socially and ecologically progressive Ben & Jerry's brand, for example, it has also used child labor in India. And while Pfizer, Inc., has donated AIDS drugs to Africa, it has received considerable criticism for its less altruistic lobbying efforts, including attempts to cut off the supply of cheaper prescription drugs from Canada.

Top Ten Republican Contributors

Pfizer, Inc.	$1,033,815
GlaxoSmithKline plc	986,752
Johnson & Johnson	402,128
Limited Brands, Inc.	289,174
Procter & Gamble	243,764
3M Company, Inc.	203,536
S. C. Johnson & Son, Inc.	193,386
J. W. Childs Associates, L.P.	192,000
Bayer AG	191,392
Bristol Myers Squibb	187,080

Top Ten Democratic Contributors

Pfizer, Inc.	$453,209
GlaxoSmithKline plc	334,248
Johnson & Johnson	225,778
Estée Lauder Companies, Inc.	131,531
Revlon	103,000
Procter & Gamble	74,881
Bristol Myers Squibb	62,083
Bayer AG	61,600
Limited Brands, Inc.	59,006
Rite Aid	58,809

1-800 Contacts Inc.

CONTRIBUTIONS: TOTAL: *$30,000* DEM: *$7,000* REP: *$23,000*
Fought and lost a highly visible case against pop-up advertising by its competitors on the Internet, couching it as trademark infringement. Was cited for board irregularities for allowing a sitting board member who was also the portfolio manager at a fund that included the company among its investments.
www.1800contacts.com

24 Hour Fitness
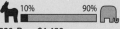
CONTRIBUTIONS: TOTAL: *$5,000* DEM: *$520* REP: *$4,480*
Privately held. In acquisition by private equity firm Forstmann Little & Co. Accused in a pending class action lawsuit of not honoring a contract renewal offer to members. Pending a gender discrimination suit brought by the Equal Employment Opportunity Commission (EEOC). Paid $3.5 million in 2003 to settle allegations of sexual harassment.
www.24hourfitness.com

3M Company, Inc.
See p. 123 in Home and Garden.

AEA Investors
See p. 52 in Finance, Insurance, and Real Estate.

Alberto-Culver

CONTRIBUTIONS: TOTAL: *$69,500* DEM: *$308* REP: *$69,192*

Paid a $114,000 fine to the Environmental Protection Agency (EPA) for violations and improper disposal of hazardous waste. Has a written nondiscrimination policy covering sexual orientation but not gender identity. Refuses insurance coverage to employees' domestic partners. www.alberto.com

Aramis

No contributions. Subsidiary of Estée Lauder Companies, Inc. (p. 110). Was a part of a lawsuit filed against several cosmetic companies for its involvement in alleged price-fixing schemes. www.esteelauder.com

Aubrey Organics

No contributions. Privately held. Produces 100% organic products. Has been certified organic since 1994. No animal testing. Uses recycled products in packaging. www.aubrey-organics.com

Aveda

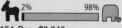

CONTRIBUTIONS: TOTAL: *$14,500* DEM: *$14,500* REP: *$0*

Subsidiary of Estée Lauder Companies, Inc. (p. 110). Before being acquired by Estée Lauder Companies, Inc., Aveda was one of the most progressive companies in the United States, with stellar environmental policy, labor practices, and outreach. Continues to hold itself to high standards, complying with the International Organization for Standardizations' 14001 environmental management framework and the Coalition for Environmentally Responsible Economies (CERES) principles. www.aveda.com

Avon Products Inc.

CONTRIBUTIONS: TOTAL: *$7,000* DEM: *$154* REP: *$6,846*

Employs more women in management than any other Fortune 500 company. No animal testing. Meets and seeks to exceed environmental regulations and product safety laws in the countries it operates in. The Avon Products Foundation focuses on women's and children's issues. The Avon Worldwide Fund for Women funds breast cancer research and women's health. Has a written nondiscrimination policy covering sexual orientation but not gender identity. Offers insurance coverage to employees' domestic partners. www.avon.com

Bally Total Fitness Holding Corporation

CONTRIBUTIONS: TOTAL: *$1,500* DEM: *$1,500* REP: *$0*

Forced employees to sign "procedurally unconscionable" arbitration agreements in 2003. Served with several class action suits in 2004 for allegedly misrepresenting earnings and misleading its investors. www.ballyfitness.com

Bath & Body Works

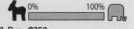 100%   0%

CONTRIBUTIONS: TOTAL: *$11,000* DEM: *$11,000* REP: *$0*

Subsidiary of Limited Brands, Inc. (p. 17). Its CEO donated only to Democratic concerns, in contrast to its parent company's heavily Republican contribution record. www.bathandbodyworks.com

Bausch & Lomb Incorporated

 0%   100%

CONTRIBUTIONS: TOTAL: *$750* DEM: *$0* REP: *$750*

Paid $12.5 million to settle a class action lawsuit for misstatements and omissions regarding the company's financial health. Paid $42 million to shareholders and a $10,000 fine to the SEC in 1997 for allegedly overstating profits in 1993. Family-forward programs include family leave, phaseback for new mothers, 77% paid child care, pretax set-asides, adoption aid, alternative work schedules, and a full-time work–family manager and staff. Has a written nondiscrimination policy covering gender identity and sexual orientation. Offers health insurance to employees' domestic partners. www.bausch.com

Bayer AG

24%   76%

CONTRIBUTIONS: TOTAL: *$253,500* DEM: *$61,601* REP: *$191,393*

Foreign owned. Fined $66 million in 2004 for involvement in an illegal price-fixing conspiracy. Pled guilty and paid a $50 million fine in 1997 for conspiracy to fix prices in the citric acid market. Paid a $257 million settlement relating to the sale of Cipro and Adalat to Kaiser HMO. Settled more than 500 cases out of court related to its inflated pricing of the cholesterol-lowering drug Baycol. Was implicated in a United Nations–revealed scandal for its activity in the Democratic Republic of Congo during that country's civil war. Faced demands for compensation from 24 Peruvian families whose children were accidentally poisoned and killed in 1999 by a Bayer pesticide. Polluted water in a South African town with a known carcinogen. Price-gouged after September 11, 2001, when the United States sought Cipro (an anthrax antidote) in mass quantities. Implicated in HIV/AIDS-tainted blood scandal, and accused of dumping tainted blood-clotting medicines in developing country markets. Sponsors a microfinance program in China, promotes science and environmental education for children, supports a diabetes prevention program, and donates polyurethane for child's prostheses. www.bayer.de

Bayer Corporation

24%   76%

CONTRIBUTIONS: TOTAL: *$253,500* DEM: *$61,601* REP: *$191,393*

Subsidiary of Bayer AG (p. 106). Fined by the Occupational Safety and Health Administration (OSHA) for exposing workers to carcinogenic chemicals at a Bayer plant in Houston in 2000. Does not have a written nondiscrimination policy. Offers health insurance coverage to employees' domestic partners. www.bayerus.com

Beiersdorf AG

CONTRIBUTIONS: TOTAL: *$1,000* DEM: *$154* REP: *$846*

Foreign owned. Sponsors social projects in East Africa, including youth clubs and AIDS awareness activities. Finances projects yearly in Indonesia, such as construction of a library in 2001 and a children's home in 2003. Has programs for environmental protection, occupational safety, and sustainability. www.beiersdorf.com

Beiersdorf, Inc.

CONTRIBUTIONS: TOTAL: *$1,000* DEM: *$154* REP: *$846*

Subsidiary of Beiersdorf AG (p. 107). www.bdfusa.com

Benefit Cosmetics

CONTRIBUTIONS: TOTAL: *$1,250* DEM: *$1,250* REP: *$0*

Subsidiary of LVMH Moët Hennessy Louis Vuitton SA (p. 88). www.benefitcosmetics.com

Bobbi Brown

No contributions. Subsidiary of Estée Lauder Companies, Inc. (p. 110). www.bobbibrown.com

Body Shop International PLC, The

No contributions. Has sourced from countries with widespread, well-documented human and labor rights abuses. Outreach supports environmental and animal protection as well as human and civil rights. Has a written nondiscrimination policy covering sexual orientation but not gender identity. Offers insurance coverage to employees' domestic partners. www.thebodyshopinternational.com

Braun

No contributions. Subsidiary of the Gillette Co. (p. 110); parent, Procter & Gamble (p. 116). www.braun.com

Bristol Myers Squibb

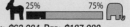

CONTRIBUTIONS: TOTAL: *$249,204* DEM: *$62,084* REP: *$187,080*

Embroiled in the federal drug importation scandal and suits alleging higher-than-average wholesale pricing. Brought a highly publicized suit against South Africa to restrict the powers of the minister of health to set aside drug patents. Distributes more than $500 million in products and donations to philanthropic causes through its foundation. Its Secure the Future program pledged $115 million over a five-year period to help alleviate the HIV/AIDS crisis in sub-Saharan and western Africa as well as smaller programs worldwide. Has a written nondiscrimination policy covering sexual orientation. www.bms.com

Bumble + Bumble

No contributions. Subsidiary of Estée Lauder Companies, Inc. (p. 110). www.bumbleandbumble.com

Burt's Bees
No contributions. Subsidiary of AEA Investors (p. 52). www.burtsbees.com

Chanel, Inc.

100%   0%

CONTRIBUTIONS: TOTAL: *$7,000* DEM: *$7,000* REP: *$0*

Settled a class action lawsuit alleging that cosmetics manufacturers and retailers colluded to set prices at consumers' expense, resulting in identical pricing from store to store and few, if any, markdowns. www.chanel.com

Church & Dwight Co., Inc.
See p. 125 in Home and Garden.

CIBA Vision Corporation
No contributions. Subsidiary of Novartis AG (p. 115). Settled an antitrust suit for price-fixing in 1997. www.cibavision.com

Clinique
100%   0%

CONTRIBUTIONS: TOTAL: *$1,500* DEM: *$1,500* REP: *$0*

Subsidiary of Estée Lauder Companies, Inc. (p. 110). www.clinique.com

Colgate-Palmolive Co.
0%   100%

CONTRIBUTIONS: TOTAL: *$600* DEM: *$0* REP: *$600*

Charged with sexual and racial discrimination in a noteworthy case in 1999. Settled an employment discrimination and retaliation case in 1998. Committed to sustainable development and environmental concerns in packaging, using 50% recycled plastic in its soap product bottles and elimination of paper cartons for toothpaste products. Considered a family-friendly employer. Sponsors International Labor Organization standards and monitoring functions. Foundation supports dental health education for children. Has a written nondiscrimination policy covering sexual orientation but not gender identity. Offers insurance coverage to employees' domestic partners. www.colgate.com

Conair Corporation
No contributions. Former CEO Leandro Rizzuto pled guilty to pocketing $3 million in kickbacks from the company's product distributors. www.conair.com

Coty, Inc.
No contributions. www.coty.com

Cover Girl
No contributions. Subsidiary of Procter & Gamble (p. 116). Has a written nondiscrimination policy covering sexual orientation but not gender identity. Offers insurance coverage to employees' domestic partners. www.covergirl.com

Crunch Fitness
No contributions. Subsidiary of Bally Total Fitness Holding Corporation (p. 105). www.crunch.com

Curves International

CONTRIBUTIONS: TOTAL: *$121,607* DEM: *$0* REP: *$121,607*

This faith-based, private company is the largest fitness franchise business in the world; approximately 90% of the locations are owned by women. The founders are major contributors to conservative causes, including antigay and prolife groups. Outreach supports a charity-matching program that gives up to $1,000 annually for needy communities. www.curves.com

CVS Corporation

CONTRIBUTIONS: TOTAL: *$75,958* DEM: *$45,104* REP: *$30,854*

Sued for breach of fiduciary duty for selling customers' prescription records without their consent. Supports educational reform and school improvement. Disperses three-year $75,000 grants to educators. Funded an alternative high school in Rhode Island encouraging students to gain work experience related to their educational interests. Has a written nondiscrimination policy covering sexual orientation but not gender identity. Offers health insurance coverage to employees' domestic partners. www.cvs.com

Dial Corporation
CONTRIBUTIONS: TOTAL: *$49,000* DEM: *$9,330* REP: *$39,654*

Subsidiary of Henkel KGaA (p. 129). Activists allege that the company continues to engage in animal testing despite its promise to abstain. Received citations from OSHA for safety violations at its plants. Agreed to pay $10 million to settle sexual harassment charges in 2003. Received numerous certificates of recognition from sanitation districts in Los Angeles for consistent compliance with wastewater discharge. www.dialcorp.com

Dr. Bronners Magic Soap
No contributions. Currently suing the Department of Agriculture for permission to continue the use of the "organic" label on its products. Recent charitable giving to social and environmental causes has roughly matched total after-tax income. www.drbronner.com

Drugstore.com
No contributions. Several pending class action lawsuits allege artificial inflation of share prices. Outreach focuses on improving the health and well-being of the communities where the company has physical operations. www.drugstore.com

Eckerd Drug
No contributions. Subsidiary of CVS Corporation (p. 109). Partly owned by the Jean Coutu Group (p. 111). www.eckerd.com

Energizer Holdings, Inc.
See p. 40 in Computers and Electronics.

Equinox Fitness Clubs
No contributions. Subsidiary of J. W. Childs Associates, L.P. (p. 86). www.equinoxfitness.com

Estée Lauder Companies, Inc.
79% 21%

CONTRIBUTIONS: TOTAL: *$166,000* DEM: *$131,531* REP: *$34,469*

Earns high marks for its refusal to test products on animals and for its longtime extension of health care benefits to its employees' same-sex partners. Criticized for its refusal to sign the Compact for Safer Cosmetics, although it has taken some steps on its own to make its products safer. Has been charged with dumping hazardous waste in two cases. Has supported sustainable development and breast cancer awareness projects. Largest corporate sponsor of the Breast Cancer Research Foundation, founded by Evelyn H. Lauder in 1993. www.elcompanies.com

Estée Lauder Cosmetics
No contributions. Subsidiary of Estée Lauder Companies, Inc. (p. 110). www.esteelauder.com

Gillette Co., The
36% 64%

CONTRIBUTIONS: TOTAL: *$66,500* DEM: *$23,968* REP: *$42,489*

Subsidiary of Procter & Gamble (p. 116). A coalition of labor activists and community groups protested vendor practices, alleging discrimination against migrant workers, in July 2005. Outreach supports youth and community programs in Boston, including a program for teenage boys convicted of nonviolent crimes. Has a written nondiscrimination policy covering sexual orientation but not gender identity. Offers insurance coverage to employees' domestic partners. www.gillette.com

GlaxoSmithKline plc

25% 75%

CONTRIBUTIONS: TOTAL: *$1,321,000* DEM: *$334,248* REP: *$986,752*

A pending lawsuit against the company and other drugmakers alleges that they fraudulently reported higher prices to Medi-Cal for medications, inflating the actual charge to doctors and pharmacies. Agreed to pay $150 million to settle federal claims of fraud related to the marketing and pricing of two of its antinausea medications. In 2005, the FDA seized millions of pills of doubtful quality from company facilities in Tennessee and Puerto Rico. The New York attorney general accused GlaxoSmithKline plc of concealing negative information about tests of Paxil in children and adolescents; the company settled the case out of court for $2.5 million. Its Global Community Partnerships program partners with organizations in the developing world to help improve the health and education of underserved communities. www.gsk.com

GlaxoSmithKline USA   25%   75%
CONTRIBUTIONS: TOTAL: *$1,316,000* DEM: *$334,248* REP: *$981,752*
Subsidiary of GlaxoSmithKline plc (p. 110). Outreach supports improving access to health care and education in underserved communities. Has a written nondiscrimination policy covering sexual orientation and plans to include gender identity. Offers insurance coverage to employees' domestic partners. www.gsk.com

GNC Corp. (General Nutrition Centers)   48%   52%
CONTRIBUTIONS: TOTAL: *$11,167* DEM: *$5,334* REP: *$5,833*
Subsidiary of Apollo Advisors LP (p. 54). www.gnc.com

Gold's Gym   10%   90%
CONTRIBUTIONS: TOTAL: *$1,000* DEM: *$104* REP: *$896*
Subsidiary of TRT Holdings, Inc. (p. 204). www.goldsgym.com

Gorilla Sports
No contributions. Subsidiary of Bally Total Fitness Holding Corporation (p. 105). www.gorillasports.com

Guerlain
No contributions. Subsidiary of LVMH Moët Hennessy Louis Vuitton SA (p. 88). www.guerlain.com

Hain Celestial Group
See p. 83 in Food and Beverage.

Henkel KgaA
See p. 129 in Home and Garden.

Jason Natural Products, Inc.
No contributions. Subsidiary of Hain Celestial Group (p. 83). www.jason-natural.com

Jean Coutu Group, The   19%   81%
CONTRIBUTIONS: TOTAL: *$6,200* DEM: *$1,175* REP: *$5,026*
Outreach includes $20 million to African AIDS sufferers. Supports work in areas of global disease and poverty, education, and Quebec charities. www.jeancoutu.com

Jean Coutu Group USA, The (Brooks Pharmacy)   19%   81%
CONTRIBUTIONS: TOTAL: *$6,200* DEM: *$1,175* REP: *$5,026*
Subsidiary of the Jean Coutu Group (p. 111). www.jeancoutu.com

Jewel-Osco
See p. 86 in Food and Beverage.

John Paul Mitchell Systems

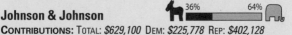

CONTRIBUTIONS: TOTAL: *$3,500* DEM: *$1,500* REP: *$0*

First hair care company to publicly oppose animal testing. Uses solar panels to generate electricity in Hawaii. Its CEO made a $2,000 contribution to Nader for President in 2004. Outreach supports St. Jude Children's Research Hospital, Red Cross Tsunami Relief, Mothers against Drunk Drivers (MADD), and People for the Ethical Treatment of Animals (PETA). www.paulmitchell.com

Johnson & Johnson

CONTRIBUTIONS: TOTAL: *$629,100* DEM: *$225,778* REP: *$402,128*

A major lobbying force, spending millions to affect Medicare policy and to fight two California propositions that would lower prescription drug prices for uninsured residents. Also charged with misleading customers about several of its products, including Acuvue lenses and Retin-A skin care. Tests products on animals (though some of this research is government mandated); is a sponsor of the Johns Hopkins Center for Alternatives to Animal Testing. Has promoted the use of green energy. Targeted by several environmental groups for using harmful chemicals in its products, including allowing trace amounts of lead in its baby powder. Charitable contributions include climate change and diversity initiatives. Has a nondiscrimination policy covering sexual orientation and gender identity. Offers insurance coverage to employees' domestic partners. www.jnj.com

J. W. Childs Associates, L.P.

See p. 86 in Food and Beverage.

Kiehl's

CONTRIBUTIONS: TOTAL: *$4,750* DEM: *$500* REP: *$4,250*

Subsidiary of L'Oréal SA (p. 113). www.kiehls.com

Kimberly-Clark Corporation

No contributions. Was cited in a 2004 Natural Resources Defense Council report for clear-cutting and destroying one of America's last great stands of native forest in Tennessee. In 2004, the FDA banned Kotex products produced in the Philippines for failure to meet U.S. standards. Has sourced from countries with widespread, well-documented human and labor rights abuses; encourages sweatshop labor with its supplier practices. Places 4% of its supplier budget with women- and minority-owned companies. Included in *Fortune* magazine's list of the "100 Best Companies to Work For." Has a written nondiscrimination policy covering sexual orientation but not gender identity. Offers insurance coverage to employees' domestic partners. www.kimberly-clark.com

Kiss My Face Corp.

CONTRIBUTIONS: TOTAL: *$300* DEM: *$300* REP: *$0*

A leader in providing natural and organic bath and beauty products since the 1980s. The company does not engage in animal testing. www.kissmyface.com

Lancôme US

No contributions. Subsidiary of L'Oréal SA (p. 113). www.lancome.com

Limited Brands, Inc.

See p. 17 in Clothing, Shoes, and Accessories.

L'Occitane

No contributions. Manufactures products in and has sourced from countries with widespread, well-documented human and labor rights abuses. Uses recycled packaging and organic ingredients. www.loccitane.com

Longs Drug Stores Corporation

CONTRIBUTIONS: TOTAL: *$2,200* DEM: *$722* REP: *$1,478*

Paid $11 million in 2004 to settle two class action lawsuits alleging failure to pay overtime wages. A California state audit found that stores sold thousands of unapproved pesticides in 2004 and withheld records from regulators. Outreach provides communities with flu shots and supports the American Diabetes Association, the Arthritis Foundation, and the American Heart Association. Has a written nondiscrimination policy covering sexual orientation but not gender identity. Refuses insurance coverage to employees' domestic partners. www.longs.com

L'Oréal SA

CONTRIBUTIONS: TOTAL: *$4,750* DEM: *$500* REP: *$4,250*

Foreign owned. Employs an environmental policy that monitors water and energy consumption and reductions. Has a noted occupational safety record that has received awards in the United States. Outreach focuses on community-based projects and a UNESCO project to encourage women to take up science professions. Has a written nondiscrimination policy covering sexual orientation but not gender identity. Refuses insurance coverage to employees' domestic partners. www.loreal.com

L'Oréal USA

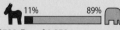

CONTRIBUTIONS: TOTAL: *$4,750* DEM: *$500* REP: *$4,250*

Subsidiary of L'Oréal SA (p. 113). Settled a class action lawsuit alleging cosmetics manufacturers and retailers colluded to set prices at consumers' expense, resulting in identical pricing from store to store and few, if any, markdowns. www.loreal.com

Luxottica Group, S.p.A.

CONTRIBUTIONS: TOTAL: *$1,000* DEM: *$1,000* REP: *$0*

A pending class action lawsuit alleges price-fixing and collusion with a controlling shareholder. Three of its executives settled insider-trading charges related to the company's buyout of the U.S. Shoe Corporation. www.luxottica.it

Luxottica Retail (U.S.)

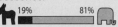

CONTRIBUTIONS: TOTAL: *$1,000* DEM: *$1,000* REP: *$0*

Subsidiary of Luxottica Group, S.p.A. (p. 114). www.luxottica.com

LVMH Inc. (U.S.)

See p. 19 in Clothing, Shoes, and Accessories.

MAC Cosmetics

No contributions. Subsidiary of Estée Lauder Companies, Inc. (p. 110). Since 1994, the MAC AIDS Fund has promoted HIV/AIDS education, awareness, and prevention and has raised $31 million for AIDS research. www.maccosmetics.com

Macy's

See p. 19 in Clothing, Shoes, and Accessories.

Mary Kay Cosmetics

CONTRIBUTIONS: TOTAL: *$35,250* DEM: *$6,574* REP: *$28,676*

Received the first Fashion and the Environment Award for Environmental Excellence from the United Nations Environment Program. Initiating a moratorium on animal testing. Has given more than $1 million to breast cancer research, nearly $200,000 to the Susan Komen Breast Cancer Foundation, and $70,000 to the American Cancer Society. www.marykay.com

Matrix

No contributions. Subsidiary of L'Oréal SA (p. 113). www.matrix.com

Max Factor

No contributions. Subsidiary of Procter & Gamble (p. 116). Has a written nondiscrimination policy covering sexual orientation but not gender identity. Offers insurance coverage to employees' domestic partners. www.maxfactor.com

Maybelline New York/Garnier

No contributions. Subsidiary of L'Oréal SA (p. 113). www.maybelline.com

McNeil Consumer & Specialty Pharmaceuticals

No contributions. Subsidiary of Johnson & Johnson (p. 112). Filed a lawsuit to counter the Sugar Association's lawsuit over an advertising campaign that connects Splenda to sugar. www.themakersoftylenol.com

Neutrogena
No contributions. Subsidiary of Johnson & Johnson (p. 112). www.neutrogena.com

Novartis AG

CONTRIBUTIONS: TOTAL: *$250* DEM: *$21* REP: *$227*

Has a written nondiscrimination policy covering sexual orientation but not gender identity. Offers insurance coverage to employees' domestic partners. www.novartis.com

Osco Drug
No contributions. Subsidiary of Albertsons, Inc. (p. 72). www.jewel-osco.com

P&G-Clairol, Inc.

CONTRIBUTIONS: TOTAL: *$4,000* DEM: *$308* REP: *$3,692*

Subsidiary of Procter & Gamble (p. 116). Has a written nondiscrimination policy covering sexual orientation but not gender identity. Offers insurance coverage to employees' domestic partners. www.clairol.com

Pantene

CONTRIBUTIONS: TOTAL: *$2,000* DEM: *$2,000* REP: *$0*

Subsidiary of Procter & Gamble (p. 116). Has a written nondiscrimination policy covering sexual orientation but not gender identity. Offers insurance coverage to employees' domestic partners. www.pantene.com

Parfums Christian Dior
No contributions. Subsidiary of LVMH Moët Hennessy Louis Vuitton SA (p. 88). www.dior.com

Parfums Givenchy
No contributions. Subsidiary of LVMH Moët Hennessy Louis Vuitton SA (p. 88). www.givenchy.com

Pearle Vision

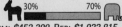

CONTRIBUTIONS: TOTAL: *$1,000* DEM: *$1,000* REP: *$0*

Subsidiary of Luxottica Retail (U.S.) (p. 114). Outreach supports Give the Gift of Sight Foundation. www.pearlevision.com

Pfizer, Inc.

CONTRIBUTIONS: TOTAL: *$1,488,410* DEM: *$453,209* REP: *$1,033,815*

Blockbuster drugs such as Lipitor, Zoloft, and Viagra have made Pfizer, Inc., the world's largest pharmaceutical company, as well as a major player in big pharmaceutical lobbying. Has sought to restrict patents on AIDS drugs in Africa, to cut off the importation of drugs from Canada (inspiring a boycott from senior citizen groups), and to stop the passage of a California proposition that would lower prescription drug prices to the poor, elderly, and uninsured. Has also come under fire for making false claims about several of its own products, such as

Bextra—which was ordered off the shelves by the FDA—and Celebrex—which has been linked to heart attacks. Charitable giving projects include the funding of Africa's largest training program for AIDS workers and some drug donations. Has a written nondiscrimination policy covering sexual orientation and gender identity. Offers insurance coverage to employees' domestic partners. www.pfizer.com

PharmaCare Management Services

CONTRIBUTIONS: TOTAL: *$800* DEM: *$0* REP: *$800*
Subsidiary of CVS Corporation (p. 109). www.pharmacare.com

Playtex Products, Inc.

CONTRIBUTIONS: TOTAL: *$2,000* DEM: *$0* REP: *$2,000*
Subsidiary of Sara Lee Corporation (p. 95).
www.playtexproductsinc.com

Procter & Gamble

CONTRIBUTIONS: TOTAL: *$318,689* DEM: *$74,881* REP: *$243,764*
One facility was listed among the top polluters in 2002 EPA's Toxic Release Inventory data. Paid $82,000 to settle a lawsuit alleging air pollution violations. The American Environmental Safety Institute has brought a pending suit alleging failure to warn consumers about lead in toothpaste products. Subsidiary the Iams Company (p. 129) has been targeted by PETA for its use of animals in research. Has a minority supplier program. Markets fair-trade-certified coffee products through its Millstone brand. Named one of the "Top 100 Employers for the Class of 2004" by *Black Collegian* magazine and ranked 45th on *Fortune* magazine's list of the "50 Best Companies for Minorities" in 2004. Has a written nondiscrimination policy covering sexual orientation but not gender identity. Offers insurance coverage to employees' domestic partners. www.pg.com

Reckitt Benckiser Inc.

See p. 135 in Home and Garden.

Redken

No contributions. Subsidiary of L'Oréal SA (p. 113).
www.redken.com

Regis Corporation

CONTRIBUTIONS: TOTAL: *$4,050* DEM: *$0* REP: *$4,050*
Subsidiary Supercuts Inc. agreed to pay $3.5 million to end a government lawsuit that it discriminated against black employees. A pending lawsuit alleges 20 Supercuts hair salons in Chicago illegally imposed an "English-only" rule that discriminated against Spanish-speaking workers. Outreach supports breast cancer research, education, and prevention. Refuses

insurance coverage to employees' domestic partners.
www.regiscorp.com

Revlon

94%   6%

CONTRIBUTIONS: TOTAL: *$109,400* DEM: *$103,000* REP: *$6,400*
Outreach supports women's health. Has a written nondiscrimination policy covering sexual orientation but not gender identity.
www.revlon.com

Rite Aid
51%   49%

CONTRIBUTIONS: TOTAL: *$114,500* DEM: *$58,809* REP: *$55,691*
Settled a class action suit for $318 million for alleged accounting fraud resulting in the indictment of several company executives. Was ordered to pay $250,000 to a woman who became permanently disabled after following incorrect advice on a company-produced pamphlet enclosed with her prescription medication. Outreach supports Children's Miracle Network and focuses on improving the lives of those in communities where Rite Aid does business. Has a written nondiscrimination policy covering sexual orientation but not gender identity. Refuses insurance coverage to employees' domestic partners.
www.riteaid.com

Sally Beauty Company, Inc.
0%   100%

CONTRIBUTIONS: TOTAL: *$1,000* DEM: *$0* REP: *$1,000*
Subsidiary of Alberto-Culver (p. 105). A pending class action lawsuit seeks to recover deductions from its vendors for advertising and public education. www.sallybeauty.com

Schick-Wilkinson Sword
No contributions. Subsidiary of Energizer Holdings, Inc. (p. 40).
www.shaving.com

S. C. Johnson & Son, Inc.
See p. 136 in Home and Garden.

Sephora
No contributions. Subsidiary of LVMH Moët Hennessy Louis Vuitton SA (p. 88). www.sephora.com

Shaklee Corporation
See p. 137 in Home and Garden.

Spectrum Brands, Inc. (formerly Rayovac Corporation)
See p. 48 in Computers and Electronics.

Stila
100%   0%

CONTRIBUTIONS: TOTAL: *$2,000* DEM: *$2,000* REP: *$0*
Subsidiary of Estée Lauder Companies, Inc. (p. 110).
www.stilacosmetics.com

Tom's of Maine

CONTRIBUTIONS: TOTAL: *$2,100* DEM: *$2,100* REP: *$0*

Outreach supports environmental protection, nutrition education for children, and dental health. www.tomsofmaine.com

Town Sports International, Inc.

CONTRIBUTIONS: TOTAL: *$2,500* DEM: *$260* REP: *$2,240*

A pending class action lawsuit alleges failure to pay managers for hours worked and for overtime. www.mysportsclubs.com

Trans-India Products, Inc. (ShiKai)

No contributions. Products carry the "no animal ingredients, no animal testing" label endorsed by animal rights groups. www.shikai.com

TRT Holdings, Inc.

See p. 204 in Travel and Leisure.

Tupperware Corporation

See p. 138 in Home and Garden.

Ulta

No contributions. www.ulta.com

Unilever

CONTRIBUTIONS: TOTAL: *$3,500* DEM: *$367* REP: *$3,114*

One of the world's largest makers of consumer products, with brands running the gamut of food, beauty, and household items. Environmental offenses include a 7.4-ton mercury dump in India (Unilever did the cleanup but was accused of failing to compensate villagers for the damages). Has come under fire for testing products on animals and its use of, and research into, genetically modified crops. Under pressure from the Campaign for Safe Cosmetics, Unilever agreed to remove controversial chemical compounds known as phthalates from its products. The company's charitable giving is extensive and has benefited many environmental and energy conservation campaigns. www.unilever.com

Unilever Cosmetics International

No contributions. Subsidiary of Unilever (p. 118). www.unilever.com

Unilever North America

CONTRIBUTIONS: TOTAL: *$3,500* DEM: *$367* REP: *$3,114*

Subsidiary of Unilever (p. 118). www.unileverna.com

Wahl Clipper Corp

CONTRIBUTIONS: TOTAL: *$550* DEM: *$0* REP: *$550*

Outreach supports HIV/AIDS education. www.wahl.com

Walgreen Co.

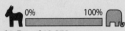

43%   57%

CONTRIBUTIONS: TOTAL: *$123,000* DEM: *$52,379* REP: *$70,622*

A pending racial discrimination suit alleges discriminatory employment practices involving black managers and pharmacists. Settled a 2002 suit alleging mistakes in filling prescriptions stemming from a 2002 incident where a child's Ritalin prescription was mistakenly filled with Methadone, resulting in the child's permanent brain damage. Outreach supports health and social services initiatives. Has a written nondiscrimination policy covering sexual orientation and gender identity. Offers insurance coverage to employees' domestic partners. www.walgreens.com

Wyeth

0%   100%

CONTRIBUTIONS: TOTAL: *$19,850* DEM: *$0* REP: *$19,850*

Has been involved in nearly $17 billion in litigation over its former diet drugs Pondimin and Redux. Placed in the EPA's Significant Noncompliance category for multiple violations and exceeding monthly effluent limits for five consecutive quarters. Fined $51,000 after a discharge resulted in a major fish kill in Pennsylvania in 2003. Fined $125,000 by the EPA for a release of mercury effluent in 1990. Found in 1991 to be in violation of the World Health Organization/UNICEF International Code of Marketing of Breast-milk Substitutes for its marketing of products in the Third World. Donates medicines to international aid groups for emergencies and global health care, and is involved with AmeriCares, Project HOPE, and Heart to Heart International. *Working Mother* magazine has selected Wyeth for eight years in a row as one of the 100 best companies for working mothers. www.wyeth.com

Home and Garden

In the United States, the home and garden represent a private, tranquil sanctuary against the chaos of the outer world. Trouble is, our private sanctuaries actually require pesticides, chemical byproducts, unsustainably and recklessly harvested timber, and underpaid third world labor.

The home and garden sector impacts the political scene far more than one might guess. Tracing this impact, however, requires following the sector further than the new refrigerator or garden hose you need. Over the years General Electric Company (see p. 58 in Finance, Insurance, and Real Estate), which otherwise "brings good things to life," has drawn criticism for dumping PCBs in New York's Hudson River and producing antipersonnel mine components. In addition to being a billion-dollar weapons manufacturer, it also owns a majority stake in NBC, which some critics have claimed wasn't sufficiently critical of the administration's justifications for going to war in Iraq—and which, according to the *New York Times,* was enlisted in 2001 to help appeal an order that the company begin a costly cleanup of the Hudson River.

Even those companies that limit their products to the kitchen or rose bed find themselves battling regulators and defending against ever more savvy consumers. Leading pesticide manufacturers, for instance, formed the benign-sounding Responsible Industry for a Sound Environment political action committee—clearly a misleading name. Spending millions each year on lobbyists, groups like this fight to limit regulation of their products and in some cases to obscure data and lawsuits suggesting the damage these products can cause. Meanwhile, the lumber and paper industries not only have a powerful lobby but have enlisted politicians to frame their controversial practices as a jobs-versus-owls debate. This even as the sector itself exports and outsources more and more jobs to Mexico and elsewhere.

Nevertheless, there have been some phenomenal successes among activist groups. As the world's largest supplier of home improvement products, Home Depot, Inc. (p. 129), found itself up against a vast and ongoing protest for its sale of rainforest lumber. Fearing a broader backlash, the company eventually reversed many of its policies and has since taken up the cause of sustainable harvesting. Even General Electric Company has begun moving—glacially, some say—toward a greener business.

Top Ten Republican Contributors

Home Depot, Inc.	$558,733
Georgia-Pacific Corporation	261,981
3M Company, Inc.	203,536
S. C. Johnson & Son, Inc.	193,386
Scotts Miracle-Gro Co.	180,010
Williams-Sonoma, Inc.	114,000
Whirlpool Corporation	73,999
Nutro Products, Inc.	53,000
Maytag Corporation	43,499
Pier 1 Imports, Inc.	41,086

Top Ten Democratic Contributors

Home Depot, Inc.	$116,162
Bed Bath & Beyond	109,243
Georgia-Pacific Corporation	97,007
Martha Stewart Living Omnimedia, Inc.	77,809
Mattel, Inc.	54,990
Euromarket Designs, Inc. (Crate and Barrel)	49,910
3M Company, Inc.	37,595
Container Store, The	33,805
Clorox Company, The	25,985
S. C. Johnson & Son, Inc.	24,971

3M Company, Inc. 16% 84%

CONTRIBUTIONS: TOTAL: *$241,131* DEM: *$37,595* REP: *$203,536*

In 2005, the American Association of Retired Persons (AARP) and employees filed an age discrimination suit claiming the company's Six Sigma quality control program and labor practices were discriminatory. Faces class action lawsuits in California alleging unfair competition and consumer protection violations. Hit with more than 388,000 suits over failures with its dust masks and similar products. Lost a major lawsuit over breast implant failures in 1994 and subsequently settled a class action with other manufacturers. In 2002, the Environmental Protection Agency (EPA) listed six facilities in the top emitters of toxic pollutants. Faces suits in Minnesota and Alabama over perfluorochemical contamination. Foundation supports education, sustainability, and health and human services, including disaster relief. Supports employee volunteerism. Has received Occupational Safety and Health Administration (OSHA) star certification for voluntary occupational safety programs. Reduced its greenhouse gas emissions by 24% from 1990 to 2003. Has a written nondiscrimination policy covering sexual orientation but not gender identity. Refuses insurance coverage to employees' domestic partners.
www.mmm.com

Aaron Brothers, Inc.

No contributions. Subsidiary of Michaels Stores, Inc. (p. 132). In 2002, paid $5 million and settled a wage-and-hour class action suit. www.aaronbros.com

Ace Hardware Corporation

No contributions. Foundation supports cancer research and medical equipment purchase. Disaster relief and children's health care needs are funded in partnership with the American Red Cross. Has a written nondiscrimination policy covering sexual orientation but not gender identity. Refuses insurance coverage to employees' domestic partners. www.acehardware.com

Aspen Pet Products, Inc.

No contributions. Subsidiary of WKI Holding Company, Inc. (p. 139). www.aspenpet.com

BabyCenter, L.L.C.

🐴 100% ▬▬▬▬▬▬ 0% 🐘

CONTRIBUTIONS: TOTAL: *$2,500* DEM: *$2,500* REP: *$0*

Subsidiary of Johnson & Johnson (p. 112). www.babycenter.com

BabyUniverse, Inc.

See p. 5 in Clothing, Shoes, and Accessories.

Bed Bath & Beyond

🐴 97% ▬▬▬▬▬▬ 3% 🐘

CONTRIBUTIONS: TOTAL: *$112,500* DEM: *$109,243* REP: *$3,257*

Was implicated in the recent Securities and Exchange Commission (SEC) chargeback scandals. Accused by the AFL-CIO of keeping Overnight Trucking, the nation's largest labor law violator, in business because of its supplier–vendor relationship. Contributes 1% of consumer purchases to individual college education funds through the UPromise program. Has a written nondiscrimination policy covering sexual orientation but not gender identity. Refuses health insurance coverage to employees' domestic partners. www.bedbathandbeyond.com

Black & Decker Corporation, The

🐴 100% ▬▬▬▬▬▬ 0% 🐘

CONTRIBUTIONS: TOTAL: *$1,000* DEM: *$1,000* REP: *$0*

Agreed to settle Federal Trade Commission (FTC) charges of unfair competition and false advertising for mislabeling products made overseas as "Made in USA." Settled FTC charges and paid $575,000 in 1999 over misrepresentation of the fire dangers of the Spacesaver toaster. Has a written nondiscrimination policy covering sexual orientation but not gender identity. Refuses insurance coverage to employees' domestic partners. www.bdk.com

Bombay Company, Inc., The

No contributions. Settled a wage-and-hour class action lawsuit in 2003, paying $1.35 million. Sells a limited edition stuffed bear for St. Jude Children's Research Hospital and donates 10% of sales to the charity. www.bombaycompany.com

Bright Horizons Family Solutions, Inc.

 100%   0%

CONTRIBUTIONS: TOTAL: *$3,500* DEM: *$3,500* REP: *$0*

Included in *Fortune* magazine's list of the "100 Best Companies to Work For"; its profile noted that employees are paid 50% above the industry standard. Has a written nondiscrimination policy covering sexual orientation and gender identity. Offers insurance coverage to employees' domestic partners. www.brighthorizons.com

Brookstone, Inc.

See p. 37 in Computers and Electronics.

Brown-Forman Corporation

See p. 74 in Food and Beverage.

Cargill, Incorporated

See p. 75 in Food and Beverage.

Central Garden & Pet Company

No contributions. Among several companies who in 2003 agreed to a $10 million settlement for 1,500 personal injury claims, after a fire in a warehouse containing its fertilizers and pesticides produced a toxic cloud 1 mile wide by 30 miles long over parts of Phoenix. Outreach includes sponsorship for no-kill animal rescue foundations and the "Dogs4Diabetics" program. www.centralgardenandpet.com

Church & Dwight Co., Inc.

 31%   69%

CONTRIBUTIONS: TOTAL: *$4,250* DEM: *$1,308* REP: *$2,942*

Paid $3,732 to OSHA for three "serious" health and safety violations at its New Jersey factory. Aggressively promotes the environmental benefits of its products, many based on baking soda rather than the traditional solvents using volatile organic compounds. Has a written nondiscrimination policy covering sexual orientation but not gender identity. Offers insurance coverage to employees' domestic partners. www.churchdwight.com

Circuit City Stores, Inc.

See p. 38 in Computers and Electronics.

Clorox Company, The

 69%   31%

CONTRIBUTIONS: TOTAL: *$37,500* DEM: *$25,985* REP: *$11,515*

In 2004, a Denver medical researcher contradicted, under oath, the company's health claims of its antimold cleaning products. The EPA cited its Bedford Park, Illinois, plant in 2003 for federal Clean Air Act violations. Foundation seeks to improve the quality of life in the communities where its employees live and work. Gave $300,000 to a children's educational space and science center in Oakland, California. Has a written nondiscrimination policy covering sexual orientation but not gender identity. Offers insurance coverage to employees' domestic partners. www.clorox.com

Conair Corporation
See p. 108 in Health and Beauty.

Container Store, The
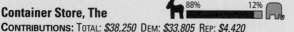
CONTRIBUTIONS: TOTAL: *$38,250* DEM: *$33,805* REP: *$4,420*

Rated since 2000 in the top five of *Fortune* magazine's annual list of the "100 Best Companies to Work For." Reasons include wages above the industry standard and benefits for part-time employees. Offers flexible scheduling for parents. Outreach activities include a community school supply drive for students. Offers insurance coverage to employees' domestic partners. www.containerstore.com

Cost Plus, Inc.

CONTRIBUTIONS: TOTAL: *$1,000* DEM: *$1,000* REP: *$0*

Paid $2.1 million in 2001 to settle a wage-and-hour lawsuit. Pressured by conservation groups to stop manufacturing goods from endangered rainforest timber. Stores invite special education and at-risk youth to learn about their businesses and shadow workers. www.costplusworldmarket.com

Doane Pet Care Company
No contributions. Acquired in 2005 by the Ontario Teachers' Pension Plan. Violated federal law in 2004 by impeding employee attempts to organize and failing to negotiate in good faith. In 2001, the South Carolina Board of Health and Environmental Control levied a $4,000 fine for violations and failure to monitor particulate emissions. In 1999, recalled dog food contaminated with a fungal toxin responsible for the death of 25 dogs. www.doanepetcare.com

Do It Best Corp.
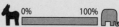
CONTRIBUTIONS: TOTAL: *$15,750* DEM: *$0* REP: *$15,750*

Supports Habit for Humanity, and many co-op members support Habitat in their own communities, contributing $430,000 in materials to the program. Also supports Big Brothers/Big Sisters and the United Way. www.doitbest.com

Drs. Foster & Smith, Inc.

CONTRIBUTIONS: TOTAL: *$4,000* DEM: *$0* REP: *$4,000*

Named in a lawsuit alleging trademark infringement and false advertising for selling medicine, not approved by the Food and

Drug Administration (FDA), that was manufactured specifically for foreign countries. Outreach includes education about pet health and care, as well as donations to support research into neuromuscular diseases. www.drsfostersmith.com

Eight in One Pet Products, Inc.
No contributions. Received an FDA warning in 2002 regarding its production of adulterated pet drugs. Cited by the state of Idaho in 2002 for animal feed ingredient violations. www.eightinonepet.com

Euromarket Designs, Inc. (Crate and Barrel)
76% 24%

CONTRIBUTIONS: TOTAL: *$65,300* DEM: *$49,910* REP: *$15,340*
Stopped stocking products made in Burma in 2001 after revelations of human and labor rights violations there. Part-time employees receive profit sharing, paid vacation, 401(k), and other benefits usually reserved for full-time workers. Has a written nondiscrimination policy covering sexual orientation but not gender identity. Offers insurance coverage to employees' domestic partners. www.crateandbarrel.com

Excelligence Learning Corporation
No contributions. Formerly LearningStar Corporation. Outreach includes donations of supplies and toys to elementary school children in need. www.excelligencelearning.com

Expo Design Center
No contributions. Subsidiary of Home Depot, Inc. (p. 129). www.expo.com

Fiskars Brands, Inc.
No contributions. Subsidiary of Finland-based Fiskars Corporation. Donates supplies to charity efforts such as a quilt-making competition/auction and a celebrity scrapbook fund-raiser. www.fiskars.com/US

Fortune Brands, Inc.
See p. 81 in Food and Beverage.

Garden Ridge Corporation
No contributions. The teamsters union in Texas complained in 2002 of unfair wages and hazardous work conditions at the company's distribution center. www.gardenridge.com

General Electric Company
See p. 58 in Finance, Insurance, and Real Estate.

Georgia Lighting, Inc.
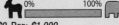
0% 100%

CONTRIBUTIONS: TOTAL: *$1,000* DEM: *$0* REP: *$1,000*
Subsidiary of Home Depot, Inc. (p. 129). www.georgialighting.com

Georgia-Pacific Corporation

CONTRIBUTIONS: TOTAL: *$358,988* DEM: *$97,007* REP: *$261,981*

Paid $22 million to settle a class action lawsuit filed by community residents who suffered injuries sustained from a blast at a company plant in 1997. Has settled numerous claims arising out of pollution from paper mills. Cited by the EPA for alleged clean-air violations at the company's manufacturing plant in Minnesota. Repeatedly cited by OSHA for worker safety violations. Boycotted by activists for buying wood from and deforesting endangered old-growth forests in Asia, North America, and Latin America. Educational, community enrichment, and environmental outreach extends into communities in which the company has a presence. Has a written nondiscrimination policy covering sexual orientation but not gender identity. Refuses insurance coverage to employees' domestic partners. www.gp.com

Gerber Products Company

CONTRIBUTIONS: TOTAL: *$250* DEM: *$21* REP: *$227*

Subsidiary of Novartis AG (p. 115). A pending class action suit alleges false advertising and misrepresentation of nutritional benefits in the promotion of Gerber Graduates Fruit Juice Snacks. Forced Guatemala to allow imports of baby food products despite laws intended to promote breast-feeding. In 1995, the Environmental Working Group found pesticide residue in some baby food products. Is a charter supporter of the EPA's Pesticide Environmental Stewardship Program to reduce risks pesticide use on human health and the environment. www.gerber.com

Good Home Company

No contributions. Privately held. All its products, cosmetics, and cleaning supplies are certified as not tested on animals. www.goodhomeco.com

Gund, Inc.

No contributions. Outreach includes matching funds donated to children's hospitals in the United States. www.gund.com

Hartmann, Inc.

CONTRIBUTIONS: TOTAL: *$300* DEM: *$124* REP: *$176*

Subsidiary of Brown-Forman Corporation (p. 74). www.hartmann.com

Hartz Mountain Corporation, The

No contributions. Named as a defendant in two wrongful injury/death suits filed by employees and their families alleging violations of OSHA regulations. Under a 2002 agreement with the EPA, enacted measures to reduce potential risks to animals caused from the use of two flea and tick products that were inciting boycotts from consumers and advocacy groups.

Outreach includes support for humane organizations and educational programs for pets in communities across the United States. www.hartz.com

Hasbro, Inc.
See p. 151 in Media and Entertainment

Henkel KGaA
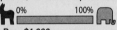
19%   81%

CONTRIBUTIONS: TOTAL: *$49,000* DEM: *$9,330* REP: *$39,654*

One of several companies faced with still-pending class action lawsuits for using slave labor from Nazi concentration camps. Claims that it no longer conducts testing on animals, choosing instead to use tissue cultures and human volunteers. Some branches of the company have ISO 14001 certification. www.henkel.com/www.henkel.us

Hill's Pet Nutrition, Inc.
0%   100%

CONTRIBUTIONS: TOTAL: *$600* DEM: *$0* REP: *$600*

Subsidiary of Colgate-Palmolive Co. (p. 108). www.hillspet.com

Hobby Lobby Stores, Inc.
0%   100%

CONTRIBUTIONS: TOTAL: *$4,000* DEM: *$0* REP: *$4,000*

Gives a 10% discount to school, church, and Boy and Girl Scout groups. Most of its charitable outreach is focused on Christian evangelicalism. www.hobbylobby.com

Home Depot, Inc.
17%   83%

CONTRIBUTIONS: TOTAL: *$674,895* DEM: *$116,162* REP: *$558,733*

America's second-largest retailer is also a major contributor to Republican campaigns, particularly President Bush's. Pushes for lower import tariffs and relaxed energy efficiency standards for its products. Also fighting multiple unfair labor practice suits, including dozens of charges filed by the U.S. Equal Employment Opportunity Commission (EEOC) alleging age, sex, and race discrimination. Agreed in 2000 to phase out its sales of lumber cut from old-growth forests. Many communities have fought to keep the big-box chain out of their towns, arguing that it promotes sprawl and wipes out competition from small businesses. Proponents counter that the stores create hundreds of jobs. Supports many children's sports and education programs. Has a written nondiscrimination policy covering sexual orientation but not gender identity. Offers insurance coverage to employees' domestic partners. www.homedepot.com

Iams Company, The

0%   100%

CONTRIBUTIONS: TOTAL: *$2,200* DEM: *$0* REP: *$2,200*

Subsidiary of Procter & Gamble (p. 116). People for the Ethical Treatment of Animals (PETA) called for a boycott following an undercover investigation in 2003 that found cruel practices at the company's testing facilities. Named in multiple lawsuits over false and misleading nutritional claims made by the company for its products. The British Advertising Standards Authority upheld two complaints that ads made "exaggerated" and "misleading" nutritional claims. Has a written nondiscrimination policy covering sexual orientation but not gender identity. Offers insurance coverage to employees' domestic partners. www.iams.com

IKEA International A/S
No contributions. Foreign owned. Forced to suspend construction because of environmental law violations at its St. Petersburg store. Offers insurance coverage to employees' domestic partners. www.ikea.com

IKEA North America
No contributions. Subsidiary of foreign-owned Ikea International A/S (p. 130). Multiple cases regarding environmental and other impacts of construction of its superstores. Several cases involving the illegal or improper demolition of historic properties. www.ikea.com

Jarden Corporation
See p. 174 in Sporting Goods.

Jo-Ann Stores, Inc.
No contributions. Ordered to pay $545,000 in 2003 to settle wage-and-hour claims brought by warehouse employees denied overtime. Paid $6.5 million in 2002 to settle a wage-and-hour suit brought by workers in California. Offers a stock ownership plan to employees. Partners with Save the Children and supports the United Way. Donated $19,000 to teachers in 10 states to support classroom projects. Publishes a craft-a-month calendar, donating 100% of net profits to charitable organizations, most recently $112,000 to the Red Cross. Has a written nondiscrimination policy covering sexual orientation but not gender identity. www.joann.com

Kimberly-Clark Corporation
See p. 112 in Health and Beauty.

KinderCare Learning Centers, Inc.
No contributions. Subsidiary of Knowledge Learning Corporation (p. 184). www.kindercare.com

Learning Care Group, Inc.
0% | 100%
CONTRIBUTIONS: TOTAL: *$5,250* DEM: *$0* REP: *$5,250*
Formerly Childtime Learning Centers. www.child-time.com

Lenox, Inc.
41% | 59%
CONTRIBUTIONS: TOTAL: *$1,654* DEM: *$683* REP: *$971*
Subsidiary of Brown-Forman Corporation (p. 74). www.lenox.com

Limited Brands, Inc.
See p. 17 in Clothing, Shoes, and Accessories.

Linens 'n Things, Inc.
CONTRIBUTIONS: TOTAL: *$1,750* DEM: *$1,750* REP: *$0*

Paid a $4 million settlement in a lawsuit brought by store managers denied overtime pay. Partners with the I Do Foundation by donating a percentage of the purchases made by and for engaged couples to charity. www.lnt.com

Lowe's Companies Inc.
CONTRIBUTIONS: TOTAL: *$9,250* DEM: *$0* REP: *$9,250*

A March 2004 lawsuit brought by the EEOC alleged racial discrimination against job applicants from 2002 to 2003. Founded the Home Safety Council and made a five-year, $10 million commitment to Habitat for Humanity. Has a written nondiscrimination policy covering sexual orientation but not gender identity. Refuses insurance coverage to employees' domestic partners. www.lowes.com

Manhattan Group, LLC
No contributions. The Canadian Labor Congress called a boycott against the company for its supplier relationships in Indonesia after the invasion of East Timor in 1999. Among 51 retailers that donated merchandise to Gifts in Kind International's 2003 toy drive. www.manhattantoy.com

Martha Stewart Living Omnimedia, Inc.
CONTRIBUTIONS: TOTAL: *$83,200* DEM: *$77,809* REP: *$5,391*

Offers three paid volunteer days per employee per year. Foundation supports women, families, and children, promoting community and domestic arts. www.marthastewart.com

Mattel, Inc.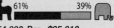
CONTRIBUTIONS: TOTAL: *$90,000* DEM: *$54,990* REP: *$35,010*

Refused to remove polyvinyl chloride from its toys despite its links to cancer and other illnesses. Has sourced from and has operations in countries with widespread, well-documented human and labor rights abuses. Philanthropy supports children's programs and community enhancement. Has a written nondiscrimination policy covering sexual orientation but not gender identity. Offers insurance coverage to employees' domestic partners. www.mattel.com

Maytag Corporation
CONTRIBUTIONS: TOTAL: *$47,500* DEM: *$4,001* REP: *$43,500*

Paid $47,500 in 2003 to the EPA for the cleanup of hazardous materials dumped in a Tennessee Superfund site. Cited by OSHA in 2005 and paid $67,500 in fines for failing to protect workers from improperly maintained and unguarded machinery.

Received the EPA's Energy Star Partner of the Year award for manufacturing energy-efficient products and reducing greenhouse gas emissions. Has a written nondiscrimination policy covering sexual orientation but not gender identity. Refuses insurance coverage to employees' domestic partners. www.maytagcorp.com

Menards, Inc.
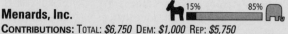
CONTRIBUTIONS: TOTAL: *$6,750* DEM: *$1,000* REP: *$5,750*
Ordered in 2005 to pay $2 million in fines for illegally dumping pollutants into the Chippewa River. Has received more citations from Wisconsin's Department of Natural Resources than any other company. In 2003, the Minnesota attorney general alleged that company sold mulch that was contaminated with toxic preservatives as "ideal for playgrounds." Paid $1.7 million in a 1997 plea agreement to settle hazardous waste charges. Fined $42,500 by OSHA in 1998 for 37 violations following the death of a 22-year-old worker. Agreed in 2000 to meet demands to phase out wood procured from endangered forests. Offers employees "instant profit sharing." Charitable outreach sponsors a professional race car team and cosponsors an annual winter coat drive in the Chicago area. www.menards.com

Meow Mix Company, The

CONTRIBUTIONS: TOTAL: *$5,000* DEM: *$0* REP: *$5,000*
Subsidiary of J. W. Childs Associates, L.P. (p. 86). www.meowmix.com

Method
No contributions. All products are certified as cruelty-free, not tested on animals. Products are biodegradable and nontoxic, contain no phosphates or bleach, and are packaged in recyclable plastic. www.methodhome.com

Michaels Stores, Inc.
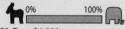
CONTRIBUTIONS: TOTAL: *$4,000* DEM: *$0* REP: *$4,000*
Controlled by Sam and Charles Wyly (board chair), among the top 10 George W. Bush supporters, who paid for the anti–John Kerry Swift Boat ads and the $2.5 million "whispering" campaign against John McCain in the 2000 Republican primary. Settled a wage-and-hour class action suit brought in 2002 by California store managers denied overtime. Has a written nondiscrimination policy covering sexual orientation but not gender identity. www.michaels.com

Natural Life Pet Products
No contributions. Recognized by PETA as not testing on animals. Outreach includes work with the Doris Day Foundation, the American Heart Association, and Special Olympics. Member of the Co-op America Business Network, a group of busi-

nesses embracing socially and environmentally responsible practices. www.nlpp.com

Newell Rubbermaid, Inc.

CONTRIBUTIONS: TOTAL: *$15,000* DEM: *$0* REP: *$15,000*

One of the country's largest producers of greenhouse gases. Subsidiary Graco Children's Products Inc. agreed in 2005 to pay a record $4 million to settle charges that it belatedly reported problems with car seats, high chairs, strollers, and other products that resulted in hundreds of injuries and at least six deaths. Supports Victory Junction Gang Camp, which seeks to enrich the lives of children with chronic or life-threatening illnesses. Has a written nondiscrimination policy covering sexual orientation but not gender identity. Refuses insurance coverage to employees' domestic partners. www.newellco.com

Nutro Products, Inc.

CONTRIBUTIONS: TOTAL: *$53,000* DEM: *$0* REP: *$53,000*

Named in multiple lawsuits over false and misleading nutritional claims made by the company for its products. Criticized for contracting with research labs that allow harsh treatment of and poor conditions for animals used in testing. www.nutroproducts.com

Oil-Dri Corporation of America

CONTRIBUTIONS: TOTAL: *$18,000* DEM: *$500* REP: *$17,500*

Received a permit to operate a Nevada clay mine and cat litter processing plant, after posting a $1.5 million security bond, an amount opponents said was low considering prior environmental violations. Has a written nondiscrimination policy covering sexual orientation but not gender identity. www.oildri.com

Old Mother Hubbard Dog Food Co., Inc.

No contributions. Subsidiary of Sears, Roebuck and Co. (p. 145). Claims it does not test on animals, though PETA cites a lack of written confirmation of company policies. www.omhpet.com

Orchard Supply Hardware Corporation

No contributions. Subsidiary of Sears, Roebuck and Co. (p. 145). Has a written nondiscrimination policy covering sexual orientation and gender identity. Offers insurance coverage to employees' domestic partners. www.osh.com

Pactiv Corporation

CONTRIBUTIONS: TOTAL: *$500* DEM: *$0* REP: *$500*

Former subsidiary of Tenneco, Inc. Fined $1 million in 2004 and expected to spend up to $5 million more to bring its plant in line with clean-air codes. One of several manufacturers asked to pay a portion of a $200 million settlement in a class action lawsuit alleging price-fixing of cardboard. Paid a $3.5 million settlement in 2003 to a worker who sustained second- and third-degree electrical burns while installing a security gate. In 2001, settled charges of wrongfully treating injured workers. Supports Chicago-area charities. www.pactiv.com

PB Teen
No contributions. Subsidiary of Williams-Sonoma, Inc. (p. 139). www.pbteen.com

Pet Appeal, Inc.
No contributions. Makes 70%-organic pet food. Contributes a portion of profits to its Pet & Soul Foundation, which supports programs that promote the health-giving relationship between pets and their owners. www.castorpolluxpet.com

Pet Central, Inc.
No contributions. Donates merchandise to charitable fundraisers and supports humane societies, rescue groups, and assistance dog–training programs. www.waggers.com

PETCO Animal Supplies Stores, Inc.
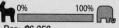
CONTRIBUTIONS: TOTAL: *$7,000* DEM: *$555* REP: *$6,420*
Subsidiary of Texas Pacific Group (p. 168). Agreed in 2004 to pay more than $900,000 to settle lawsuits over mistreating animals and overcharging customers in four California counties. Settled a lawsuit in 2003 alleging failure to pay overtime. PETA agreed to end its boycott in 2005 after the company agreed to stop selling large birds. www.petco.com

Petguard, Inc.
No contributions. Products are made without chemical additives, preservatives, animal by-products, or genetically modified organisms. Does not test on animals. www.petguard.com

PETsMART, Inc.
CONTRIBUTIONS: TOTAL: *$6,250* DEM: *$0* REP: *$6,250*
Cited by the EPA in 2001 and fined $44,550 for selling products whose labels claimed they would repel animals. Activists have called for a boycott until animal sales cease. Supports in-store animal adoption efforts. Has a written nondiscrimination policy covering sexual orientation but not gender identity. Offers insurance coverage to employees' domestic partners. www.petsmart.com

Pet Valu, Inc.
No contributions. Recalled several products in 1999 for suspected salmonella contamination. Individual stores donate merchandise to local rescue operations and shelters. www.petvalu.com

Pier 1 Imports, Inc.

CONTRIBUTIONS: TOTAL: *$41,500* DEM: *$393* REP: *$41,086*

Fined $175,000 in 2004 for storing hazardous waste. In 2000, its former CFO was fined $75,000 and censured by the SEC after he hid $20 million in company losses in 1995. Supports UNICEF, donating 100% of the proceeds from sale of UNICEF holiday cards, amounting to $1.8 million in 2002. Has donated substantially to the Susan G. Komen Breast Cancer Foundation. Has a written nondiscrimination policy covering sexual orientation. www.pier1.com

Pottery Barn

No contributions. Subsidiary of Williams-Sonoma, Inc. (p. 139). Brought a lawsuit against former secretary of state Colin Powell for injunctive relief after Powell used the company's name connected to a negative concept in his recent book. www.potterybarn.com

Pottery Barn Kids

No contributions. Subsidiary of Williams-Sonoma, Inc. (p. 139). www.potterybarnkids.com

Procter & Gamble

See p. 116 in Health and Beauty.

RC2 Corporation

No contributions. Merged in 2004 with the First Years, Inc. Donated merchandise to Gifts in Kind International's 2003 toy drive. www.rc2corp.com

Reckitt Benckiser Inc.

No contributions. Settled charges in 2004 claiming Energine Spot Remover contained excessive volatile organic compounds and agreed to pay $165,000 in penalties. Claims to oppose animal testing in products or raw materials unless legally required, though a boycott in the United Kingdom was called due to its animal testing. Has a comprehensive environmental initiative, focusing on sustainability and biodiversity. Greenhouse gas output has been decreasing incrementally since 2001. In 2005, reengineered several of its products to decrease the use of plastic in packaging. Donates more than $1 million annually to organizations such as Habitat for Humanity, the United Way, and Save the Children. Matches employees' charitable gifts. Has a written nondiscrimination policy that covers sexual orientation but not gender identity. www.reckitt.com

Redbarn Pet Products, Inc.

No contributions. Uses only natural preservatives. www.redbarninc.com

Restoration Hardware, Inc.

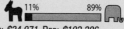

100%   0%

CONTRIBUTIONS: TOTAL: *$200* DEM: *$200* REP: *$0*

Has a written nondiscrimination policy covering sexual orientation but not gender identity. Offers insurance coverage to employees' domestic partners.
www.restorationhardware.com

Russ Berrie and Company, Inc.

No contributions. Russell Berrie Foundation supports Jewish communal life and religious tolerance, the arts, awards for health care, and research, including a donation of more than $20 million to Columbia University for a Diabetic Retinopathy Program and Medical Science Pavilion. www.russberrie.com

S. C. Johnson & Son, Inc.

11%   89%

CONTRIBUTIONS: TOTAL: *$218,357* DEM: *$24,971* REP: *$193,386*

Stopped using chlorofluorocarbons three years before being required to do so by law. Uses methane gas derived from a landfill as an electricity source for its largest Wisconsin plant. Paid nearly $1 million to settle charges that it failed in 2001 to comply with New York state child safety packaging requirements for its roach killer. Wholly owned Subsidiary Drackett Products is known to test on animals. Subsidiary Johnson Financial Group, Inc., settled an EEOC-led lawsuit in 2005 for $450,000 for pregnancy discrimination. Cosponsors an educational campaign to end malaria in sub-Saharan Africa. Has comprehensive, company-wide recycling policies. Has contributed $140 million in the last decade to efforts ranging from the Nature Conservancy to building schools in Latin America. Consistently recognized as among the top companies nationally for women and minorities. Offers paid sabbaticals, flexible scheduling, and on-site child care. Has a written nondiscrimination policy covering sexual orientation and gender identity. Offers insurance coverage to employees' domestic partners.
www.scjohnson.com

Scotts Miracle-Gro Co.

0%   100%

CONTRIBUTIONS: TOTAL: *$180,701* DEM: *$691* REP: *$180,010*

Formerly Scotts Company. Continued to process vermiculite with asbestos content for a decade despite five employee deaths allegedly from asbestos exposure. Announced plans to phase out the use of vermiculite in its products in 2001. Processing of vermiculite continues, with the company's assurance that asbestos levels are too low to be a health risk. Fined $300,000 and required to give $900,000 to a pesticide disposal project in New York state in 2002, for distributing pesticides. Friends of the Earth called for a boycott of its peat-containing compost products in 2001, citing the disappearance and need for conservation of bogs. Gives $40,000 a year to community gardeners; supports the Farms for City Kids program in Vermont.

Partners with Keep America Beautiful, U.S. Botanic Garden, New York Botanical Garden, Franklin Park Conservatory, and Global Environmental Management Initiative. www.scotts.com

Sears, Roebuck and Co.
See p. 145 in Major Retailers.

Seventh Generation, Inc.
CONTRIBUTIONS: TOTAL: *$4,476* DEM: *$4,476* REP: *$0*

Largest manufacturer of nontoxic household products, including cleaners, paper goods, and diapers. Products are biodegradable, do not contain animal matter, and are not tested on animals. Introduced chlorine-free diapers in 2003, after urging one of its suppliers to begin providing unbleached raw materials. Has begun using rail instead of truck transport for some shipping. In 2003, donated $25,000 cash and $5,000 in matching gifts and merchandise to socially and environmentally conscious organizations. www.seventhgeneration.com

Shaklee Corporation
CONTRIBUTIONS: TOTAL: *$5,000* DEM: *$4,372* REP: *$628*

Named by PETA as one of many companies that do not test on animals. Partners with the Whale Conservation Institute and Wild Dolphin Project; is part of the Climate Neutral Network, a coalition of companies seeking to have zero net impact on the environment. www.shaklee.com

Sharper Image Corporation
See p. 47 in Computers and Electronics.

Sherwin-Williams Company, The
CONTRIBUTIONS: TOTAL: *$39,000* DEM: *$0* REP: *$39,000*

Paid $4.7 million in fines in 1997 after the EPA found its Chicago manufacturing site was polluted; agreed to cover the state's oversight and planning costs. One of several companies cited in a pending antitrust class action suit alleging price-fixing. One of several paint manufacturers alleged to have sold toxic, lead-based paint in recent pending lawsuits. Has a written nondiscrimination policy covering sexual orientation but not gender identity. Refuses insurance coverage to employees' domestic partners. www.sherwinwilliams.com

Sitstay Goout Inc.
No contributions. Donates to dog rescue operations. www.sitstay.com

Spectrum Brands, Inc.
See p. 48 in Computers and Electronics.

Stanley Works, The

0%   100%

CONTRIBUTIONS: TOTAL: *$5,000* DEM: *$0* REP: *$5,000*

Targeted by an SEC investigation in 2003 over questionable accounting practices. Has a favorable employee gain-sharing program. Has a written nondiscrimination policy covering sexual orientation but not gender identity. www.stanleyworks.com

Toshiba America, Inc.; Toshiba Corporation

See p. 49 in Computers and Electronics.

Toys "R" Us, Inc.

No contributions. Agreed in 1999 to a $40.5 million settlement in a lawsuit brought by 44 states alleging misuse of market power for pressuring suppliers and restricting toy sales to other retailers. As settlement in a privacy lawsuit in 2000, terminated an arrangement the company had with a third-party data firm that allowed access to the personal information of online customers. Outreach supports children's education and literacy. Has a written nondiscrimination policy covering sexual orientation and gender identity. Refuses insurance coverage to employees' domestic partners. www.toysrus.com

True Value Company

No contributions. A cooperative of independently owned stores. Was fined $75,000 by the EPA in 2001 for failing to secure hazardous waste permits and initiate regular inspections of its Chicago-area paint manufacturing plant. www.truevaluecompany.com

Tupperware Corporation

4%   96%

CONTRIBUTIONS: TOTAL: *$13,500* DEM: *$500* REP: *$13,000*

Outreach efforts support children and women's issues and matches employee donations supporting disaster response. www.tupperware.com

Ty Inc.

No contributions. www.ty.com

WD-40 Company

No contributions. Uses recycled materials in its packaging and is developing products that extend the lives of machinery. Outreach supports education, health, and human services. Matches employees' charitable gifts and supports volunteerism. www.wd40.com

Wellmark International, Inc.

No contributions. Formerly known as Zoecon. In 2000, the New York State Department of Environmental Conservation rejected the company's request to remove warning labels from its Methoprene pesticide products. www.wellmarkinternational.com

Whirlpool Corporation

22%   78%

CONTRIBUTIONS: TOTAL: *$94,500* DEM: *$20,501* REP: *$74,000*

Paid an $80,000 settlement to the Ohio EPA for hazardous waste and pollution permit violations. Currently pending a racial discrimination lawsuit brought by a multiracial employee group alleging discrimination against blacks at its Tennessee facility. Outreach supports family self-sufficiency for community building. Listed six years running as one of the "100 Best Corporate Citizens" by *Business Ethics* magazine. Has a written nondiscrimination policy covering sexual orientation and gender identity. Offers insurance coverage to employees' domestic partners. www.whirlpoolcorp.com

White Barn Candle Co., The

No contributions. Subsidiary of Limited Brands, Inc. (p. 17). www.limitedbrands.com

Williams-Sonoma, Inc.

0%   100%

CONTRIBUTIONS: TOTAL: *$114,000* DEM: *$0* REP: *$114,000*

A pending class action lawsuit brought by employees in California alleges improper classification and failure to pay overtime. No longer stocks products made in Burma in a direct response to the human rights violations there. Claims to use ethical sourcing methods by establishing relationships with socially responsible vendors. Uses paper procurement practices that promote sustainability of forests and other natural resources. Has an ambitious recycling outreach program. Has a written nondiscrimination policy covering sexual orientation but not gender identity. Offers health insurance coverage to employees' domestic partners. www.williams-sonomainc.com

Williams-Sonoma Stores

No contributions. Subsidiary of Williams-Sonoma, Inc. (p. 139). Has a written nondiscrimination policy covering sexual orientation not gender identity. Offers insurance coverage to employees' domestic partners. www.williams-sonoma.com

WKI Holding Company, Inc.

0%   100%

CONTRIBUTIONS: TOTAL: *$2,000* DEM: *$0* REP: *$2,000*

Sponsors the Pillsbury Bake-Off. www.worldkitchen.com

Woolrich, Inc.

See p. 30 in Clothing, Shoes, and Accessories.

Z Gallerie, Inc.

No contributions. Has partnered with the Pancreatic Cancer Action Network. www.zgallerie.com

Major Retailers

The fight for market share has forced major retailers to grow ever larger; as with many growth industries, this expansion tends to put them at odds with local communities, environmentalists, labor unions, and smaller businesses unable to compete on the same level. It follows, then, that the sector spends millions on lobbying and public relations. The sector has pushed at both federal and local levels for imminent domain rights, massive tax breaks, and the revision of local ordinances barring giant stores. Proponents of the big-box store and other major retailer operations argue that these institutions benefit both the consumer and the state, bringing in new jobs and taxes.

In the major retailer sector, Wal-Mart Stores, Inc., understandably dominates the headlines. From sprawl to outsourcing, monopolization, labor abuses, and cuts to health insurance and other employee benefits, the multibillion-dollar big-box store has found itself enmeshed in just about every issue relevant to the sector at large.

The spread of major retail chains has generally gone hand-in-hand with big business–friendly legislation, but the government has pushed back at times. Recently legislators have noted the trend among major retailers to move away from providing health insurance for their employees. With funding for Medicaid and other public health insurance programs becoming scarce, some members of Congress have proposed asking these large employers—which often employ thousands of uninsured employees—to do their share rather than abandoning their responsibility for their employees to public services provided by taxpayers.

Top Ten Republican Contributors

United Parcel Service, Inc.	$2,073,930
Wal-Mart Stores, Inc.	1,654,949
FedEx Holding Corporation	1,513,085
Sears Holdings Corporation	246,537
Target Corporation	245,821
EBay Inc.	133,071
OfficeMax Incorporated	57,921
Staples, Inc.	14,006
Office Depot, Inc.	8,840
Costco Wholesale Corporation	2,000

Top Ten Democratic Contributors

United Parcel Service, Inc.	$859,900
FedEx Holding Corporation	643,465
Wal-Mart Stores, Inc.	453,651
Costco Wholesale Corporation	224,303
EBay Inc.	175,183
Sears Holdings Corporation	98,362
Target Corporation	50,419
Staples, Inc.	18,994
OfficeMax Incorporated	7,618
Office Depot, Inc.	1,110

Ahold USA, Inc.
See p. 71 in Food and Beverage.

Amazon.com, Inc.
See p. 149 in Media and Entertainment.

Costco Wholesale Corporation 🐴 99% ▰▰▰▰▰▰ 1% 🐘
CONTRIBUTIONS: TOTAL: *$226,303* DEM: *$224,303* REP: *$2,000*
Fought several publicized battles to build controversial high-impact stores, including one in New Mexico that included destroying a historic building housing a series of invaluable murals. Its workers are among the highest paid in the retail industry. Is considered union-friendly, having negotiated generous contracts with many of the unions representing its workforce. Has a written nondiscrimination policy covering sexual orientation but not gender identity. Offers insurance coverage to employees' domestic partners. www.costco.com

EBay Inc. 🐴 57% ▰▰▰▰▱▱ 43% 🐘
CONTRIBUTIONS: TOTAL: *$308,254* DEM: *$175,183* REP: *$133,071*
The company PAC contributes two-thirds of its revenue to Republican causes, but its individual contributions are predominantly Democratic. Was awarded the Smithsonian Award by *Computerworld* magazine for "creating a new global mar-

ketplace and trading community," thereby improving society. Has a written nondiscrimination policy covering sexual orientation but not gender identity. Offers insurance coverage to employees' domestic partners. www.ebay.com

Federated Department Stores
See p. 11 in Clothing, Shoes, and Accessories.

FedEx Holding Corporation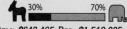
CONTRIBUTIONS: TOTAL: *$2,156,550* DEM: *$643,465* REP: *$1,513,085*
May be best known for its overnight delivery service, but also enjoys major military contracts as the Defense Department's number one supplier of air charter services. The company's campaign contributions strongly favor Republican candidates. Has made significant investments in hybrid delivery trucks and solar power; also made *Fortune* magazine's list of the "100 Best Companies to Work For." Has a nondiscrimination policy covering sexual orientation but not gender identity. Some FedEx subsidiaries offer insurance coverage to employees' domestic partners. www.fedex.com

Home Depot, Inc.
See p. 129 in Home and Garden.

Kmart Corporation
No contributions. Subsidiary of Kmart Holding Corporation (p. 143); parent, Sears Holdings Corporation (p. 144). Has been accused of supporting sweatshop labor, most famously in 1996 for its Kathy Lee Gifford clothing line. Charged by the Securities and Exchange Commission (SEC) in 2004 with fraud for reportedly misstating its earnings to investors. Agreed to stop selling handguns and ammunition at its stores in 2001. Corporate giving includes $10 million annually to schools. Has sourced from countries with widespread, well-documented human and labor rights abuses. Has a written nondiscrimination policy covering sexual orientation but not gender identity. Plans to offer insurance coverage to employees' domestic partners. www.kmart.com

Kmart Holding Corporation
No contributions. Subsidiary of Sears Holdings Corporation (p. 144). See subsidiary Kmart Corporation (p. 143) for complete listing. Outreach supports children's health initiatives and toy distribution programs.

Kroger Co., The
See p. 88 in Food and Beverage.

Macy's
See p. 19 in Clothing, Shoes, and Accessories.

Mail Boxes Etc., Inc.

No contributions. Subsidiary of United Parcel Service, Inc. (p. 145). Its purchase in 2003 by United Parcel Service, Inc., spawned lawsuits by franchisees. Foundation supports activities for underprivileged and sick children. www.mbe.com

Office Depot, Inc.

11%   89%

CONTRIBUTIONS: TOTAL: *$10,000* DEM: *$1,110* REP: *$8,840*

Paid $4.75 million to settle charges of selling office products to the government that were manufactured in countries without reciprocal trade agreements with the United States. Settled a class action suit alleging failure to pay overtime to assistant store managers. Listed by the National Association for Female Executives as one of the top 30 companies for female executives, with steady increases in female senior management. Has a written nondiscrimination policy covering sexual orientation but not gender identity. Offers insurance coverage to employees' domestic partners. www.officedepot.com

OfficeMax Incorporated

12%   88%

CONTRIBUTIONS: TOTAL: *$65,539* DEM: *$7,618* REP: *$57,921*

Sued by the state of Ohio in 2005 for violating consumer laws and engaging in unfair and deceptive practices. Has an "unsatisfactory" rating with the Better Business Bureau. Facing several class action suits filed in 2005 on behalf of shareholders for misrepresenting earnings prompting the departure of several top-level executives. Pressure from environmental groups induced then–parent company Boise Cascade to establish a landmark environmental policy, ending purchase of logs from endangered areas and giving preference to suppliers working certified, well-managed forests. Outreach supports education, civic improvement, and the arts. Has a written nondiscrimination policy covering sexual orientation but not gender identity. Refuses insurance coverage to employees' domestic partners. www.officemax.com

Petters Group Worldwide, LLC

See p. 46 in Computers and Electronics.

Royal Ahold, N.V.

See p. 94 in Food and Beverage.

Sears Holdings Corporation

28%   72%

CONTRIBUTIONS: TOTAL: *$345,850* DEM: *$98,363* REP: *$246,537*

Cut most employee benefits, eliminated tuition reimbursement plans, and initiated a policy tying employee pay to profits. See individual subsidiaries for more specifics: Sears, Roebuck and Co. (p. 145), Kmart Corporation (p. 143), Lands' End, Inc. (p. 16), and Orchard Supply Hardware Corporation (p. 133). www.searshc.com

Sears, Roebuck and Co.

No contributions. Subsidiary of Sears Holding Corporation (p. 144). One of 26 retailers that agreed to a $20 million settlement of a class action lawsuit by garment workers in Saipan alleging sweatshop practices. Currently facing litigation from 200 franchised dealers who will lose business when Kmart stores begins selling Sears hardware. Indicted in 2004 for illegal contributions to Tom DeLay. Sued in 2002 by the state of New Jersey for violations of the Consumer Fraud Act at Sears Auto Centers. Has sourced from countries with widespread, well-documented human and labor rights abuses. Outreach supports home maintenance education for low-income families. Has a written nondiscrimination policy covering sexual orientation and gender identity. Offers insurance coverage to employees' domestic partners. www.sears.com

Staples, Inc.

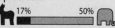

58%   50%

CONTRIBUTIONS: TOTAL: *$33,000* DEM: *$18,994* REP: *$14,006*

Adopted a proconsumer environmental policy after environmental groups protested against its lax recycling policies. Provides financial support for environmental causes and education. Has a written nondiscrimination policy covering sexual orientation and gender identity. Offers insurance coverage to employees' domestic partners. www.staples.com

Target Corporation

17%   50%

CONTRIBUTIONS: TOTAL: *$296,240* DEM: *$50,419* REP: *$245,821*

One of 26 retailers that agreed to a $20 million settlement with garment workers in Saipan for alleged sweatshop practices. Agreed to pay a $1.9 million settlement to immigrant janitors for failure to pay overtime, Social Security, and other taxes. Has sourced from countries with widespread, well-documented human and labor rights abuses. Foundation supports education, the arts, and social services. Has a written nondiscrimination policy covering sexual orientation but not gender identity. Offers insurance coverage to employees' domestic partners. www.targetcorp.com

UBid, Inc.

No contributions. Bought in 2003 by Petters Group Worldwide, LLC (p. 46). Has hosted auctions of celebrity memorabilia to raise funds for cancer and diabetes research. www.ubid.com

United Parcel Service, Inc.

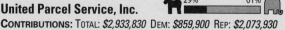

29%   61%

CONTRIBUTIONS: TOTAL: *$2,933,830* DEM: *$859,900* REP: *$2,073,930*

Fined $72,000 for willful and serious safety violations resulting in the fatal electrocution of an employee. Paid $1.6 million in attorneys' fees and was forced to pay into union workers' retirement accounts for violation of federal law. Recognized for efforts in ethnic and gender diversity. Outreach supports environmental stewardship and the United Way. Has a written nondiscrimination policy covering sexual orientation but not gender identity. Offers insurance coverage to employees' domestic partners. www.ups.com

Wal-Mart Stores, Inc.

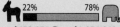

CONTRIBUTIONS: TOTAL: *$2,108,600* DEM: *$453,651* REP: *$1,654,949*

Notorious for its refusal to allow workers to unionize, its dismal record on employee compensation, and its poor benefits program. Gave more to political campaigns in 2004 than any other company, with contributions overwhelmingly favoring Republican candidates. The company's lobbying campaigns include increasing tax cuts, eliminating the estate tax, and greasing the wheels for trade with China. Paid an $11 million settlement to avoid federal criminal charges stemming from government crackdowns on employers using illegal alien contractors. Faces the largest civil rights class action lawsuit in U.S. history over alleged sexual discrimination in its hiring and promotional practices. Blamed for consuming vast tracks of farmland and natural habitat, as well as promoting sprawl, destroying local businesses, contaminating groundwater with parking lot runoff, and encouraging car dependency. Charitable giving exceeded $170 million in 2004. Has a written nondiscrimination policy covering sexual orientation but not gender identity. Refuses insurance coverage to employees' domestic partners. www.walmartstores.com

Media and Entertainment

So many channels, so many websites, so many books, so many newspapers and magazines nowadays—no wonder the public has been slow to notice the tiny number of corporate giants behind many of them.

Media consolidation may be the granddaddy of all political issues. As the so-called free press consolidates itself under a handful of enormous companies, its ability to guard the public interest becomes increasingly undermined by bean counters and earnings statements. With the demise of independence and variety comes the neglect of all else: honest and balanced news coverage of widening class disparity, the environment, corporate malfeasance, political maneuvering, and so on.

Nevertheless, public debate about the state of the media has largely centered on the red herring of liberal versus conservative bias. The question of political bias, though occasionally pertinent, shifts the public's focus from the larger issue of media corporatization. The chain of effects is rarely direct—seldom does the head of Viacom, Inc. (see p. 154), tap out a directive to its local school board reporter in Boise—but corporate culture and policy trickles down all the same. Writing in 1938, but envisioning precisely the present day, the renowned press critic George Seldes noted, "The most stupid boast in the history of present-day journalism is that of the writer who says, 'I have never been given orders; I am free to do as I like.'"

The dramatic shrinking of media diversity picked up pace in the 1990s, even as the Internet promised to expand the number of voices. The heavily lobbied Telecommunications Act of 1996—a love letter to media giants—led to unprecedented concentration of the media, and the climate has only grown more permissive since. Critics have noted the particular danger in having an industry coddled by the very administration it purports to report on. Then there are moments when corporate policy and journalistic cravenness collide, as when the CEO of General Electric Company (which owns NBC; see p. 58 in Finance, Insurance, and Real Estate) instructed NBC News to call the 2000 election for George W. Bush, following Fox News' premature announcement. Even the much-heralded democratization of the digital realm finds itself under fire as the media lobby has sought to limit peer-to-peer networks, fair use, and Internet service provider (ISP) choice for broadband.

Though the Bush administration has gone out of its way to support media conglomeration, the matter hardly breaks down by party. It was President Bill Clinton who supported deregulation in the 1990s, and Rupert Murdoch was so taken with Al Gore's friendliness to the industry that the arch-conservative supported him in his 2000 run for president.

From the responsible consumer standpoint, affecting change in the media is tricky; tuning out the corporate media entirely threatens to harm the citizen more than the company. Supporting the independent press—and publishers, film companies, music labels, and so forth—is a start, as is an awareness of the connection between media outlets and their parent companies.

Top Ten Republican Contributors

General Electric Company	$1,013,039
Viacom, Inc.	250,065
Blockbuster Inc.	240,645
News Corporation, Ltd., The	235,601
American Express Company	226,885
Walt Disney Company, The	193,052
Amazon.com, Inc.	73,506
Mattel, Inc.	35,010
Cinemark	25,679
Discovery Communications, Inc./ Discovery Channel Store	14,642

Top Ten Democratic Contributors

General Electric Company	$562,011
Walt Disney Company, The	226,948
News Corporation, Ltd., The	219,910
Viacom, Inc.	178,139
American Express Company	155,865
Blockbuster Inc.	154,855
Barnes & Noble Inc.	80,000
Discovery Communications, Inc./ Discovery Channel Store	72,308
Bad Boy Worldwide Entertainment Group	69,495
Hasbro, Inc.	66,750

AEA Investors

See p. 52 in Finance, Insurance, and Real Estate.

Amazon.com, Inc.

39%   61%

CONTRIBUTIONS: TOTAL: *$120,750* DEM: *$47,244* REP: *$73,506*

Settled a class action lawsuit in 2005 alleging falsification of financial and other statements about the company's finances and prospects. Settled a class action lawsuit accusing it of fraud and violations of privacy, agreeing to pay $1.9 million in fines and retributions to individuals. Has a written nondiscrimination policy covering sexual orientation but not gender identity. Offers insurance coverage to employees' domestic partners. www.amazon.com

AMC Entertainment Inc.

No contributions. Owns one-quarter of MovieTickets.com (p. 152). Lost a suit filed by the Department of Justice alleging violations of the Americans with Disabilities Act over theater seating. Forgave nearly $20 million in loans to two executive officers despite workforce reductions and higher-than-predicted losses. www.amctheatres.com

American Express Company
See p. 53 in Finance, Insurance, and Real Estate.

Bad Boy Records
No contributions. Subsidiary of Bad Boy Worldwide Entertainment Group (p. 150). www.badboyonline.com

Bad Boy Worldwide Entertainment Group
CONTRIBUTIONS: TOTAL: *$69,500* DEM: *$69,500* REP: *$0*
Company outreach supports education, internship programs, and initiatives for inner-city youth. www.badboyonline.com

Barnes & Noble Inc.
CONTRIBUTIONS: TOTAL: *$88,000* DEM: *$80,000* REP: *$0*
In 2001, Barnes & Noble Inc. and Border's Group Inc. (p. 151) paid $2 million in fines after they were found to have unfairly competed with independent booksellers. Outreach efforts include sponsoring literacy programs, higher learning, and the arts. Has a written nondiscrimination policy covering sexual orientation but not gender identity. Offers health insurance coverage to employees' domestic partners.
www.barnesandnobleinc.com

Blockbuster Inc.
CONTRIBUTIONS: TOTAL: *$395,500* DEM: *$154,855* REP: *$240,645*
Removed NC-17 titles from its shelves in 2000. Criticized for squeezing locally owned video rental stores out of the business. Its "no more late fees" campaign earned a fine and restitution order when a judge ruled that the "restocking charge" constituted a late fee. Store in the occupied West Bank has earned boycott calls from pro-Palestinian groups. Outreach includes support for the National Association for the Advancement of Colored People (NAACP) and the Boys & Girls Clubs of America. Has a written nondiscrimination policy covering sexual orientation but not gender identity. Offers insurance to employees' domestic partners.

BMG Direct Marketing Inc.
CONTRIBUTIONS: TOTAL: *$4,250* DEM: *$4,250* REP: *$0*
One of 16 music industry companies agreeing to a $143 million settlement in a price-fixing scheme following an action by the Federal Trade Commission (FTC). The settlement resulted in refunds to customers and donations of music CDs to libraries and not-for-profit organizations. Paid a $10 million settlement in a lawsuit alleging payola and other fraud. www.bmg.com

Books-A-Million Inc.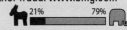
CONTRIBUTIONS: TOTAL: *$9,750* DEM: *$3,750* REP: *$6,000*
Absorbed Crown Books in 2001. www.booksamillion.com

Borders Group Inc.
No contributions. In 2001, Barnes & Noble Inc. (p. 150) and Border's Group Inc. paid $2 million in fines after they were found to have unfairly competed with independent booksellers. Settled a lawsuit in 2002 alleging failure to compensate employees for logged overtime. Foundation supports literacy programs, education, and the fine and performing arts, particularly music. Has a written nondiscrimination policy covering sexual orientation and gender identity. Offers health insurance coverage to employees' domestic partners. www.bordersgroupinc.com

Carmike Cinemas
No contributions. Settled a lawsuit alleging its theater seating violates regulations of the Americans with Disabilities Act. www.carmike.com

Cinemark
21% / 79%

CONTRIBUTIONS: TOTAL: *$32,429* DEM: *$6,750* REP: *$25,679*

Settled a lawsuit alleging its theater seating violates regulations of the Americans with Disabilities Act. www.cinemark.com

Columbia House Company
100% / 0%

CONTRIBUTIONS: TOTAL: *$4,250* DEM: *$4,250* REP: *$0*

Subsidiary of BMG Direct Marketing Inc. (p. 150). Fined $1.6 million for more than 600 health and safety violations at its Indiana plant. www.columbiahouse.com

Discovery Communications, Inc./Discovery Channel Store
83% / 17%

CONTRIBUTIONS: TOTAL: *$87,000* DEM: *$72,308* REP: *$14,642*

Outreach includes educational programming in the United States and third world countries. Has a written nondiscrimination policy covering sexual orientation but not gender identity. Offers insurance coverage to employees' domestic partners. www.discovery.com

General Electric Company
See p. 58 in Finance, Insurance, and Real Estate.

Hasbro, Inc.
97% / 3%

CONTRIBUTIONS: TOTAL: *$69,000* DEM: *$66,750* REP: *$2,250*

In 2003, Hasbro, Inc., and two British retail store chains were fined by the British Office of Fair Trading for price-fixing of toys and games. Adopted a labor code of conduct in response to a Chinese supplier having been found to violate human and labor rights. Makes philanthropic donations to programs supporting children's issues and has a employee matching program. Has a written nondiscrimination policy covering sexual orientation but not gender identity. Offers insurance coverage to employees' domestic partners. www.hasbro.com

IAC/InterActiveCorp

81%   19%

CONTRIBUTIONS: TOTAL: *$56,093* DEM: *$45,645* REP: *$10,448*

Currently named in a pending class action lawsuit alleging misrepresentation and other violations of federal securities laws. Has a written nondiscrimination policy covering sexual orientation but not gender identity. Offers insurance coverage to employees' domestic partners. www.iac.com

Knowledge Universe, Inc.

See p. 184 in Telecommunications and Internet.

Landmark Theatre Corp.

No contributions. Subsidiary of 2929 Entertainment. www.landmarktheatres.com

LeapFrog Enterprises, Inc.

See p. 43 in Computers and Electronics.

Loews Cineplex Entertainment Corporation

No contributions. Sued for alleged violations of the Americans with Disabilities Act due to lack of captioning for movies. Sued along with Sony Theaters by the owner of three Manhattan movie theaters for violation of the Sherman Antitrust Act. www.loewscineplex.com

Mattel, Inc.

See p. 131 in Home and Garden.

Movie Gallery Inc.

0%   100%

CONTRIBUTIONS: TOTAL: *$6,200* DEM: *$0* REP: *$6,200*

Adheres to the Video Software Dealer's Association "Pledge to Parents" that limits the rental of violent and sexualized video games to children. Philanthropy includes college scholarships. www.moviegallery.com

MovieTickets.com

0%   100%

CONTRIBUTIONS: TOTAL: *$9,250* DEM: *$0* REP: *$9,250*

Joint venture of AMC Entertainment Inc. (p. 149), Cineplex Galaxy, Hollywood Media, Marcus Corp., National Amusements, America Online, Inc. (p. 180), and Viacom (p. 154). www.movietickets.com

MTS, Incorporated

100%   0%

CONTRIBUTIONS: TOTAL: *$250* DEM: *$250* REP: *$0*

Fined by the FTC for exposing customers' personal information to other individual users on its website. One of 16 music industry companies agreeing to a $143 million settlement in a price-fixing scheme. Offers insurance coverage to employees' domestic partners. www.towerrecords.com

MusicLand Group Inc., The
No contributions. One of 16 music industry companies agreeing to a $143 million settlement in a price-fixing scheme.
www.musicland.com

Netflix

CONTRIBUTIONS: TOTAL: *$18,000* DEM: *$13,000* REP: *$5,000*

Several pending lawsuits and class actions brought by investors allege securities fraud, misrepresentation, and material omissions regarding operations and performance.
ir.netflix.com

News Corporation, Ltd., The

CONTRIBUTIONS: TOTAL: *$455,510* DEM: *$219,910* REP: *$235,601*

Accused of championing conservative causes, including President Bush's policies on Iraq. Often held as a prime example of the dangers of media consolidation, and has successfully lobbied to relax restrictions on concentrated media ownership. Was criticized for complying with Chinese free speech restrictions in order to expand its lucrative operations there. Along with DirecTV, named in a lawsuit by a Venezuelan company seeking to bar the companies from consolidating Latin American satellite interests. Has a written nondiscrimination policy covering sexual orientation. Offers insurance coverage to employees' domestic partners. www.newscorp.com

Powell's Books, Inc.

CONTRIBUTIONS: TOTAL: *$53,250* DEM: *$53,250* REP: *$0*

The largest independent bookstore in the United States. Its online arm is held up as the green alternative to Amazon.com, Inc. (p. 149) and Barnes & Noble Inc. (p. 150). Gives 100% of its campaign contributions to Democrats. Criticized for its prolonged and contentious negotiations with union members. Outreach includes adults' and children's literacy programs, civil rights issues, and free speech causes in the communities in which it has a presence. Has a written nondiscrimination policy covering sexual orientation but not gender identity.
www.powells.com

Regal Entertainment Group

CONTRIBUTIONS: TOTAL: *$2,000* DEM: *$2,000* REP: *$0*

In 2004, the U.S. Supreme Court upheld a ruling that "stadium-style" seating violates disability access laws. In 2004, a National Labor Relations Board (NLRB) judge ordered Regal Cinemas to reinstate unionized projectionists locked out since 1997, provide back pay, and enter into contract negotiations. In 1998, subsidiary Edward's Cinemas was required by court order to pay unpaid overtime to managers.
www.regalcinemas.com

Sony Corporation; Sony of America, Inc.
See p. 47 in Computers and Electronics.

Thomson
No contributions. Foreign owned. Sued by the Recording Industry Association of America (RIAA) for illegally copying and distributing pirated CDs. Its ethics charter states a commitment to embracing diversity and ensuring the environment's and public's health. www.thomson.net

Ticketmaster
No contributions. Subsidiary of IAC/InterActiveCorp (p. 152). Settled a 2003 lawsuit alleging anticompetitive practices such as exclusive contracts with venues. Has faced at least a dozen antitrust lawsuits and a congressional investigation. Has picked up a long list of enemy bands, venues, and small-ticket concessions. Has a written nondiscrimination policy covering sexual orientation but not gender identity. Offers insurance coverage to employees' domestic partners. www.ticketmaster.com

Tivo Inc.
No contributions. www.tivo.com

Tower Records
No contributions. Subsidiary of MTS, Incorporated (p. 152). In 2005, the FTC charged that Tower Records and MTS, Incorporated, misrepresented their safeguards for personal customer data. In 2004, settled FTC charges that a security flaw in the Tower Records website exposed the personal information of customers. One of 16 music industry companies agreeing to a $143 million settlement in a price-fixing scheme following an action by the FTC. The settlement resulted in refunds to customers and donations of music CDs to libraries and not-for-profit organizations. Offers insurance coverage to employees' domestic partners. www.towerrecords.com

Trans World Entertainment Corporation
92% | 8%

CONTRIBUTIONS: TOTAL: *$3,250* DEM: *$3,000* REP: *$250*
One of 16 music industry companies agreeing to a $143 million settlement in a price-fixing scheme. Has a written nondiscrimination policy covering sexual orientation but not gender identity. www.twec.com/corpsite

Viacom, Inc.
42% | 58%

CONTRIBUTIONS: TOTAL **$428,024** DEM: *$178,139* REP: *$250,065*
Viacom Outdoor subsidiary paid $14 million to three small billboard operators after being found guilty of racketeering violations. Multiple indecency settlements to the Federal Communications Commission (FCC), most recently paying $3.5 mil-

lion, not including the $550,000 proposed for Janet Jackson's "wardrobe malfunction" during the 2005 Super Bowl halftime show. Agreed to pay $1 million to the FCC for violations of limits on advertising in children's television programs on Nickelodeon. Foundation serves communities where employees live and work by supporting social causes. KNOW HIV/AIDS public education program is in partnership with the Henry J. Kaiser Family Foundation. Has a written nondiscrimination policy covering sexual orientation and gender identity. Offers insurance coverage to employees' domestic partners. www.viacom.com

Virgin Entertainment Group Inc.

No contributions. Subsidiary of foreign-owned Virgin Group Ltd. (p. 155). Has a written nondiscrimination policy covering sexual orientation but not gender identity. Offers insurance coverage to employees' domestic partners. www.virgin.com/us/entertainment

Virgin Group Ltd.

No contributions. Foreign owned. Philanthropic global and local outreach efforts include programs to research and fight HIV/AIDS, tuberculosis, and malaria. www.virgin.com

Walt Disney Company, The

54%   46%

CONTRIBUTIONS: TOTAL: *$420,000* DEM: *$226,948* REP: *$193,052*

Gave ex-president Michael Ovitz a $140 million severance package after his 14-month tenure (and successfully defended that move in court in 2005). Charged with contracting with sweatshop laborers, especially in China. Ordered Miramax to hold distribution of *Fahrenheit 9/11,* allegedly to preserve tax cuts the company enjoyed in Jeb Bush's Florida. Weathered an eight-year boycott by Christian groups protesting its "Gay Days" at Disney parks and extension of health benefits to same-sex couples. Has notable waste minimization, recycling, and water conservation programs at its parks and hotels. Has a written nondiscrimination policy covering sexual orientation and plans to cover gender identity. Offers insurance coverage to employees' domestic partners. www.disney.go.com

Restaurants

With 12 million workers—nearly 9% of total employ-ment in the United States—the restaurant industry employs more people than any other private sector. Given that it added 260,000 jobs a year over the last decade, employed more immigrants than any other industry, and comprised 4% of the gross domestic product (this isn't even counting the enormous impact it has on the agriculture, manufacturing, and trans-portation sectors), it's no surprise Congress pays special attention to the restaurant lobby.

That lobby is involved with a variety of social and policy issues, from obesity to public smoking to mini-mum wage to immigration. Even tort reform has found advocates in the lobby, which hopes to limit its expo-sure to litigation stemming from harmful foods. Facing a growing "war on obesity," the sector and its lobby has attempted to shift the blame from unhealthy foods to unhealthy lifestyles. Fearing a backlash similar to the one suffered by big tobacco, industry representatives have gone state to state working to ban health-related lawsuits. An effort has been made to couch the matter as a "personal responsibility" issue, suggesting that such suits would merely be the recourse of overeaters who wanted someone to blame; in fact, the more likely litigation would relate to undisclosed health informa-tion about common ingredients.

As the nation's biggest employer of immigrants, the sector advocated strongly for the recent and widely praised McCain-Kennedy immigration bill, which seeks to address the exploitation of illegal workers, among other things.

In the past, the restaurant lobby has been criticized for joining forces with the alcohol lobby to fight the lowering of the blood alcohol content level for deter-mining drunk-driving violations. At a local level, the industry has also fought the wave of antismoking ordinances to hit restaurants and bars recently.

Top Ten Republican Contributors

Outback Steakhouse, Inc.	$585,476
Wendy's International, Inc.	474,630
Yum! Brands, Inc.	251,705
Darden Restaurants, Inc.	249,342
Ilitch Holdings, Inc.	113,994
Castle Harlan, Inc.	109,417
Brinker International, Inc.	108,029
CBRL Group, Inc.	103,285
McCormick & Schmick's Seafood Restaurants, Inc.	75,792
Domino's Pizza, Inc.	62,489

Top Ten Democratic Contributors

Texas Pacific Group	$264,435
Sonic Corp.	100,956
Triarc Companies, Inc.	67,975
Ilitch Holdings, Inc.	58,510
Nathan's Famous, Inc.	45,750
Yum! Brands, Inc.	29,952
Darden Restaurants, Inc.	21,992
Palm Management Corp.	21,170
Wendy's International, Inc.	18,662
Brinker International, Inc.	16,472

AFC Enterprises, Inc.

 63% — 37%

CONTRIBUTIONS: TOTAL: *$5,000* DEM: *$3,174* REP: *$1,826*

Currently pending a settlement decision in a class action lawsuit brought by shareholders; the company agreed to pay $517,000 for plaintiffs' legal fees and, awaiting court approval, a settlement of $17 million. Listed on *Fortune* magazine's list of best companies for minorities. Foundation provides resources to national and international charities. Has a written nondiscrimination policy covering sexual orientation but not gender identity. Refuses insurance coverage to employees' domestic partners. www.afce.com

Applebee's International, Inc.

 6% — 94%

CONTRIBUTIONS: TOTAL: *$14,750* DEM: *$816* REP: *$13,935*

Identified in an NBC *Dateline* segment as having 446 critical violations of food safety regulations, the fifth-worst violator of the 100 restaurants surveyed. Settled a racial discrimination lawsuit in 2003 and instituted a written nondiscrimination policy covering discrimination on the basis of race and sexual orientation but not gender identity. Donated "ambiance" decorations to a soldiers' mess in Iraq. Offers health insurance coverage to employees' domestic partners. www.applebees.com

Arby's, LLC

No contributions. Subsidiary of Triarc Companies, Inc. (p. 168). Sued by the Disabled Rights Action Committee for violations of the Americans with Disabilities Act; numerous restaurants were found to lack ramps, adequate seating, and parking. Outreach supports education and youth development. www.arbys.com

Auntie Anne's, Inc.

0% 100%

CONTRIBUTIONS: TOTAL: *$5,000* DEM: *$0* REP: *$5,000*
Outreach supports children's and Christian causes. www.auntieannes.com

Berkshire Hathaway

See p. 54 in Finance, Insurance, and Real Estate.

Blimpie International, Inc.

100% 0%

CONTRIBUTIONS: TOTAL: *$2,000* DEM: *$2,000* REP: *$0*
www.blimpie.com

Boston Market Corporation

No contributions. Subsidiary of McDonald's Corporation (p. 165). The United Auto Workers (UAW) has called a consumer boycott because of unfair labor and supplier practices. Has a written nondiscrimination policy covering sexual orientation but not gender identity. Offers insurance coverage to employees' domestic partners. www.bostonmarket.com

Brinker International, Inc.

13% 87%

CONTRIBUTIONS: TOTAL: *$124,500* DEM: *$16,472* REP: *$108,029*
Settled multiple class action lawsuits filed by diners who were infected with salmonella at a Chicago-area Chili's in 2004. Chili's subsidiary identified in an NBC *Dateline* segment as having 402 critical violations of food safety regulations, the seventh-worst violator of the 100 restaurants surveyed. Outreach supports children, education, artistic, and family causes; does not support religious organizations. Has a written nondiscrimination policy covering sexual orientation. Offers insurance coverage to employees' domestic partners. www.brinker.com

Burger King Corporation

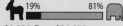

19% 81%

CONTRIBUTIONS: TOTAL: *$43,000* DEM: *$8,030* REP: *$34,970*
Subsidiary of Texas Pacific Group (p. 168). Fired without cause or severance at least 27 employees in its affiliated restaurants in Honduras, many of them single mothers, after rumors were circulated that they were organizing to demand better working conditions. Targeted by a lawsuit in California alleging multiple violations including failure to notify consumers purchasing French fries that they contain elevated levels of the cancer-

causing chemical acrylamide. Paid $30 million to settle a 2001 lawsuit for breach of contract. Settled a lawsuit alleging wage and hour violations for failure to pay overtime compensation and incorrectly categorizing employees. Paid $400,000 in settlements for a sexual harassment case. Identified in an NBC *Dateline* segment as having 241 critical violations of food safety regulations. Foundation supports community charities, specifically youth education programs. Donates food products through Second Harvest. www.burgerking.com

California Pizza Kitchen, Inc.

CONTRIBUTIONS: TOTAL: *$8,000* DEM: *$0* REP: *$8,000*

Partnered with Kraft Foods Inc. (p. 87), a subsidiary of Altria Group (p. 72), on its frozen pizza line. A pending class action lawsuit brought by employees alleges overtime and labor violations. Outreach supports communities in which the company has a presence. Has a written nondiscrimination policy covering sexual orientation but not gender identity. Offers insurance coverage to employees' domestic partners. www.cpk.com

Capricorn Management, G.P.

See p. 75 in Food and Beverage.

Carl's Jr.

No contributions. Subsidiary of CKE Restaurants, Inc. (p. 162). www.carlsjr.com

Carlson Companies, Inc.

See p. 192 in Travel and Leisure.

Carlson Restaurants Worldwide, Inc.

CONTRIBUTIONS: TOTAL: *$22,000* DEM: *$2,000* REP: *$20,000*

Subsidiary of the Carlson Companies, Inc. (p. 192). www.carlson.com

Castle Harlan, Inc.

CONTRIBUTIONS: TOTAL: *$120,250* DEM: *$10,834* REP: *$109,417*

Philanthropy supports public education groups. www.castleharlan.com

CBRL Group, Inc.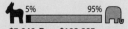

CONTRIBUTIONS: TOTAL: *$108,325* DEM: *$5,040* REP: *$103,285*

Paid nearly $9 million in 2004 to settle five suits involving 40 plaintiffs who alleged racial discrimination and labor violations. Sued in 2004 by the Equal Employment Opportunity Commission (EEOC) for sexual discrimination against its employees. Received national attention in 1991 when protesters closed stores after 11 workers were fired for sexual preference in accordance with a company policy requiring "normal heterosexual values." Now has a written nondiscrimination policy covering sexual orientation but not gender identity. Refuses insurance coverage to employees' domestic partners. www.cbrlgroup.com

CEC Entertainment, Inc.

CONTRIBUTIONS: TOTAL: *$27,000* DEM: *$0* REP: *$27,000*

Paid $4.5 million to settle a class action lawsuit filed by employees seeking back wages and overtime in 2003. Chuck E Cheese subsidiary paid $70,000 in damages for firing a mentally disabled man who, the defense argued, was "too retarded" to feel pain and should therefore not receive compensatory damages. The company has since increased sensitivity training for employees. www.chuckecheese.com

Cendant Corporation

See p. 192 in Travel and Leisure.

Checkers Drive-In Restaurants, Inc.

No contributions. Paid settlements in two separate sexual harassment claims filed by employees in 2005. Outreach in communities where company has a presence. www.checkers.com

Cheesecake Factory Incorporated, The

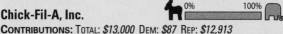

CONTRIBUTIONS: TOTAL: *$5,450* DEM: *$4,300* REP: *$1,135*

Pending a wage-and-hour class action suit brought by employees; in 2004, the company set aside $4.5 million for possible settlement. Foundation supports hunger relief and cancer research. Has a written nondiscrimination policy that excludes sexual orientation and gender identity. Refuses insurance coverage to employees' domestic partners. www.thecheesecakefactory.com

Chevys, Inc.

No contributions. Subsidiary of Real Mex Restaurants (p. 167). Outreach supports community-building organizations. www.chevys.com

Chick-Fil-A, Inc.

CONTRIBUTIONS: TOTAL: *$13,000* DEM: *$87* REP: *$12,913*

Settled (for an undisclosed sum) a religious discrimination lawsuit with a Muslim franchisee whose relationship was terminated because he refused to take part in a Christian group prayer. The company's corporate purpose includes the mandate to "glorify God." Outreach supports Christian causes, character education, children's issues, and education in communities where the company has a presence. Written nondiscrimination policy excludes sexual orientation and gender identity. Refuses insurance coverage to employees' domestic partners. www.chick-fil-a.com

Chipotle Mexican Grill, Inc.

 0% ▭ 100%

CONTRIBUTIONS: TOTAL: *$2,000* DEM: *$0* REP: *$2,000*

Subsidiary of McDonald's Corporation (p. 165). Has a written nondiscrimination policy covering sexual orientation but not gender identity. Offers insurance coverage to employees' domestic partners. www.chipotle.com

CKE Restaurants, Inc.

47% ▭ 53%

CONTRIBUTIONS: TOTAL: *$2,150* DEM: *$1,000* REP: *$1,148*

Received negative press for its ad campaign featuring a bikini-clad Paris Hilton washing a Bentley. In 2003, a class action suit was filed in California charging labor violations for denying workers vacation pay. Charitable giving program supports education and community leadership. President and CEO is active in the antiabortion movement. www.ckr.com

Cracker Barrel Old Country Store, Inc.

No contributions. Subsidiary of CBRL Group, Inc. (p. 160). Settled a lawsuit brought by the Civil Rights Division of the U.S. Department of Justice alleging a pattern of racial discrimination in employment and public accommodation. The National Association for the Advancement of Colored Persons (NAACP) alleged racial discrimination against black customers, forcing them to wait longer for seating and sit in segregated areas. www.cbrlgroup.com

Darden Restaurants, Inc.

 8% ▭ 92%

CONTRIBUTIONS: TOTAL: *$271,334* DEM: *$21,992* REP: *$249,342*

Settled multiple racial discrimination lawsuits brought by customers. Red Lobster subsidiary identified in an NBC *Dateline* segment as having 350 critical violations of food safety regulations, the eighth-worst violator of the 100 restaurants surveyed. Named one of the 30 best companies for diversity in 2005 by *Black Enterprise*. Focuses philanthropy on arts and culture, nutrition, education, and preservation of natural resources. Has a minority supplier program. Has a written nondiscrimination policy covering sexual orientation and gender identity. Offers insurance coverage to employees' domestic partners. www.dardenrestaurants.com

Denny's Corporation

 100% ▭ 0%

CONTRIBUTIONS: TOTAL: *$9,550* DEM: *$9,550* REP: *$0*

Currently pending a lawsuit brought by Arab American customers that alleges racial discrimination. Settled several high-profile racial discrimination lawsuits for $54 million. Paid $135,000 to settle a sexual discrimination lawsuit brought by the EEOC. Has been listed in *Fortune* magazine's top companies for minorities yet continues to be at the center of discrimination allegations and lawsuits. Outreach supports youth programs. www.dennys.com

Doctor's Associates Inc.

No contributions. Paid $10 million in 2001 to settle a lawsuit after a child who had consumed a Subway sandwich contracted hepatitis A and required a liver transplant. Paid a $1 million settlement to 35 others who also contracted hepatitis at the same outlet. A pending federal lawsuit alleges violations of antitrust laws. Outreach supports youth development and health education. www.subway.com

Domino's Pizza, Inc.

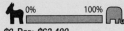

CONTRIBUTIONS: TOTAL: *$62,489* DEM: *$0* REP: *$62,489*

Paid $175,000 to a rape victim after failing to do a background check on a delivery man who had been convicted of sexual assault and other felonies. A pending class action suit alleges company-wide age discrimination. Faulted for its child labor record; its CEO stated that it has never terminated a franchise contract for child labor violations. Outreach supports minority interest groups, Special Olympics, and hunger relief. Has a written nondiscrimination policy that excludes sexual orientation and gender identity. Refuses insurance coverage to employees' domestic partners. www.dominos.com

Fresh Enterprises, Inc.

No contributions. Subsidiary of Wendy's International, Inc. (p. 168). Franchise locations participate in various local charitable causes. Does not have a written nondiscrimination policy covering sexual orientation or gender identity. Refuses insurance coverage to employees' domestic partners.
www.bajafresh.com

Hardee's Food Systems, Inc.

No contributions. Subsidiary of CKE Restaurants, Inc. (p. 162). Listed as one of the 10 worst corporations of 2004 for the introduction of its 0.66-pound "Monster Thickburger," a beef sandwich equivalent to nearly one day's normal caloric intake or five McDonald's hamburgers. Identified in an NBC *Dateline* segment as having 118 critical violations of federal food safety regulations per 100 inspections, the highest number of violations in *Dateline*'s original survey. Paid an $87,000 settlement in a child labor lawsuit. www.hardees.com

Hard Rock Cafe International, Inc.

No contributions. Subsidiary of the Rank Group PLC, a foreign-owned company. Served British beef at its Paris café in violation of the mad cow disease ban. Environmental efforts include using only environmentally safe cleaning materials and recycled paper products. Outreach includes community charities, People for the Ethical Treatment of Animals (PETA), cancer research, and Earth Day events, among others. Has a written nondiscrimination policy covering sexual orientation but not gender identity. Offers insurance coverage to employees' domestic partners. www.hardrock.com

Hooters of America, Inc.

CONTRIBUTIONS: TOTAL: *$32,000* DEM: *$0* REP: *$32,000*

Paid $2 million to settle a class action suit filed by men denied the opportunity to serve as "Hooters girls." Ordered to create gender-neutral positions, though it still maintains that "being female is reasonably necessary" to be a Hooters girl. Multiple instances of high-figure punitive damage awards to former female employees who complained of sexual harassment. Outreach includes cancer research, juvenile diabetes, and Special Olympics. www.hootersofamerica.com

IHOP Corp.

CONTRIBUTIONS: TOTAL: *$3,720* DEM: *$981* REP: *$2,739*

Settled a sexual harassment lawsuit for $180,000 in 2003. Settled a racial discrimination suit for $185,000 in 2000. Identified in an NBC *Dateline* segment as having 513 critical violations of food safety regulations, the third-worst violator of the 100 restaurants surveyed. In 2003, nine California restaurants were closed for failing to carry worker's compensation insurance. Outreach supports community building nonprofit charities. www.ihop.com

Ilitch Holdings, Inc.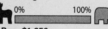

CONTRIBUTIONS: TOTAL: *$172,534* DEM: *$58,510* REP: *$113,994*

Fought with preservationists in Detroit to purchase and subsequently demolish a historic hotel to build a parking lot. Ilitch Charities for Children supports cancer research, job training, and Detroit-area charities. www.ilitchholdings.com

International Dairy Queen, Inc.

CONTRIBUTIONS: TOTAL: *$1,250* DEM: *$0* REP: *$1,250*

Subsidiary of Berkshire Hathaway (p. 54). www.dairyqueen.com

Jack in the Box Inc.

CONTRIBUTIONS: TOTAL: *$950* DEM: *$0* REP: *$950*

Violated the National Labor Relations Act in 2004 by restricting employees from talking to the Labor Relations Board. Paid millions to settle multiple lawsuits brought by customers who consumed its burgers tainted with *E. coli* in 1993. Commended for revolutionizing food safety in a fast-food environment in 2000. Foundation supports youth mentoring. www.jackinthebox.com

Kahala Corp.

No contributions. www.kahalacorp.com

Krispy Kreme Doughnuts, Inc.

0% | 100%

CONTRIBUTIONS: TOTAL: *$22,000* DEM: *$0* REP: *$22,000*

A pending class action lawsuit alleges mismanagement of employee retirement plans, resulting in huge loses. www.krispykreme.com

Landry's Restaurants, Inc.

35% | 65%

CONTRIBUTIONS: TOTAL: *$11,386* DEM: *$4,000* REP: *$7,386*

A pending class action lawsuit alleges violations of federal labor laws for requiring servers to give up a portion of tips to offset charges levied by credit card companies. Rainforest Cafe subsidiary promotes public education about conservation. Has a management foundation encouraging employee career training. www.landrysseafood.com

Little Caesar Enterprises, Inc.

No contributions. Subsidiary of Ilitch Holdings, Inc. (p. 164). Foundation feeds the homeless. www.littlecaesars.com

Logan's Roadhouse, Inc.

No contributions. Subsidiary of CBRL Group, Inc. (p. 160). www.logansroadhouse.com

Marie Callender Pie Shops, Inc.

No contributions. Subsidiary of Castle Harlan, Inc. (p. 160). The frozen food line, with the exception of pies, is licensed to ConAgra Foods, Inc. (p. 77). www.mcpies.com

McCormick & Schmick's Seafood Restaurants, Inc.

1% | 99%

CONTRIBUTIONS: TOTAL: *$76,662* DEM: *$870* REP: *$75,792*
www.mccormickandschmicks.com

McDonald's Corporation

14% | 86%

CONTRIBUTIONS: TOTAL: *$44,000* DEM: *$5,986* REP: *$38,014*

Following the popularity of *Super Size Me* and prominent obesity claim lawsuits, the company has made very little effort to include healthier options on its menu and continues to target children in advertising. The United Food and Commercial Workers union calls the company "very antiunion." Ronald McDonald House Charities support cancer research, youth programs, and HIV/AIDS research. Has a written nondiscrimination policy covering sexual orientation but not gender identity. Offers insurance coverage to employees' domestic partners. www.mcdonalds.com/corp.html

Morton's Restaurant Group, Inc.

1% | 99%

CONTRIBUTIONS: TOTAL: *$39,500* DEM: *$544* REP: *$38,957*
Subsidiary of Castle Harlan, Inc. (p. 160). www.mortons.com

Mrs. Fields' Original Cookies, Inc.
See p. 89 in Food and Beverage.

Nathan's Famous, Inc.
CONTRIBUTIONS: TOTAL: *$63,750* DEM: *$45,750* REP: *$18,000*
www.nathansfamous.com

New World Restaurant Group, Inc.
No contributions. Paid a $500,000 settlement to managers for unpaid overtime in 2003. Supports cancer research and children's charities. www.newworldrestaurantgroup.com

Outback Steakhouse, Inc.
CONTRIBUTIONS: TOTAL: *$595,650* DEM: *$10,175* REP: *$585,476*
Identified in an NBC *Dateline* segment as having 419 critical violations of food safety regulations, the sixth-worst violator of the 100 restaurants surveyed. Outreach supports U.S. troops fighting in Afghanistan and Iraq by bringing mobile catering units to them. www.outback.com

Palm Management Corp.
CONTRIBUTIONS: TOTAL: *$30,300* DEM: *$21,170* REP: *$9,130*
The EEOC ordered an overhaul of the company's employment practices in 2003, including mandatory diversity and gender discrimination training for supervisors. Participant in the Women's Foodservice Forum, which promotes career advancement for executive women. www.thepalm.com

Panda Restaurant Group, Inc.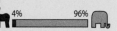
CONTRIBUTIONS: TOTAL: *$1,900* DEM: *$78* REP: *$1,822*
Outreach supports children's causes in communities where the company has a presence. www.pandarg.com

Papa John's International, Inc.
CONTRIBUTIONS: TOTAL: *$6,750* DEM: *$1,000* REP: *$5,750*
Outreach supports agricultural education, cerebral palsy research, and children's causes in communities where the company has a presence. Does not have a written nondiscrimination policy covering sexual orientation or gender identity. Refuses insurance coverage to employees' domestic partners. www.papajohns.com

P. F. Chang's China Bistro, Inc.
No contributions. Charity efforts benefit hunger relief and juvenile diabetes. www.pfchangs.com

Pick Up Stix
No contributions. Subsidiary of Carlson Restaurants Worldwide, Inc. (p. 160). www.pickupstix.com

Pizza Inn, Inc.
No contributions. www.pizzainn.com

Planet Hollywood International, Inc.
No contributions. www.planethollywood.com

Qdoba Restaurant Corporation
No contributions. Subsidiary of Jack in the Box Inc. (p. 164). Lauded for its employee training program in harassment and diversity. www.qdoba.com

Quiznos Master LLC, The
No contributions. A pending class action suit seeks reimbursement for medical bills incurred after a worker tested positive for hepatitis A and restaurant patrons had to be inoculated against the virus. www.quiznos.com

Real Mex Restaurants
No contributions. www.eltorito.com

Ruth's Chris Steak House, Inc.   7%   93%
CONTRIBUTIONS: TOTAL: *$6,375* DEM: *$468* REP: *$5,907*
Settled a precedent-setting same-sex harassment case in 1995 for an undisclosed sum. Outreach includes support for the Deafolympics. www.ruthschris.com

Sbarro, Inc.   100%   0%
CONTRIBUTIONS: TOTAL: *$2,000* DEM: *$2,000* REP: *$0*
Settled a class action suit for an undisclosed sum alleging failure to pay overtime. www.sbarro.com

Smith & Wollensky Restaurant Group, Inc., The   85%   15%
CONTRIBUTIONS: TOTAL: *$5,000* DEM: *$4,000* REP: *$1,000*
Settled a racial discrimination suit filed by immigrant workers in 2005 after a year-long shutout and picketing of New York outlets. www.smithandwollensky.com

Sonic Corp.   100%   0%
CONTRIBUTIONS: TOTAL: *$100,956* DEM: *$100,956* REP: *$0*
A pending suit brought by the EEOC alleges a pattern of pregnancy discrimination. Outreach supports educational causes within the state of Oklahoma. www.sonicdrivein.com

TDL Group Corp., The
No contributions. Subsidiary of Wendy's International, Inc. (p. 168). Outreach supports children's causes. Franchise locations participate in various local charitable causes. Does not have a written nondiscrimination policy covering sexual orientation or gender identity. Refuses insurance coverage to employees' domestic partners. www.timhortons.com

Texas Pacific Group

85% — 15%

CONTRIBUTIONS: TOTAL: *$312,395* DEM: *$264,435* REP: *$47,765*
www.tpgvc.com

T.G.I. Friday's
No contributions. Subsidiary of Carlson Restaurants Worldwide, Inc. (p. 160). Identified in an NBC *Dateline* segment as having 490 critical violations of food safety regulations, the fourth-worst violator of the 100 restaurants surveyed.
www.fridays.com

Triarc Companies, Inc.

57% — 43%

CONTRIBUTIONS: TOTAL: *$120,000* DEM: *$67,975* REP: *$52,025*
www.triarc.com

TruFoods Systems, Inc.
No contributions. www.trufoods.com

Uno Restaurant Holdings Corp.
No contributions. Violated the "whistleblowers' protection act" in a pattern of termination following employees' reporting of food safety violations. www.unos.com

Wendy's International, Inc.

4% — 96%

CONTRIBUTIONS: TOTAL: *$493,292* DEM: *$18,662* REP: *$474,630*
Has ongoing problems with disability access, settling a federal suit in 1998 only to have the issue resurface in 2003 after failing to comply with the federal order. Outreach supports adoption advocacy and education. Does not have a written nondiscrimination policy covering sexual orientation or gender identity. Refuses insurance coverage to employees' domestic partners.
www.wendys.com

White Castle System, Inc.

0% — 100%

CONTRIBUTIONS: TOTAL: *$34,750* DEM: *$0* REP: *$34,750*
www.whitecastle.com

Wolfgang Puck Worldwide, Inc.
No contributions. Licenses its frozen food products to ConAgra Foods, Inc. (p. 77) and has other licensing agreements for some of its cafés and restaurants. www.wolfgangpuck.com

Worldwide Restaurant Concepts, Inc.

0% — 100%

CONTRIBUTIONS: TOTAL: *$2,000* DEM: *$0* REP: *$2,000*
Sued in a class action by Pat & Oscar's customers who became sick after eating *E. coli*–contaminated lettuce in 2003. Settled 20 individual lawsuits brought by customers over *E. coli*–contaminated beef at Sizzler in 2003.
www.wrconcepts.com

Yum! Brands, Inc.

11%   89%

CONTRIBUTIONS: TOTAL: *$281,657* DEM: *$29,952* REP: *$251,705*

Currently facing a class action suit filed by employees for violations of overtime and wage laws. KFC was boycotted by PETA due to its animal welfare practices. Listed in *Fortune*'s "Top 50 Best Companies for Minorities" in 2004 and 2003 and *Black Enterprise*'s "30 Best Companies for Diversity" in 2005. Outreach supports education and women's and minority issues. Has a written nondiscrimination policy covering sexual orientation but not gender identity. Refuses insurance coverage to employees' domestic partners. www.yum.com

Sporting Goods

The declining level of physical activity among Americans—which is to say the explosion of the video gaming industry, for example, or the now eight-hours-per-day TV-watching average in U.S. households—isn't just a health problem. The sporting goods industry worries that a day will come when kids no longer get off their butts to buy baseball gloves and footballs.

This concern has led industry lobbyists to join the growing antiobesity movement. In particular, it has supported efforts to grow physical education programs in the nation's schools—for example, through grants to local districts and community awareness campaigns. The sector has also been involved in similarly benign initiatives to increase funding for parks and extend Daylight Savings Time.

As with any robust manufacturing industry—the sporting goods sector reported $2.1 billion in exports in 2004—trade issues draw much of the lobby's attention. The sector has worked to promote legislation favorable to inexpensive production and sales across borders. At the same time, and jumpstarted by public outcry about the athletic shoe business, the sector has begun looking closer at what goes into its production and sales. In 1995, the World Federation of the Sporting Goods Industry established its Committee on Ethics and Fair Trade to address child labor.

Sweatshop concerns in general continue to dog the industry, which conducts most of its production in developing countries. Though most major manufacturers now have written codes regarding wages, hours, and minimum age of workers, human rights groups have long noted a frequent gap between regulation and reality at many factories. While companies do perform random checks at their production facilities, critics point at the sector's intense competitiveness as the central issue; if these same companies worried less about losing their edge, they could band together to make real headway in the problem.

Top Ten Republican Contributors

New Balance Athletic Shoe, Inc.	$104,500
NIKE, Inc.	41,513
Jarden Corporation	30,019
Huffy Corporation	23,000
Fortune Brands, Inc.	22,752
Sierra Trading Post	12,000
K2 Inc.	12,000
Cabela's Incorporated	11,045
Adidas AG	9,490
Columbia Sportswear Company	6,000

Top Ten Democratic Contributors

Adidas AG	$65,010
Patagonia	42,400
NIKE, Inc.	40,986
Jarden Corporation	16,231
L. L. Bean, Inc.	15,659
VF Corporation	10,750
Trek Bicycle Corporation	8,550
Columbia Sportswear Company	7,000
Fortune Brands, Inc.	6,998
Recreational Equipment, Inc. (REI)	6,500

Acushnet Company
No contributions. Subsidiary of Fortune Brands, Inc. (p. 81).
www.acushnetcompany.com

Adidas AG
87%   13%

CONTRIBUTIONS: TOTAL: *$74,500* DEM: *$65,010* REP: *$9,490*
Foreign owned. Sold Salomon (see Amer Sports Corporation, p. 172) in late 2005. Has sourced from countries with widespread, well-documented human and labor rights abuses, and encourages sweatshop labor with its supplier practices. Among the founding companies of the Fair Labor Association, a nonprofit organization identifying industry-wide strategies to eliminate global apparel sweatshops. Is eliminating polyvinyl chlorides (PVCs), reducing toxic solvents, and controlling and monitoring its own and suppliers' use. Offers insurance coverage to employees' domestic partners. www.adidas-salomon.com

Amer Sports Corporation
No contributions. Foreign owned. Became the largest sporting goods company in the world following the May 2005 acquisition of Salomon and its subsidiary brands.
www.amersports.com

Big 5 Sporting Goods Corporation
No contributions. www.big5sportinggoods.com

Burton Snowboards
No contributions. Founder of Chill, an international nonprofit intervention program benefiting at-risk youth. www.burton.com

Cabela's Incorporated
CONTRIBUTIONS: TOTAL: *$11,100* DEM: *$55* REP: *$11,045*
Accepted public funds for a new Texas store but sued to keep its use of that money secret from taxpayers, despite Texas's Public Information Act. One of *Fortune*'s "100 Best Companies to Work For" in 2000. www.cabelas.com

Callaway Golf Company
CONTRIBUTIONS: TOTAL: *$5,000* DEM: *$5,000* REP: *$0*
Outreach in communities with a company presence, targeting at-risk youth and those underserved by health care. Has a written nondiscrimination policy covering sexual orientation but not gender identity. Offers insurance coverage to employees' domestic partners. www.callawaygolf.com

Cannondale Bicycle Corporation
No contributions. Donated new road bikes and cycling apparel to Afghan athletes to train for the 2004 Olympics in the middle of the "War on Terror." www.cannondale.com

Coleman Company Inc., The
CONTRIBUTIONS: TOTAL: *$41,250* DEM: *$14,231* REP: *$27,019*
Subsidiary of Jarden Corporation (p. 174). Supporter of outdoor conservation efforts in the United States. Offers nonprofit organizations merchandise at discounted prices. www.coleman.com

Columbia Sportswear Company
CONTRIBUTIONS: TOTAL: *$13,000* DEM: *$7,000* REP: *$6,000*
Stated publicly in 2001 that it has not produced any clothing in Burma since 1996 due to that country's well-documented, widespread human and labor rights violations. Has a written nondiscrimination policy covering sexual orientation but not gender identity. Offers insurance coverage to employees' domestic partners. www.columbia.com

Eddie Bauer, Inc.
CONTRIBUTIONS: TOTAL: *$1,000* DEM: *$0* REP: *$1,000*
Sources from countries with widespread, well-documented human and labor rights abuses and encourages sweatshop

labor with its supplier practices. Among the founding companies of the Fair Labor Association a nonprofit to eliminate global apparel sweatshops. A worker died of exhaustion at a supplier sweatshop in the Philippines. Uses prison labor in Tennessee and Washington to produce apparel and wooden furniture. Raised $1.3 million in 2000 for reforestation efforts in several U.S. states and Canadian provinces. Has a written nondiscrimination policy covering sexual orientation but not gender identity. Offers insurance coverage to employees' domestic partners. www.eddiebauer.com

Fortune Brands, Inc.
See p. 81 in Food and Beverage.

Huffy Corporation
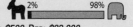
CONTRIBUTIONS: TOTAL: *$23,500* DEM: *$500* REP: *$23,000*
Paid $50,000 to the state of Wisconsin to settle allegations of air pollution violations. Paid $10 million to a man who became paralyzed and permanently disabled following a collision on a faulty bicycle, prompting recalls. Former subsidiary Washington Inventory Service, which Huffy sold in 2000 but continues to be liable for, was named in a lawsuit alleging wage and hour violations. Has a long history of union strikes. www.huffy.com

Hurley International, LLC
No contributions. Subsidiary of NIKE, Inc. (p. 175). Has a supplier-monitoring program that includes sending monitors for random visits to manufacturing locations and requires labor law compliance. Has a written nondiscrimination policy covering sexual orientation and gender identity. Offers insurance coverage to employees' domestic partners. www.hurley.com

JanSport, Inc.
No contributions. Subsidiary of the VF Corporation (p. 29). Was boycotted in 2000 and had its apparel removed from stores after activist groups revealed its sweatshop supplier in Burma. Outreach supports environmental and educational philanthropy. Has a written nondiscrimination policy covering sexual orientation but not gender identity. Refuses insurance coverage to employees' domestic partners. www.jansport.com

Jarden Corporation

CONTRIBUTIONS: TOTAL: *$46,250* DEM: *$16,231* REP: *$30,019*
www.jarden.com

K2 Inc.

CONTRIBUTIONS: TOTAL: *$12,000* DEM: *$0* REP: *$12,000*
www.k2inc.net

Kellwood Company
See p. 15 in Clothing, Shoes, and Accessories.

Leatherman Tool Group, Inc.
No contributions. Outreach supports Habitat for Humanity and the American Red Cross. www.leatherman.com

L. L. Bean, Inc.
CONTRIBUTIONS: TOTAL: *$16,000* DEM: *$15,659* , REP: *$341*
Settled a sexual harassment case in 2001, paying $215,000 for failure to prevent systemic and continuing harassment. Member of the Fair Labor Association and the Apparel Industry Partnership, systems that inspect overseas factories to assess whether they meet minimum labor standards. Outreach focuses on nature conservation and youth leadership. Has a written nondiscrimination policy covering sexual orientation but not gender identity. Offers insurance coverage to employees' domestic partners. www.llbean.com

London Fog Industries, Inc.
See p. 19 in Clothing, Shoes, and Accessories.

Marmot Mountain, LLC
No contributions. Subsidiary of K2 Inc. (p. 174). Its vendor code of conduct states that "contractors must meet or surpass the national and local labor standards in terms of minimum age, hours of work and work environment." Foundation seeks to preserve the rare marmot in the Pacific Northwest. www.marmot.com

New Balance Athletic Shoe, Inc.
CONTRIBUTIONS: TOTAL: *$107,000* DEM: *$2,500* REP: *$104,500*
Made contributions to both political conventions in 2004, though executive contributions heavily favored the GOP. Despite its "Made in the USA" image and labels, 75% of its shoes are made overseas, mostly in China. Settled a price-fixing complaint in the mid-1990s. Has a long history of labor violations in its footwear manufacturing plant in China. Outreach supports sports and health programs mostly in Boston. www.newbalance.com

NIKE, Inc.
CONTRIBUTIONS: TOTAL: *$82,500* DEM: *$40,987* REP: *$41,514*
Has taken recent steps to address complaints about labor conditions at its overseas suppliers, releasing a list of its overseas contractors for review and cofounding the Fair Labor Association. Lost a landmark "corporate parenthood" suit after it made false statements about worker conditions. Has sourced from countries with widespread, well-documented human and labor rights abuses. Member of the Joint Initiative on Corporate Accountability and Workers' Rights. Has a written nondiscrimination policy covering sexual orientation and gender

identity. Offers insurance coverage to employees' domestic partners. www.nike.com

North Face, Inc., The
No contributions. Subsidiary of the VF Corporation (p. 29). Outreach supports community development overseas, environmental causes, and outdoor recreation. Has a written nondiscrimination policy covering sexual orientation but not gender identity. Refuses insurance coverage to employees' domestic partners. www.thenorthface.com

Oakley, Inc.
See p. 22 in Clothing, Shoes, and Accessories.

O'Neill, Inc.
100% — 0%

CONTRIBUTIONS: TOTAL: *$500* DEM: *$500* REP: *$0*
Outreach includes marine education programs in the Santa Cruz, California, area. www.oneill.com

Patagonia
91% — 9%

CONTRIBUTIONS: TOTAL: *$46,500* DEM: *$42,400* REP: *$2,100*
Active in the environmental movement through community outreach and donation of 1% of company sales or 10% of profits, whichever is greater. Uses organic cotton in its clothing production. Has a clothing recycling program asking customers to return worn-out clothing to be recycled into new garments. Member of the Joint Initiative on Corporate Accountability and Workers' Rights, which works toward a goal of commonly accepted global labor standards. Member of the Fair Trade Association. Has a written nondiscrimination policy covering sexual orientation but not gender identity. Offers insurance coverage to employees' domestic partners. www.patagonia.com

PUMA AG Rudolf Dassler Sport
No contributions. Foreign owned. Has sourced from countries with widespread, well-documented human and labor rights abuses and encourages sweatshop labor with its supplier practices. www.puma.com

Quiksilver, Inc.
0% — 100%

CONTRIBUTIONS: TOTAL: *$1,500* DEM: *$0* REP: *$1,500*
Was cited for labor law, wage-and-hour, and safety violations and levied $21,800 in fines. Leader in customer privacy. Prohibits sales and marketing from using any data collected when people join mailing lists or become members at its website. Does not retain credit card numbers after transactions in Quiksilver stores. Foundation funds public education and scientific research on environmental issues. www.quiksilver.com

Rawlings Sporting Goods Company, Inc.
No contributions. Subsidiary of K2 Inc. (p. 174). www.rawlings.com

Recreational Equipment, Inc. (REI)

CONTRIBUTIONS: TOTAL: *$6,500* DEM: *$6,500* REP: *$0*

Outreach includes youth programs, environmental steward-ship, and grants to environmental projects. Has a written nondiscrimination policy covering sexual orientation but not gender identity. Offers insurance coverage to employees' domestic partners. www.rei.com

Reebok International Ltd.

CONTRIBUTIONS: TOTAL: *$74,500* DEM: *$65,010* REP: *$9,490*

Currently being acquired by Adidas AG (p. 172). China Labor Watch reported in 2002 alleged routine violations of Chinese labor law at its southern Chinese factories. Among companies founding the Fair Labor Association, a nonprofit to eliminate global apparel sweatshops. Has made notable efforts to re-duce volatile organic compounds and solvents following worker exposure in 1998. Foundation supports increasing public aware-ness of human rights issues and expanding the legal frame-work. Has a written nondiscrimination policy covering sexual orientation but not gender identity. Offers insurance coverage to employees' domestic partners. www.reebok.com

Sierra Trading Post

CONTRIBUTIONS: TOTAL: *$12,000* DEM: *$0* REP: *$12,000*

Company website states that "business ethics must be con-sistent with the faith of the owners in Jesus Christ and his teachings." www.sierratradingpost.com

Spiegel, Inc.

See p. 26 in Clothing, Shoes, and Accessories.

Sports Authority Inc., The

No contributions. Outreach includes partnerships with Boys & Girls Clubs of America and youth physical health education programs. www.sportsauthority.com

TaylorMade–Adidas Golf

No contributions. Subsidiary of Adidas AG (p. 172). Offers in-surance coverage to employees' domestic partners. www.tmag.com

Trek Bicycle Corporation

CONTRIBUTIONS: TOTAL: *$11,000* DEM: *$8,550* REP: *$2,450*

Outreach community building where the company has a pres-ence. www.trekbikes.com

VF Corporation

See p. 29 in Clothing, Shoes, and Accessories.

Victorinox AG
No contributions. Foreign owned. www.victorinox.com

Wilson Sporting Goods Co.
No contributions. Subsidiary of Amer Sports Corporation
(p. 172). Has sourced from countries with widespread, well-documented human and labor rights abuses. Uses prison labor and supports "private-prison industrialization." Outreach supports the Breast Cancer Research Foundation.
www.wilson.com

Telecommunications and Internet

Information wants to be free, we learned with the advent of the digital commons. Indeed, the Internet was trumpeted as a great democratizer—ordinary citizens free to distribute and gather all the information they please. But the question of *access* has proven that, yet again, the devil's in the details.

Indeed, the question of how citizens make their way online has emerged as a central issue in the telecommunications sector. The powerful telecommunications lobby, increasingly overlapped with that of the media and entertainment sector, has made it its business to fight for control of the Internet. Some industry experts predict that wireless Internet access will become the overarching debate within the sector in coming years. Despite Philadelphia's celebrated plans to offer free citywide wireless Internet access, the much larger trend is for the telecom industry to clamp down on such municipal networks.

As with many information technologies, the issue of class hovers quietly above the questionably level playing field. The digital divide, as it's been called, has kept the conceivably empowering Internet away from developing nations, from rural regions within the United States, and, disproportionately, from minorities. Increasingly, legislators have granted the industry power to limit government-provided access to poor and underserved communities.

It seems the primary goal within the industry—which has contributed heavily to both parties but found particular friendship in the Bush administration—is to stake out and reserve as much of the Internet as possible for commercial interests. The same holds true for radio airwaves and the television market. A number of independent organizations have cropped up to fight what they fear might be an inevitability: that the private sector, not the public, will build and determine the future of media, digital and otherwise, in years to come.

Top Ten Republican Contributors

SBC Communications Inc.	$1,767,725
Verizon Communications Inc.	1,340,972
BellSouth Corporation	816,304
Qwest Communications International Inc.	576,364
Time Warner Inc.	507,648
Comcast Corporation	462,386
Sprint Nextel Corporation	432,493
ALLTEL Corporation	339,071
AT&T Corp.	310,069
Viacom, Inc.	250,065

Top Ten Democratic Contributors

SBC Communications Inc.	$935,805
Verizon Communications Inc.	804,272
BellSouth Corporation	532,396
Comcast Corporation	388,225
Cablevision Systems Corporation	268,092
Time Warner Inc.	261,426
Qwest Communications International Inc.	250,147
EchoStar Communications Corporation	230,620
Sprint Nextel Corporation	229,807
AT&T Corp.	218,931

ALLTEL Corporation

22% | 78%

CONTRIBUTIONS: TOTAL: *$437,171* DEM: *$95,563* REP: *$339,071*
Outreach supports Amber Alert child response programs, wireless handset recycling, driver safety, and access to health care. Has a written nondiscrimination policy covering sexual orientation but not gender identity. Refuses insurance coverage to employees' domestic partners. www.alltel.com

America Online, Inc.

58% | 42%

CONTRIBUTIONS: TOTAL: *$26,550* DEM: *$15,300* REP: *$11,250*
Subsidiary of Time Warner Inc. (p. 186), previously referred to as AOL Time Warner. Agreed in 2005 to pay $1.25 million in penalties and to reform its customer service practices following an investigation by the New York attorney general. Has been charged with overbilling customers by rounding up their time online. Has a written nondiscrimination policy covering sexual orientation and plans to cover gender identity. Offers insurance coverage to employees' domestic partners. www.aol.com

AOL Access Business
No contributions. Subsidiary of America Online, Inc. (p. 180). www.aol.com

AT&T Corp.

41% 59%

CONTRIBUTIONS: TOTAL: *$529,000* DEM: *$218,931* REP: *$310,069*

A major player in the telecommunications lobby (one of Washington's most influential, outspending even the oil and gas industry), where it campaigns for industry deregulation, among other things. Charged in a class action suit for unlawfully billing non–AT&T Corp. customers through their local phone bills; paid a $500,000 fine to the Federal Communications Commission (FCC) and settled suits in multiple states. A landmark sexual discrimination suit brought by the Equal Employment Opportunity Commission (EEOC) led to widespread changes in both the company and the industry. Known for accommodating employees with disabilities. Donates technology equipment to schools; is a strong supporter of programs promoting the use of technology in education. Has a written nondiscrimination policy covering sexual orientation and gender identity. Offers health insurance to employee's domestic partners. www.att.com

BellSouth Corporation

39% 61%

CONTRIBUTIONS: TOTAL: *$1,348,700* DEM: *$532,396* REP: *$816,304*

Agreed to self-audit environmental procedures in 1999 and was levied only nominal fines by the Environmental Protection Agency (EPA) for violating public right-to-know measures and spill control regulations. Settled an EEOC lawsuit in 2003 alleging unfair promotion practices for African American workers. Agreed to pay $5.1 million in back wages to customer service workers after alleged violations of overtime laws. Foundation supports educational reform, dispersing $49 million in grants from 1986 through 2002. Places 10% of subcontracting for goods and services with minority-owned companies. Has a written nondiscrimination policy covering sexual orientation but not gender identity. Offers insurance coverage to employees' domestic partners. www.bellsouth.com

Cablevision Systems Corporation

66% 34%

CONTRIBUTIONS: TOTAL: *$405,250* DEM: *$268,092* REP: *$137,158*

A 2004 Securities and Exchange Commission (SEC) investigation followed the disclosure of three years' and $15 million worth of financial reporting errors—some the result of fabricated invoices—that led to the firing of 14 senior executives in its Rainbow Media unit. A pending class action suit alleges that it committed a fiduciary breach by forcing shareholders to exchange Rainbow Media stock for Cablevision Systems Corporation stock at a significant loss. Provides free cable television and broadband Internet access to schools. Owns Madison Square Garden, whose "Cheering for Children" program provides after-school activities. Has a written nondiscrimination policy covering sexual orientation but not gender identity. Offers insurance coverage to employees' domestic partners. www.cablevision.com

Charter Communications, Inc.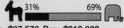
CONTRIBUTIONS: TOTAL: *$38,990* DEM: *$12,241* REP: *$26,749*

Paid a $144 million settlement to stockholders following an SEC investigation resulting in guilty pleas from the former chief financial officer, former chief operating officer, and two former senior vice presidents for felony conspiracy to defraud; the company subsequently countersued to recover legal costs. Outreach focuses on providing cable and Internet access for schools and developing online educational resources. Has a written nondiscrimination policy covering sexual orientation but not gender identity. Refuses insurance coverage to employees' domestic partners. www.charter.com

Cingular Wireless LLC
CONTRIBUTIONS: TOTAL: *$310,200* DEM: *$97,579* REP: *$212,622*

Co-owned by SBC Communications Inc. (p. 185) and BellSouth Corporation (p. 181). Paid $775,000 in consent decrees to avoid FCC fines for violating deadlines to ensure mobile 911 calls are traceable. Fined $12.1 million in 2004 for false advertising. Settled a wage-and-hour class action brought by the Department of Labor for $5.1 million. Three lawsuits alleging discrimination and hostile work environment have been filed in the last four years. Actively supports employees' union relationships, community programs combating domestic abuse and assisting disaster victims, and the Amber Alert program. Received the 2003 New Freedom Initiative Award for its support and commitment to Americans with disabilities. Has a written nondiscrimination policy covering sexual orientation but not gender identity. Offers insurance coverage to employees' domestic partners. www.cingular.com

Comcast Corporation
CONTRIBUTIONS: TOTAL: *$850,609* DEM: *$388,225* REP: *$462,384*

Often cited as an example of media consolidation, particularly during its failed 2004 bid for the Walt Disney Company (p. 155) (which would have made it the world's largest media company). Has also been one of the most resistant to union campaigns; in 2005, it received a rebuke from the National Labor Relations Board (NRLB) for interfering with its workers efforts to organize. Activist groups claim that the corporation is anti-union, ignores consumer and worker protections, and negotiates in bad faith. Participates in Cable in the Classroom, providing free cable access, programming, and support materials; helps libraries raise funds to purchase computers. Donates commercial-free educational programming to more than 10,000 schools. Has a written nondiscrimination policy covering sexual orientation but not gender identity. Offers insurance to employees' domestic partners. www.cmcsk.com

Cox Communications, Inc.

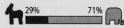

31%   69%

CONTRIBUTIONS: TOTAL: *$18,000* DEM: *$5,664* REP: *$12,336*

Subsidiary of Cox Enterprises, Inc. (p. 183). Has a written non-discrimination policy covering sexual orientation but not gender identity. Offers insurance coverage to employees' domestic partners. www.cox.com

Cox Enterprises, Inc.

29%   71%

CONTRIBUTIONS: TOTAL: *$37,000* DEM: *$10,660* REP: *$26,340*

Supports employee volunteerism and community organizations. Has a written nondiscrimination policy covering sexual orientation but not gender identity. Offers insurance coverage to employees' domestic partners. www.coxenterprises.com

Deutsche Telekom AG

45%   55%

CONTRIBUTIONS: TOTAL: *$89,500* DEM: *$40,007* REP: *$49,494*

Paid $120 million in 2005 to settle a class action suit alleging an overstatement of assets in conjunction with its 2001 VoiceStream (now T-Mobile USA, Inc.; p. 186) takeover. Fined $14.7 million by the European Commission for charging competitors more for network access than retail customers. Offers reduced rates for service to disabled and low-income customers, supports Doctors for the Third World, and provides free Internet access to German schoolchildren. Has a written nondiscrimination policy covering sexual orientation and gender identity. Offers insurance to employees' domestic partners. www.telekom.de

EarthLink, Inc.

19%   81%

CONTRIBUTIONS: TOTAL: *$10,800* DEM: *$2,000* REP: *$8,800*

"GenerationLink" program joins high school students with senior citizens to teach internet skills. Has a written nondiscrimination policy covering sexual orientation but not gender identity. Offers insurance coverage to employees' domestic partners. www.earthlink.net

EchoStar Communications Corporation

50%   50%

CONTRIBUTIONS: TOTAL: *$457,150* DEM: *$230,620* REP: *$226,530*

Paid undisclosed "millions" to settle a suit brought by Elliot Spitzer for excessive service termination fees. Privately settled a former executive's suit alleging gender discrimination for an undisclosed sum following a 2005 trial that revealed "systemic harassment and discrimination." Paid $8 million to a blind applicant who was told the company was "not equipped" to handle blind workers in an EEOC-sponsored suit. Its chairman and CEO, who holds majority voting power on the board, specifically opposed a 2005 shareholder initiative to include sexual orientation protection in written nondiscrimination policies. Has a written nondiscrimination policy that does not cover sexual orientation or gender identity. Refuses insurance coverage to employees' domestic partners. www.dishnetwork.com

IDT Corporation

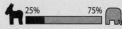

CONTRIBUTIONS: TOTAL: *$247,000* DEM: *$20,700* REP: *$226,300*

A pending 2004 class action suit filed by call center workers alleged discriminatory treatment of non-Jewish employees. Its founder is known for his work with modern Orthodox Jewish causes and was vice chair of the 2004 Republican National Convention. Company supports "Play It Smart" program, which works with student-athletes in underserved communities. Has a written nondiscrimination policy covering sexual orientation and gender identity. www.idt.net

Knowledge Learning Corporation

CONTRIBUTIONS: TOTAL: *$2,000* DEM: *$500* REP: *$1,500*

Subsidiary of Knowledge Universe, Inc. (p. 184). www.knowledgelearning.com

Knowledge Universe, Inc.

CONTRIBUTIONS: TOTAL: *$13,500* DEM: *$3,500* REP: *$10,000*

After serving time and paying upward of $1 billion in fines for securities fraud in the early 1990s, chairman Michael Milken has continued charity and community building; awarded $25,000 each to more than 100 teachers per year; founded the Prostate Cancer Foundation, the world's largest such research funding source; and founded the nonprofit, nonpartisan think tank the Milken Institute, which researches economic issues and policymaking. www.knowledgeu.com

MCI, Inc.

CONTRIBUTIONS: TOTAL: *$617,500* DEM: *$278,104* REP: *$339,397*

Subsidiary of Verizon Communications Inc. (p. 187). Changed name from WorldCom back to MCI, Inc., following an Enron-style accounting scandal that plagued the companies after their merger. Ordered to pay $625,000 in EPA fines in 1999 for violations at 153 facilities in 29 states. Sponsorship of the Heritage Gold Tournament brings in more than $1 million annually for college scholarships. Has a written nondiscrimination policy covering sexual orientation but not gender identity. Offers insurance coverage to employees' domestic partners. www.mci.com

Nextel Communications, Inc.

CONTRIBUTIONS: TOTAL: *$100,000* DEM: *$35,476* REP: *$64,524*

Being acquired by Sprint Corporation (p. 185). Charged repeatedly with unfair billing practices, mostly for misrepresenting consumer charges and padding bills with "fake fees." Sponsors professional NASCAR racing. Has a written nondiscrimination policy covering sexual orientation but not gender identity. Offers insurance coverage to employees' domestic partners. www.nextel.com

Qwest Communications International Inc.

 30%   70%

CONTRIBUTIONS: TOTAL: *$826,511* DEM: *$250,147* REP: *$576,364*

Paid a $250 million fine to the SEC for inflating revenue and concealing expenses from 1999 to 2002. Its former cochair and CEO was charged with fraud, with actions taken against 21 other officers and employees. Paid over $17 million in fines to the FCC for violation of federal law. Paid $3.75 million in 2003 to settle allegations that it fraudulently charged for unauthorized services and withheld refunds. In 2003, was among the top 50 workplaces for Latina women, according to *Latina Style* magazine. Foundation supports primary education, job preparedness training, and community economic development. Partners with the American Red Cross and the National Center for Missing & Exploited Children. Has a written nondiscrimination policy covering sexual orientation but not gender identity. Offers insurance coverage to employees' domestic partners. www.qwest.com

Samsung Electronics America, Inc.; Samsung Group
See p. 46 in Computers and Electronics.

SBC Communications Inc.

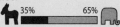 35%   65%

CONTRIBUTIONS: TOTAL: *$2,703,530* DEM: *$935,805* REP: *$1,767,725*

Spends more on state level lobbying and (mostly Republican) campaigns than any other telecommunications company: Fighting municipal wireless access programs and seeking to eliminate antitrust regulations limiting telecommunications monopolies. Settled a $40 million suit in 2004 for misleading and fraudulent advertising. Pending class action lawsuit alleges fraudulent miscalculation of pension and retirement plans. Seventeenth among 50 companies with reputations for employing and accommodating people with disabilities. Committed to placing 16.6% of supplier spending ($1.7 billion in 2002) with businesses owned by minorities, women, and veterans. Donated $5 million to promote college readiness among poor students. www.sbc.com

Sprint Nextel Corporation

 35%   65%

CONTRIBUTIONS: TOTAL: *$662,300* DEM: *$229,807* REP: *$432,493*

Paid $1.5 million to settle FTC allegations for denying service to customers considered credit risks. Corporate giving supports education, especially in Missouri. Has a used wireless equipment donation program to refurbish and distribute cell phones to charity. Has a written nondiscrimination policy covering sexual orientation and gender identity. Offers insurance coverage to employees' domestic partners. www.sprint.com

T-Mobile USA, Inc.

45% — 55%

CONTRIBUTIONS: TOTAL: *$89,500* DEM: *$40,007* REP: *$49,494*

Subsidiary of Deutsche Telekom AG (p. 183). Cited by the Communications Workers of America (CWA) as "antiworker" for retaining management while dismissing workers; has similar disputes with CWA's U.K. counterpart. Paid $4.7 million in back wages in 2003 to settle wage-and-hour violations for more than 20,000 customer service employees. Fined $1.1 million by the FCC in 2003 for missing deadlines to implement enhanced 911 service. Part of a task force to research implementing age-based restrictions on access to adult content. Has a written nondiscrimination policy covering sexual orientation and gender identity. Offers insurance coverage to employees' domestic partners. www.t-mobile.com

TDS Telecommunications Corporation

92% — 8%

CONTRIBUTIONS: TOTAL: *$13,105* DEM: *$12,000* REP: *$1,105*

Subsidiary of Telephone and Data Systems, Inc. (p. 186). Has a written nondiscrimination policy covering sexual orientation but not gender identity. Refuses insurance coverage to employees' domestic partners. www.tdstelecom.com

Telephone and Data Systems, Inc.

47% — 53%

CONTRIBUTIONS: TOTAL: *$66,105* DEM: *$35,250* REP: *$30,855*

Outreach supports various local charities. Has a written nondiscrimination policy covering sexual orientation but not gender identity. Refuses insurance coverage to employees' domestic partners. www.teldta.com

Time Warner Cable Inc.

41% — 59%

CONTRIBUTIONS: TOTAL: *$31,500* DEM: *$12,828* REP: *$18,672*

Subsidiary of Time Warner Inc. (p. 186). Has a written nondiscrimination policy covering sexual orientation and plans to cover gender identity. Offers insurance coverage to employees' domestic partners. www.timewarnercable.com

Time Warner Inc.

34% — 66%

CONTRIBUTIONS: TOTAL: *$769,074* DEM: *$261,426* REP: *$507,648*

Paid $550 million to settle a shareholder class action alleging accounting irregularities in its AOL division. Paid $2.9 million to settle a class action suit alleging violation of the Employee Retirement Income Security Act (ERISA.) Funds Americans for Tax Reform, a conservative group founded by Grover Norquist at the request of Ronald Reagan. Ranked 16th of 50 companies with the best reputation for employing and accommodating people with disabilities. Has a written nondiscrimination policy covering sexual orientation and plans to cover gender identity. Offers insurance coverage to employees' domestic partners. www.timewarner.com

United Online, Inc.
No contributions. Philanthropy supports Ronald McDonald House Charities, including donating computers and Internet access. Has a written nondiscrimination policy covering sexual orientation but not gender identity. www.unitedonline.net

United States Cellular Corporation
94% ■ 6%

CONTRIBUTIONS: TOTAL: *$8,750* DEM: *$8,250* REP: *$500*
Subsidiary of Telephone and Data Systems, Inc. (p. 186). A pending lawsuit alleges fraud and violations of consumer credit laws for misleading advertising luring customers into purchasing plans then charging large cancellation fees. Outreach supports programs serving disadvantaged youth, families, and seniors. Offers subscribers free access to wireless text–messaged Amber Alerts. www.uscellular.com

Verizon Communications Inc.
37% ■ 63%

CONTRIBUTIONS: TOTAL: *$2,147,710* DEM: *$804,272* REP: *$1,340,972*
The Communications Workers of America filed a 2003 grievance claiming members were denied participation in an early retirement buyout program. Outreach supports education, health, economic development, and the digital divide. Foundation focuses on computer literacy, especially for people with disabilities, minorities, and immigrants. Has a written nondiscrimination policy covering sexual orientation but not gender identity. Offers health insurance coverage to employees' domestic partners. www.verizon.com

Viacom, Inc.
See p. 154 in Media and Entertainment.

Vonage Holdings Corp.
37% ■ 63%

CONTRIBUTIONS: TOTAL: *$14,250* DEM: *$5,250* REP: *$9,000*
Recent outreach included sponsorship of the Live 8 concert schedule on MTV Networks. www.vonage.com

Western Wireless Corporation
17% ■ 83%

CONTRIBUTIONS: TOTAL: *$231,171* DEM: *$39,443* REP: *$189,191*
Subsidiary of ALLTEL Corporation (p. 180). In the first such act of enforcement, the FCC proposed a $200,000 fine in 2003 after the company erected an unauthorized cell tower within a historically and environmentally protected North Dakota site. (A year later, the agency backpedaled, rescinding the fine and agreeing to "mitigate" the situation.) In 1999, in exchange for

the company's agreeing to self-audit, the EPA levied only nominal fines for violating public right-to-know measures and spill control regulations. www.wwireless.com

Yahoo! Inc.

CONTRIBUTIONS: TOTAL: *$258,250* DEM: *$103,531* REP: *$154,719*

Argued recently that its posting Nazi memorabilia on a website—a practice declared by a French court to be in violation of that country's antiracism law—is constitutionally protected in the United States. Closed chat rooms to help fight child exploitation and electronic distribution of child pornography. Outreach supports various social and environmental programs throughout the world and focuses on the company's global reach as a means to help connect people to causes. Employees may volunteer on company time; donations matched up to $1,000 a year. Has a written nondiscrimination policy covering sexual orientation but not gender identity. Offers insurance coverage to employees' domestic partners. www.yahoo.com

Travel and Leisure

One story, possibly untrue, has the term *lobbyist* coming into being in Washington, D.C.'s, Willard Hotel. Reportedly, Ulysses S. Grant would take his brandy and cigars there; people who wanted his attention on a particular matter learned to wait for him to come through the hotel lobby before approaching him.

Today the hotel lobby—joined by the airline lobby, the resort lobby, the travel agents lobby, and so on—scarcely waits for anyone to arrive anywhere before approaching them. From September 11, 2001, and the Gulf Coast hurricanes to the rising prices of jet fuel and a generally sporadic economy, the sector has been looking for all the help it can get. Since most of the companies within this sector depend on the government to promote a travel-friendly climate, the bigger players focus contributions on candidates involved with transportation policy and—with the sector's substantial reliance on immigrant labor—immigration policies.

From airlines to hotels, companies in the tourism and hospitality business have given heavily to both parties historically. After September 11, 2001, however, an even greater focus was put on winning support on the travel and leisure front from the party in power.

But, perhaps more than other sectors—and no doubt owing to the ever-growing number of tourism options available to us—travel and leisure has also demonstrated a responsiveness to its customers. Ecotourism is one of the more promising ideas to come out of the sector in recent years, and its popularity has been on the increase. Though they still represent just a fraction of all vacations, "green tours" and other ecologically and socially responsible trips have proven that ethical shoppers can make a difference.

Top Ten Republican Contributors

Enterprise Rent-A-Car Company	$578,626
Tracinda Corporation	301,265
MGM Mirage	269,265
AMR Corporation (American Airlines)	239,777
Wynn Resorts, Limited	218,881
Southwest Airlines Co.	194,142
Northwest Airlines Corporation	172,496
Continental Airlines, Inc.	149,381
Marriott International, Inc.	135,904
Las Vegas Sands Corp.	132,250

Top Ten Democratic Contributors

Tracinda Corporation	$169,787
MGM Mirage	169,787
Harrah's Entertainment, Inc.	148,460
Choice Hotels International, Inc.	144,490
Global Hyatt Corporation	135,125
AMR Corporation (American Airlines)	110,873
Northwest Airlines Corporation	104,837
Sabre Holdings Corporation	104,673
Enterprise Rent-A-Car Company	92,529
Expedia, Inc.	91,496

Accor North America

No contributions. Foreign owned. Pending a class action brought by 2004 tsunami victims for lack of disaster preparedness. Paid an $11 million settlement to 53 plaintiffs bitten by bedbugs in a Motel 6. Sofitel subsidiary settled a suit in 2003 for failure to warn customers of possible exposure to smoke and hazardous chemicals. Motel 6 subsidiary has a pending wage-and-hour class action suit. Executive member of American Hotel & Lodging Association Multicultural Advisory Council, which develops initiatives to promote and recruit a racially diverse workforce. National sponsor of the 2004 Toys for Tots program. www.accor-na.com

AirTran Holdings, Inc.

CONTRIBUTIONS: TOTAL: *$2,500* DEM: *$0* REP: *$2,500*

Settled a suit in 1999 over improper maintenance of a jet in a 1996 Everglades crash under its former name ValuJet. Emphasizes community involvement in outreach, especially with organizations that benefit children. Has a written nondiscrimination policy covering sexual orientation but not gender identity. Refuses insurance coverage to employees' domestic partners. www.airtran.com

Alaska Air Group, Inc.

CONTRIBUTIONS: TOTAL: *$56,500* DEM: *$18,151* REP: *$38,349*

Involved in a series of lawsuits and safety violations relating to a January 2000 crash in which all 88 passengers and crew were killed. Pulled Christian-only prayer cards from meals when threatened with legal action. Has notable employee profit sharing and retirement plans. Has a written nondiscrimination policy covering sexual orientation but not gender identity. Offers insurance coverage to employees' domestic partners. www.alaskaair.com

American Express Company

See p. 53 in Finance, Insurance, and Real Estate.

AmeriHost Franchise Systems, Inc.

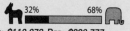

CONTRIBUTIONS: TOTAL: *$2,000* DEM: *$2,000* REP: *$0*

Subsidiary of Cendant Corporation (p. 192). www.arlingtonhospitality.com

AMR Corporation (American Airlines)

CONTRIBUTIONS: TOTAL: *$350,650* DEM: *$110,873* REP: *$239,777*

In 2002, the Federal Aviation Administration (FAA) announced it would seek $1.2 million in penalties for maintenance and safety violations. Part of the Coalition for Environmentally Responsible Economies (CERES) standard for environmental reporting. Supports the Global Sullivan Principles, which call on multinational corporations to promote human rights and uphold social and economic justice in their operations. Foundation has suspended all cash grants due to the financial crisis facing the airline industry following September 11, 2001. Has a written nondiscrimination policy covering sexual orientation and gender identity. Offers insurance coverage to employees' domestic partners. www.aa.com

Avis Group Holdings, Inc.

No contributions. Subsidiary of Cendant Corporation (p. 192). Accused in a 2003 class action of underpaying travel agent commissions. In 2001, settled a federal lawsuit alleging discrimination and violations of the American Disabilities Act (ADA). Settled a racial discrimination suit for an undisclosed sum brought by Latino drivers working at the San Francisco airport location. www.avis.com

Best Western International, Inc.

No contributions. A not-for-profit membership association. Ousted a member hotel in response to complaints of racial discrimination and then settled in federal court. Received a D grade from the 2004 National Association for the Advancement of Colored People (NAACP) lodging industry report on business practices. Does not have standardized benefits throughout membership. www.bestwestern.com

Budget Rent A Car System, Inc.
No contributions. Subsidiary of Cendant Corporation (p. 192). A pending 2003 class action suit accused the company of compensation violations for underpaying travel agent commissions. www.budget.com

Candlewood Suites
No contributions. Subsidiary of InterContinental Hotels Group PLC (p. 198). www.candlewoodsuites.com

Carlson Companies, Inc.
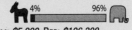
CONTRIBUTIONS: TOTAL: *$111,208* DEM: *$5,000* REP: *$106,208*
Involved in several union scuffles at its flagship Radisson in Minnetonka, Minnesota. Cofounder of the World Childhood Foundation. Supports volunteerism. National foundation focuses support on children at risk, mentoring, and education, mainly in Minnesota. Has a written nondiscrimination policy covering sexual orientation but not gender identity. Offers insurance coverage to employees' domestic partners. www.carlson.com

Carlson Cruises Worldwide
No contributions. Subsidiary of Carlson Companies, Inc. (p. 192). www.carlson.com/consumer_cruises.cfm

Carlson Hotels Worldwide
No contributions. Subsidiary of Carlson Companies, Inc. (p. 192). www.carlson.com/consumer_hotels.cfm

Carlson Leisure Group
No contributions. Subsidiary of Carlson Companies, Inc. (p. 192). www.carlson.com/consumer_travel.cfm

Carnival Corporation

CONTRIBUTIONS: TOTAL: *$185,950* DEM: *$79,349* REP: *$106,591*
Paid a $200,000 settlement in 2003 for questionable compliance with ballast water management requirements. Paid an $18 million fine in 2002 after pleading guilty to six false statements associated with discharging waste and falsifying record books. Settled a negligence lawsuit with an undisclosed payment estimated at up to $57 million in the death of 16 passengers and three crew members in an air crash. www.carnivalcorp.com

Cendant Corporation

CONTRIBUTIONS: TOTAL: *$196,750* DEM: *$69,520* REP: *$127,230*
Paid more than $2.8 billion in settlements for securities irregularities; vice chairman was sentenced to 10 years in prison.

Legal counsel used what is now referred to as the "dumb CEO defense." Subject of a class action suit for forced referrals to its own subsidiary companies charging excessive rates for reports required for real estate transactions at its subsidiary Coldwell Banker Real Estate Corporation (p. 56). Subsidiary Trendwest Resorts, Inc., settled with the state of California over deceptive sales practices in timeshare contracts. Has a minimal employee volunteer program. Supports literacy initiatives through subsidiary Budget Rent A Car System, Inc. (p. 192). Has a written nondiscrimination policy covering sexual orientation but not gender identity. Offers insurance coverage to employees' domestic partners. www.cendant.com

Choice Hotels International, Inc.

72%   28%

CONTRIBUTIONS: TOTAL: *$199,500* DEM: *$144,490* REP: *$53,010*

Repeatedly recognized as a progressive employer. Committed to employee development, diversity initiatives, and minority ownership incentives. Supports employee volunteerism. Has a charitable matching program. Foundation supports food aid, tourism, education, and enhancing quality of life in areas where the company has a presence. Has a written nondiscrimination policy covering sexual orientation but not gender identity. www.choicehotels.com

Clarion

No contributions. Subsidiary of Choice Hotels International, Inc. (p. 193). Settled a federal disability discrimination suit brought on behalf of housekeepers in Arizona. www.clarionhotel.com

Classic Residence by Hyatt

91%   9%

CONTRIBUTIONS: TOTAL: *$74,500* DEM: *$67,730* REP: *$6,770*

Subsidiary of Global Hyatt Corporation (p. 196). www.hyattclassic.com

Comfort Inn

No contributions. Subsidiary of Choice Hotels International, Inc. (p. 193). Settled a federal lawsuit alleging a pattern of race bias practiced against African American guests in 2002. www.comfortinn.com

Comfort Suites

No contributions. Subsidiary of Choice Hotels International, Inc. (p. 193). www.comfortsuites.com

Conrad Hospitality, LLC

No contributions. Subsidiary of Hilton Hotels Corporation (p. 197). www.conradhotels.com

Continental Airlines, Inc.

24% | 76%

CONTRIBUTIONS: TOTAL: *$194,629* DEM: *$45,248* REP: *$149,381*

Paid $825,000 to settle a sexual harassment suit in 1997 that has shaped employment law surrounding internet and electronic harassment and led to several settled defamation suits. Has a pending age discrimination suit. Supports community organizations in the arts, culture, sports, education, health, and medicine. Has suspended community service and outreach efforts following September 11, 2001. Has a written nondiscrimination policy covering sexual orientation but not gender identity. Offers insurance coverage to employees' domestic partners. www.continental.com

Country Inns & Suites by Carlson

No contributions. Subsidiary of Carlson Hotels Worldwide (p. 192). www.countryinns.com

Courtyard

No contributions. Subsidiary of Marriott International, Inc. (p. 199). www.marriott.com/courtyard

Crowne Plaza Hotels & Resorts

No contributions. Subsidiary of InterContinental Hotels Group PLC (p. 198). www.crowneplaza.com

Days Inn Worldwide, Inc.

12% | 88%

CONTRIBUTIONS: TOTAL: *$4,400* DEM: *$519* REP: *$3,881*

Subsidiary of Cendant Corporation (p. 192). Settled a price-gouging lawsuit brought by the state of Florida alleging that consumers were overcharged for basic necessities during a hurricane state of emergency. Admitted in a 1999 federal lawsuit that it knowingly built an Illinois inn without proper disability access. www.daysinn.com

Delta Air Lines, Inc.

33% | 67%

CONTRIBUTIONS: TOTAL: *$180,750* DEM: *$60,116* REP: *$120,635*

Targeted in a $1 billion class action suit for its practice of penalizing travelers who deplane without completing a multistop ticket. Paid a $150,000 settlement in an Equal Employment Opportunity Commission (EEOC) case alleging discrimination against pregnant employees. Granted $1.7 million to fund flight training for women and minorities. Has a written nondiscrimination policy covering sexual orientation but not gender identity. Offers insurance coverage to employees' domestic partners. www.delta.com

Dollar Thrifty Automotive Group, Inc.

44% | 66%

CONTRIBUTIONS: TOTAL: *$51,250* DEM: *$22,738* REP: *$28,512*

Provides grants to nonprofit organizations supporting economic and neighborhood revitalization in areas where employees and customers reside. www.dtag.com

Doubletree Corporation
No contributions. Subsidiary of Hilton Hotels Corporation (p. 197). www.doubletree.com

Econo Lodge
No contributions. Subsidiary of Choice Hotels International, Inc. (p. 193). www.econolodge.com

Embassy Suites Hotels
No contributions. Subsidiary of Hilton Hotels Corporation (p. 197). www.embassysuites.com

Enterprise Rent-A-Car Company

 14%   86%

CONTRIBUTIONS: TOTAL: *$671,154* DEM: *$92,528* REP: *$578,626*
Pending wrongful termination suit estimated at $4 million. Settled a major class action suit alleging violations of the ADA at its rental locations. Supports community strengthening with employee matching and volunteer programs, and a grant and charitable donation program. Has a written nondiscrimination policy covering sexual orientation but not gender identity. Offers insurance coverage to employees' domestic partners. www.enterprise.com

Expedia, Inc.

 91%   9%

CONTRIBUTIONS: TOTAL: *$100,700* DEM: *$91,496* REP: *$9,204*
A pending securities fraud class action suit brought by investors alleges gross misrepresentation leading to sustained loss in its spinoff from IAC/InterActiveCorp (p. 152). Community Grant Program supports employee-elected charities. Has an employee volunteer program. Partnered with IAC Travel, donating $22,000 to a hurricane relief fund. Has a written nondiscrimination policy covering sexual orientation but not gender identity. Offers insurance coverage to employees' domestic partners. www.expedia.com

Fairfield Inn
No contributions. Subsidiary of Marriott International, Inc. (p. 199). www.marriott.com/fairfieldinn

Fairmont Hotels & Resorts Inc.
No contributions. Forbids political contributions of any kind using company funds, but encourages political activity and involvement by its employees. Has a written nondiscrimination policy covering sexual orientation but not gender identity. www.fairmont.com

Four Points by Sheraton
No contributions. Subsidiary of Starwood Hotels & Resorts Worldwide, Inc. (p. 203). www.starwoodhotels.com/fourpoints

Four Seasons Hotels Inc.

CONTRIBUTIONS: TOTAL: *$500* DEM: *$500* REP: *$0*

Was sued for alleged misappropriation and unauthorized use of the likeness of Elvis Presley. Listed in *Fortune* magazine as one of the "100 Best Companies to Work For." Has a written nondiscrimination policy covering sexual orientation but not gender identity. Offers insurance coverage to employees' domestic partners. www.fshr.com

Frontier Airlines, Inc.

CONTRIBUTIONS: TOTAL: *$1,500* DEM: *$1,000* REP: *$500*

Allegedly broke privacy laws in 2002 and 2003 by giving passenger data to the Transportation Security Administration and its contractors. Paid a $100,000 fine for failure to provide space in aircraft cabins for wheelchairs. Supports community improvement in cities it serves, with both funding and employee volunteer programs. www.frontierairlines.com

General Electric Company

See p. 58 in Finance, Insurance, and Real Estate.

Global Hyatt Corporation

CONTRIBUTIONS: TOTAL: *$151,500* DEM: *$135,125* REP: *$16,375*

Franchisees have faced individual suits for labor issues and code infractions. Recognized for diversity policies in recruiting and employing minorities. Outreach includes blood drives and mentoring programs. Supports volunteerism, donating 81,000 hours in 2003. Has a written nondiscrimination policy covering sexual orientation but not gender identity. Offers insurance coverage to employees' domestic partners. www.hyatt.com

Hampton Inn

No contributions. Subsidiary of Hilton Hotels Corporation (p. 197). www.hamptoninn.com

Hard Rock Cafe International, Inc.

See p. 163 in Restaurants.

Harrah's Entertainment, Inc.

CONTRIBUTIONS: TOTAL: *$256,560* DEM: *$148,460* REP: *$108,100*

Found guilty of invasion of privacy and intentional infliction of emotional distress by a former employee in a sexual discrimination case. Donates 1% of profits to civic and charitable causes focusing on minority issues, Alzheimer's disease, and seniors' issues. Supports employee volunteerism and has a matching grant program supporting educational institutions. Has a written non discrimination policy covering sexual orientation, and there are plans to cover gender identity. Soon to offer insurance coverage to employees' domestic partners as of 2006. www.harrahs.com

Hertz Corporation, The
No contributions. Subsidiary of Ford Motor Company (p. 214), who recently announced its intention to sell to a group of private equity firms. Has a written nondiscrimination policy covering sexual orientation and gender identity. Offers insurance coverage to employees' domestic partners. www.hertz.com

Hilton Garden Inn
No contributions. Subsidiary of Hilton Hotels Corporation (p. 197). www.hiltongardeninn.com

Hilton Grand Vacations Company, LLC
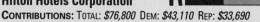
0%   100%
CONTRIBUTIONS: TOTAL: *$800* DEM: *$0* REP: *$800*
Subsidiary of Hilton Hotels Corporation (p. 197). www.hiltongrandvacations.com

Hilton Hotels Corporation
56%   44%
CONTRIBUTIONS: TOTAL: *$76,800* DEM: *$43,110* REP: *$33,690*
Settled suits resulting from inhalation and exposure to black mold at its Hawaiian Village hotel in Honolulu. Has a written nondiscrimination policy covering sexual orientation but not gender identity. Offers insurance coverage to employees' domestic partners. www.hiltonworldwide.com

Holiday Inn Express
No contributions. Subsidiary of InterContinental Hotels Group PLC (p. 198). www.hiexpress.com

Holiday Inn Hotels & Resorts
No contributions. Subsidiary of InterContinental Hotels Group PLC (p. 198). www.holiday-inn.com

Homewood Suites by Hilton
No contributions. Subsidiary of Hilton Hotels Corporation (p. 197). www.homewoodsuites.com

Hooters of America, Inc.
See p. 164 in Restaurants.

HowardJohnson International, Inc.
No contributions. Subsidiary of Cendant Corporation (p. 192). In 2005, a child who drowned at an Orlando hotel, with an eight-year history of violations, was not found for two hours due to murky pool water. www.howardjohnson.com

HVM L.L.C. (Extended Stay Hotels)
No contributions. Paid $5.2 million to settle a class action suit alleging violation of overtime laws and failure to pay overtime wages. www.extendedstayhotels.com

Hyatt Hotels Corporation

CONTRIBUTIONS: TOTAL: *$1,000* DEM: *$0* REP: *$1,000*
Subsidiary of Global Hyatt Corporation (p. 196).

Hyatt International Corporation

No contributions. Subsidiary of Global Hyatt Corporation (p. 196). www.hyatt.com

InterContinental Hotels & Resorts

No contributions. Subsidiary of InterContinental Hotels Group PLC (p. 198). www.intercontinental.com

InterContinental Hotels Group PLC

CONTRIBUTIONS: TOTAL: *$40,200* DEM: *$10,148* REP: *$30,052*
Fought a personal injury and wrongful death case brought against the company in Egypt. Partners with UNICEF to provide educational opportunities for children. Claims to be apolitical on its website. Founding member of International Hotels Environmental Initiative. Complies only with the labor laws of the countries in which it operates. Does not have a written nondiscrimination policy covering sexual orientation or gender identity. Refuses insurance coverage to employees' domestic partners. www.ihgplc.com

JetBlue Airways Corporation

CONTRIBUTIONS: TOTAL: *$26,250* DEM: *$14,930* REP: *$11,320*
The CEO has performed every job at JetBlue Airways Corporation, from baggage handler to ticketing agent, to better understand the demands made on employees. Has a written nondiscrimination policy covering sexual orientation but not gender identity. Offers insurance to employees' domestic partners. www.jetblue.com

JW Marriott Hotels & Resorts

No contributions. Subsidiary of Marriott International, Inc. (p. 199). www.marriott.com/jwmarriott

Knights Franchise Systems, Inc. (Knights Inn)

No contributions. Subsidiary of Cendant Corporation (p. 192). www.knightsinn.com

Landry's Restaurants, Inc.

See p. 165 in Restaurants.

La Quinta Corporation

No contributions. Does not have a written nondiscrimination policy covering sexual orientation or gender identity. Refuses insurance coverage to employees' domestic partners. www.lq.com

Las Vegas Sands Corp.

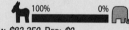

CONTRIBUTIONS: TOTAL: *$132,250* DEM: *$0* REP: *$132,250*

Settled a suit by paying $1 million in fines for "fixing" promotional contests to favor certain Asian high rollers. A complaint filed by Common Cause alleged the CEO funneled $80,000 in political contributions through unlicensed companies to a local Republican candidate for County Commission. Foundation supports youth education programs and minority empowerment. Offers on-site day care, wellness programs, and extensive benefits for employees. www.lasvegassands.com

Loews Corporation

See p. 61 in Finance, Insurance, and Real Estate.

Loews Hotels Holding Corporation

CONTRIBUTIONS: TOTAL: *$82,250* DEM: *$82,250* REP: *$0*

Subsidiary of Loews Corporation (p. 61). Provides pet amenities and services as part of its Very Important Pets program. www.loewshotels.com

Luxury Collection, The

No contributions. Subsidiary of Starwood Hotels & Resorts Worldwide, Inc. (p. 203). www.starwoodhotels.com/luxury

MainStay Suites

No contributions. Subsidiary of Choice Hotels International, Inc. (p. 193). www.mainstaysuites.com

Marriott Conference Centers

No contributions. Subsidiary of Marriott International, Inc. (p. 199). www.marriott.com/conferencecenters

Marriott ExecuStay

No contributions. Subsidiary of Marriott International, Inc. (p. 199). www.execustay.com

Marriott Executive Apartments

No contributions. Subsidiary of Marriott International, Inc. (p. 199). www.marriott.com/execapartments

Marriott Hotels & Resorts

No contributions. Subsidiary of Marriott International, Inc. (p. 199). www.marriott.com/marriott

Marriott International, Inc.

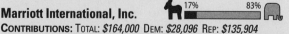

CONTRIBUTIONS: TOTAL: *$164,000* DEM: *$28,096* REP: *$135,904*

Listed as one of *Fortune* magazine's "Best Companies for Minorities" several years in a row despite a 2001 court finding that it had allowed a hostile work environment for minority workers. Paid $70,000 to settle a negligence suit following the death of a 14-year-old boy at one of its California theme parks.

Foundation supports "school to work" programs for youth with disabilities. Offers welfare recipients full-time work with benefits on completion of a company training program. Has a written nondiscrimination policy covering sexual orientation but not gender identity. Offers insurance to employees' domestic partners. www.marriott.com

Marriott Vacation Club International

37% 63%

CONTRIBUTIONS: TOTAL: *$1,500* DEM: *$556* REP: *$944*
Subsidiary of Marriott International, Inc. (p. 199). www.marriott.com/vacationclub

MGM Grand Hotel, LLC

50% 50%

CONTRIBUTIONS: TOTAL: *$8,000* DEM: *$4,000* REP: *$4,000*
Subsidiary of MGM Mirage (p. 200). www.mgmgrand.com

MGM Mirage

39% 61%

CONTRIBUTIONS: TOTAL: *$439,051* DEM: *$169,787* REP: *$269,264*
Subsidiary of Tracinda Corporation (p. 204). Has a written nondiscrimination policy covering sexual orientation but not gender identity. Offers insurance to employees' domestic partners. www.mgmmirage.com

Mirage Resorts, Incorporated

40% 60%

CONTRIBUTIONS: TOTAL: *$10,000* DEM: *$4,000* REP: *$6,000*
Subsidiary of MGM Mirage (p. 200). Paid a $40,000 penalty to the Federal Elections Committee for violations of the Federal Elections Campaign Act in association with contributions to William Gormley's 2000 senate campaign. www.mirage.com

Motel 6

No contributions. Subsidiary of Accor North America (p. 190). In 2004 settled federal government claims of violations of the ADA. A pending wage-and-hour class action suit alleges a failure to pay overtime and misclassification. A federal appeals court upheld $358,000 in damages for two Idaho couples who sued for age discrimination after they were abruptly fired as Motel 6 managers and replaced by younger, lower-paid couples. www.motel6.com

North America Sofitel Corporation

No contributions. Subsidiary of Accor North America (p. 190). Settled a California lawsuit for failure to adequately warn customers about tobacco smoke and other chemical exposure. Successfully resisted unionization of housekeepers in its San Francisco hotel. www.sofitel.com

Northwest Airlines Corporation

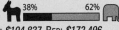
38% 62%

CONTRIBUTIONS: TOTAL: *$277,333* DEM: *$104,837* REP: *$172,496*
Targeted in a $1 billion class action lawsuit for its practice of penalizing travelers who deplane without completing a multi-

stop ticket. Paid $7.1 million to settle a class action lawsuit brought by passengers stranded on planes for several hours due to a blizzard. Lost a major class action age discrimination suit brought by current and former women cabin attendants and their unions. Supports community improvement through AirCares and KidCares mileage donation programs. Has a written nondiscrimination policy covering sexual orientation but not gender identity. Offers insurance coverage to employees' domestic partners. www.nwa.com

Omni Hotels Corporation

0%   100%

CONTRIBUTIONS: TOTAL: *$3,000* DEM: *$0* REP: *$3,000*

Subsidiary of TRT Holdings, Inc. (p. 204). Sued for discrimination and violation of the ADA. Ranked 10 of the 10 best hotels for families according to *Child* magazine in 2003. Has a written nondiscrimination policy covering sexual orientation but not gender identity. Refuses insurance coverage to employees' domestic partners. www.omnihotels.com

Orbitz, LLC

52%   48%

CONTRIBUTIONS: TOTAL: *$2,850* DEM: *$1,486* REP: *$1,364*

Subsidiary of Cendant Corporation (p. 192). Sued by the cities of Los Angeles and Philadelphia for not collecting room taxes. www.orbitz.com

Park Inn

No contributions. Subsidiary of Carlson Hotels Worldwide (p. 192). www.parkinn.com

Park Plaza Hotels & Resorts

No contributions. Subsidiary of Carlson Hotels Worldwide (p. 192). www.parkplaza.com

Quality

No contributions. Subsidiary of Choice Hotels International, Inc. (p. 193). Has settled several lawsuits in the last decade over access laws and violations of the Americans with Disabilities Act. www.qualityinn.com

Radisson Hotels & Resorts

No contributions. Subsidiary of Carlson Hotels Worldwide (p. 192). Settled for $625,000 an EEOC-led sexual harassment lawsuit brought on behalf of women housekeepers in Rochester in 2005. Settled a racial discrimination class action lawsuit for an undisclosed sum in 2003, brought by the EEOC on behalf of black employees in its Memphis accounting, catering, and reservations departments. www.radisson.com

Ramada Franchise Systems, Inc.

No contributions. Subsidiary of Cendant Corporation (p. 192). Agreed to make its website more accessible to the blind and visually impaired in response to charges by the state of New York. www.ramada.com

Red Roof Inns
No contributions. Subsidiary of Accor North America (p. 190). www.redroof.com

Regent International Hotels
No contributions. Subsidiary of Carlson Hotels Worldwide (p. 192). www.regenthotels.com

Renaissance Hotels & Resorts
No contributions. Subsidiary of Marriott International, Inc. (p. 199). www.marriott.com/renaissancehotels

Residence Inn
No contributions. Subsidiary of Marriott International, Inc. (p. 199). www.marriott.com/residenceinn

Ritz-Carlton Hotel Company, L.L.C., The
No contributions. Subsidiary of Marriott International, Inc. (p. 199). www.ritzcarlton.com

Rodeway Inn
No contributions. Subsidiary of Choice Hotels International, Inc. (p. 193). www.rodeway.com

Royal Caribbean Cruises Ltd.
54% | 46%

CONTRIBUTIONS: TOTAL: *$160,500* DEM: *$85,936* REP: *$74,554*
Paid an $18.4 million settlement in class action lawsuit alleging failure to pay overtime wages. Supports efforts to restore and maintain marine environments and to promote awareness and respect for marine life. www.royalcaribbean.com

Sabre Holdings Corporation
45% | 55%

CONTRIBUTIONS: TOTAL: *$234,795* DEM: *$104,673* REP: *$130,122*
Spun off in 1999 from AMR Corporation (p. 191), the parent company to American Airlines (p. 191), to avoid continued accusations of bias to one airline. Has a written nondiscrimination policy covering sexual orientation but not gender identity. Offers insurance coverage to employees' domestic partners. www.sabre-holdings.com

Sheraton Hotels & Resorts
No contributions. Subsidiary of Starwood Hotels & Resorts Worldwide, Inc. (p. 203). www.starwoodhotels.com/sheraton

Sinclair Oil Corporation
See p. 221 in Vehicles, Parts, and Gas.

Sleep Inn
No contributions. Subsidiary of Choice Hotels International, Inc. (p. 193). www.sleepinn.com

Southwest Airlines Co.

CONTRIBUTIONS: TOTAL: *$237,500* DEM: *$43,358* REP: *$194,142*

One of six companies awarded the Corporate Conscience Award for its creative workforce retention following September 11, 2001. Recognized for its employee-friendly policies and working culture. Has a written nondiscrimination policy covering sexual orientation but not gender identity. Offers insurance coverage to employees' domestic partners.
www.southwest.com

SpringHill Suites

No contributions. Subsidiary of Marriott International, Inc. (p. 199). www.marriott.com/springhill

St. Regis Hotels & Resorts

No contributions. Subsidiary of Starwood Hotels & Resorts Worldwide, Inc. (p. 203). www.starwoodhotels.com/stregis

Starwood Hotels & Resorts Worldwide, Inc.

CONTRIBUTIONS: TOTAL: *$26,000* DEM: *$26,000* REP: *$0*

Fined for receiving kickbacks from vendors. Agreed to acquire Le Meridien Hotels & Resorts, Ltd. Community outreach encourages employee volunteerism and mentoring. Partners with Habitat for Humanity and the Juvenile Diabetes Research Foundation. Has a written nondiscrimination policy covering sexual orientation but not gender identity. Offers insurance coverage to employees' domestic partners. www.starwoodhotels.com

Staybridge Suites

No contributions. Subsidiary of InterContinental Hotels Group PLC (p. 198). www.staybridge.com

Studio 6

No contributions. Subsidiary of Accor North America (p. 190). www.staystudio6.com

Super 8 Motels, Inc.

No contributions. Subsidiary of Cendant Corporation (p. 192). Offers free accommodations during the holidays to eligible customers visiting friends or relatives in distant nursing homes, hospitals, veterans' homes, or treatment facilities.
www.super8.com

Texas Pacific Group

See p. 168 in Restaurants.

TownePlace Suites

No contributions. Subsidiary of Marriott International, Inc. (p. 199). www.marriott.com/towneplace

Tracinda Corporation

CONTRIBUTIONS: TOTAL: *$471,051* DEM: *$169,787* REP: *$301,264*

Privately owned. MGM Mirage (p. 200) subsidiary has separate benefits and environmental statements. Involved in too many claims, actions, and suits to list. Sold its interest in Metro-Goldwyn-Mayer Inc. for the third time in April 2005.

Travelocity.com L.P.

CONTRIBUTIONS: TOTAL: *$9,670* DEM: *$9,670* REP: *$0*

Subsidiary of Sabre Holdings Corporation (p. 202).
www.travelocity.com

Travelodge Hotels, Inc.

No contributions. Subsidiary of Cendant Corporation (p. 192).
www.travelodge.com

TRT Holdings, Inc.

CONTRIBUTIONS: TOTAL: *$96,750* DEM: *$104* REP: *$96,646*

Privately owned. Implicated in a bribery scandal resulting in an $875,000 summary judgment ruling in 1997.

Trump Entertainment Resorts, Inc.

CONTRIBUTIONS: TOTAL: *$63,250* DEM: *$38,440* REP: *$24,810*

Mired in bankruptcy reorganization and Securities and Exchange Commission (SEC) violations and investigations, but CEO Donald Trump's public persona remains in the clear. Paid a record $250,000 in fines for lobbying violations for its alleged scheme to derail expansion of Native American gambling to the Catskills. Settled a suit for discriminating against employees with disabilities. www.trump.com

UAL Corporation (United Airlines)

CONTRIBUTIONS: TOTAL: *$166,500* DEM: *$76,002* REP: *$90,498*

Shed its pension/retirement obligations to its employees in bankruptcy court. A pending lawsuit involves multiple labor violations and alleged racial discrimination. Foundation supports community improvement with a focus on education, health, diversity, arts, and culture. Has an employee volunteer and charitable gifting program. Has a written nondiscrimination policy covering sexual orientation but not gender identity. Offers insurance coverage to employees' domestic partners.
www.united.com

US Airways Group, Inc.

CONTRIBUTIONS: TOTAL: *$75,500* DEM: *$13,985* REP: *$61,516*

Pending a merger with America West Holdings Corporation at press time. Scrapped employee pension plans following an extensive court battle. Fought a suit against a disabled employee who claimed violations of the ADA, appealing all the way to the Supreme Court. Supports social responsibility and diversity projects through employee volunteerism and contributions of air transportation. Has a written nondiscrimination policy covering sexual orientation and gender identity. Offers insurance coverage to employees' domestic partners. www.usairways.com

Vanguard Car Rental USA Inc.

50%   50%

CONTRIBUTIONS: TOTAL: *$21,000* DEM: *$10,540* REP: *$10,460*
Privately held. Settled a Justice Department probe into disability rights violations with promises of increasing wheelchair accessibility. www.vanguardcar.com

Virgin Group Ltd.
See p. 155 in Media and Entertainment.

Westin Hotels & Resorts
No contributions. Subsidiary of Starwood Hotels & Resorts Worldwide, Inc. (p. 203). Has a written nondiscrimination policy covering sexual orientation but not gender identity. Offers insurance coverage to employees' domestic partners. www.starwoodhotels.com/westin

W Hotels Worldwide
No contributions. Subsidiary of Starwood Hotels & Resorts Worldwide, Inc. (p. 203). www.starwoodhotels.com/whotels

Wingate Inns International
No contributions. Subsidiary of Cendant Corporation (p. 192). www.wingateinns.com

Wyndham International, Inc.

94%   6%

CONTRIBUTIONS: TOTAL: *$32,000* DEM: *$30,000* REP: *$2,000*
Implicated in a class action suit alleging securities fraud and tax evasion in its affiliation with Patriot American Hospitality. Received a number one ranking on the NAACP's lodging industry report for its commitment to corporate diversity. Outreach includes partnership with the Susan B. Komen Foundation to fight breast cancer. www.wyndham.com

Wynn Resorts, Limited

7%   93%

CONTRIBUTIONS: TOTAL: *$234,881* DEM: *$16,000* REP: *$218,881*
Known for bankrolling the Mirage with Michael Milken–backed junk bonds, his extensive art collection, and his troubles with rival Donald Trump, CEO Stephen Wynn is politically active nationally and locally. Has been implicated and fined in several cases alleging improper handling of political contributions. Minimally committed to employee volunteerism. Written nondiscrimination policy does not cover sexual orientation or gender identity. Refuses insurance coverage to employees' domestic partners. www.wynnresorts.com

Vehicles, Parts, and Gas

The auto industry's main ingredient isn't so much steel and fiberglass as Teflon. For decades the sector has weathered a barrage of would-be bad statistics, bad policy, and bad press. Unlike, say, the tobacco industry, U.S. automakers have yet to suffer a major legal or PR defeat, even as gas prices climb, dependence on foreign oil grows, and greenhouse gases gather.

It's the lobby, stupid. For years now, and against public opinion, the U.S. auto lobby has kept Congress from increasing fuel efficiency standards. It has also worked to dilute safety standards and pushed for import quotas from Japan. It has learned to get around fuel efficiency standards by marketing SUVs, which are required to meet less rigorous standards, as passenger vehicles. It has even joined the tort reform movement popularized under the current business-friendly administration, working to limit liability in class action suits, for instance.

Both automakers and auto dealers—an even larger lobby—have given predominantly to Republicans over the years. Ties between carmakers and the Bush administration in particular are close, as *U.S. News & World Report* has detailed: Chief of Staff Andrew Card was formerly General Motors Corporation's top lobbyist and head of a trade group of major domestic automakers. Jacqueline Glassman, chief counsel for the National Highway Traffic Safety Administration, was once a top lawyer for DaimlerChrysler AG. In a few cases—cases where lives were actually lost—the money trail from lobby to government has been too glaring for the public to ignore. In 2000, when Firestone sat through accident after accident before recalling its faulty tires, it was eventually noted that the very officials guiding National Highway and Traffic Safety Administration (NHTSA) policy were the ones benefiting most from the auto lobby.

The response to this and other potential setbacks has been a sophisticated PR campaign. Despite overwhelming data to the contrary, the Alliance of Auto Manufacturers has claimed that the higher percentage of deaths in SUV accidents (compared to car accidents) came from lower seatbelt usage; similar distortions have been made about rollover tendency. At the same time, an even more insidious greenwashing trend has spread throughout the sector. Even as Ford Motor Company—which has the worst fuel efficiency of any U.S. automaker—worked feverishly to gut California's clean air regulations, it publicly trumpeted its commitment to "clean-running" vehicles.

Top Ten Republican Contributors

Valero Energy Corporation	$707,949
Exxon Mobil Corporation	703,211
General Motors Corporation	575,145
Ford Motor Company	523,030
DaimlerChrysler AG	501,680
Ashland Inc.	339,167
Chevron Corporation	334,739
Marathon Petroleum Company LLC	240,588
ConocoPhillips	235,428
Goodyear Tire & Rubber Company, The	217,962

Top Ten Democratic Contributors

DaimlerChrysler AG	$238,171
General Motors Corporation	210,426
Ford Motor Company	139,021
Amerada Hess Corporation	133,500
Valero Energy Corporation	104,052
BP p.l.c.	94,122
Bridgestone Americas Holding, Inc.	57,540
Marathon Petroleum Company LLC	46,513
Chevron Corporation	43,562
Ashland Inc.	41,659

Advance Auto Parts, Inc.

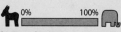

CONTRIBUTIONS: TOTAL: *$18,000* DEM: *$0* REP: *$18,000*

Paid $6.8 million to settle a class action racial discrimination suit filed on behalf of 5,000 black employees of subsidiary Western Auto in 2003. Outreach supports youth alcohol education, children's causes, and diabetes research. Does not have a written nondiscrimination policy covering sexual orientation or gender identity. Refuses insurance coverage to employees' domestic partners. www.advance-auto.com

Amerada Hess Corporation

CONTRIBUTIONS: TOTAL: *$138,500* DEM: *$133,500* REP: *$5,000*

Faces several pending lawsuits for contamination of groundwater supplies with MTBE. Fined for environmental violations in Texas in 2004. Outreach supports health and education in communities where the company has a presence. Has a written nondiscrimination policy covering sexual orientation but not gender identity. Refuses insurance coverage to employees' domestic partners. www.hess.com

AMERCO

CONTRIBUTIONS: TOTAL: *$13,050* DEM: *$10,000* REP: *$3,050*

Holding company for U-Haul International, Inc. Outreach supports hunger relief and housing. www.amerco.com

AM General, LLC

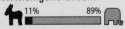

CONTRIBUTIONS: TOTAL: *$64,500* DEM: *$30,007* REP: *$34,494*

Does not have a written nondiscrimination policy covering sexual orientation or gender identity. www.amgeneral.com

Ashland Inc.

CONTRIBUTIONS: TOTAL: *$380,825* DEM: *$41,659* REP: *$339,166*

Paid $9.4 million in environmental fines and $3.5 million to injured workers following a 1997 oil refinery explosion caused by flammable waste system leaks. Cited 10 times by the Arkansas Environmental Quality Department since 1997. Fined $650,000 by the Environmental Protection Agency (EPA) in 2004 for hazardous waste violations in Michigan. Paid a $60,000 fine to the Ohio EPA in 2000. In 1998 the EPA levied $32.5 million in fines for air and water pollution violations at petroleum refineries in Ohio, Kentucky, and Minnesota. Former CEO and chairman received a $7.6 million severance payout, plus $300,000 a year for life, in a forced resignation in 2002 after he violated company policy with his romantic involvement with a subordinate. Has a supplier diversity program. Supports community organizations focusing on children's education, mentoring, and literacy. Has an employee-matching charitable contribution program. Has a written nondiscrimination policy covering sexual orientation but not gender identity. Offers insurance coverage to employees' domestic partners. www.ashland.com

AUDI AG

No contributions. Subsidiary of Volkswagen AG (p. 222). Outreach supports environmental protection and ecological responsibility. Has a written nondiscrimination policy covering sexual orientation and plans to cover gender identity. Offers insurance coverage to employees' domestic partners. www.audi.com

AutoNation, Inc.

CONTRIBUTIONS: TOTAL: *$65,000* DEM: *$5,000* REP: *$60,000*

Ordered in arbitration to pay $130,000 in damages in 2002 to an employee who was fired after reporting practices that defrauded customers. That same year, another California dealership's license was suspended and put on probation for defrauding consumers, and four employees pleaded no contest to claims they conspired to cheat customers by hiding charges. Outreach supports Big Brothers/Big Sisters, the National Association for the Advancement of Colored People (NAACP), Habitat for Humanity, the United Way, and the Urban League. Has a written nondiscrimination policy that does not cover sexual orientation or gender identity. Refuses insurance coverage to employees' domestic partners. www.corp.autonation.com

AutoZone, Inc.

16% █████████ 84%

CONTRIBUTIONS: TOTAL: *$38,000* DEM: *$6,006* REP: *$31,994*

Currently facing a $12 million lawsuit alleging illegal dumping and breach of California's hazardous waste laws at 400 stores statewide. Outreach supports programs and projects focused on education, human services, and civic endeavors. Annually awards fifteen $2,500 scholarships to graduating high school seniors. Has a written nondiscrimination policy covering sexual orientation but not gender identity. Refuses insurance coverage to employees' domestic partners. www.autozone.com

Bayerische Motoren Werke AG

No contributions. Foreign owned. Paid a $2 million punitive damage award to a single customer who challenged a nationwide policy of nondisclosure of damage to "new" vehicles. Volunteer participant in the United Nations Global Compact on human rights and the United Nations Environmental Mobility Forum. Outreach supports traffic safety programs, sustainable development, educational projects, HIV/AIDS research, alternate fuel, and environmental research. www.bmw.com

BP p.l.c.

37% █████████ 63%

CONTRIBUTIONS: TOTAL: *$250,999* DEM: *$94,122* REP: *$156,877*

Foreign owned. Paid $21.3 million in fines, the largest fine ever levied by the Occupational Safety and Health Administration (OSHA), after 15 workers died and 170 were injured in a 2005 Texas refinery fire linked to more than 300 safety violations. On probation while OSHA considers relaying findings to the Department of Justice for criminal proceedings. A 2004 incident at the same refinery killed two, injured one, and resulted in a $102,500 fine. A 1998 Human Rights Watch report found BP p.l.c. complicitous in Colombian human rights violations committed by its security officers, who had ties with the Colombian military. Paid $81 million in 2005 to settle a lawsuit over Los Angeles refinery emissions violations, which forced local schools to close three times to protect students from harmful emissions. Paid $414 million in 2003 for alleged violations at the same facility. Fined $1.42 million—a state record—in early 2005 for safety violations at an Alaska oilfield. Has a comprehensive diversity initiative. Outreach focuses on community initiatives—fund-raising, construction of homes, health education, educating children in rural areas—in worldwide locations where the company has a presence. Has a written nondiscrimination policy covering sexual orientation and gender identity. Offers insurance coverage to employees' domestic partners. www.bp.com

Bridgestone Americas Holding, Inc.

32% 68%

CONTRIBUTIONS: TOTAL: *$178,750* DEM: *$57,540* REP: *$121,210*

Involved in the infamous recall of 2000–2001, when at least 271 people were killed on account of faulty Firestone Wilderness ATX and AT tires that induced rollovers of Ford Explorers. In October 2003, Bridgestone-Firestone agreed to pay $240 million to Ford Motor Company (p. 214) to settle claims related to the recall. At the time of press, some lawsuits against both companies are still pending. Has a written nondiscrimination policy covering sexual orientation but not gender identity. Refuses insurance coverage to employees' domestic partners. www.bridgestone-firestone.com

Chevron Corporation

12% 88%

CONTRIBUTIONS: TOTAL: *$378,300* DEM: *$43,561* REP: *$334,739*

Paid $100,000 to the EPA in August 2005 for discharging 140,000 cubic yards of dredge material, in violation of the Clean Water Act. Implicated in violent events, human rights violations, and other reported acts in Nigeria's oil-rich Niger Delta. Has a written nondiscrimination policy covering sexual orientation and gender identity. Offers insurance coverage to employees' domestic partners. www.chevron.com

CITGO Petroleum Corporation

0% 100%

CONTRIBUTIONS: TOTAL: *$500* DEM: *$0* REP: *$500*

Subsidiary of 7-Eleven, Inc. (p. 71), and PDV America, Inc. (p. 220). Paid $3.6 million in fines in 2004 for federal Clean Air Act violations. Assessed a $1.7 million fine and required to make $20 million in required improvements in 2004 to a Texas refinery. Cited by the EPA in 2001 for violations at an Illinois refinery, including failing to implement emissions monitoring procedures. Spent $320 million on improvements to pollution controls at refineries in 2004. Outreach supports the Muscular Dystrophy Association, the United Way, and the Nature Conservancy. Has a written nondiscrimination policy that does not cover sexual orientation or gender identity. www.citgo.com

Clorox Company, The

See p. 125 in Home and Garden.

ConocoPhillips

14% 86%

CONTRIBUTIONS: TOTAL: *$273,500* DEM: *$38,072* REP: *$235,428*

Paid $64.5 million in 2005 to settle a class action suit brought by 20,000 Louisiana residents whose health suffered due to refinery emissions. Settled a $100 million class action lawsuit brought by Pensacola residents, some of whose property was bought and condemned by the EPA. Settled with the EPA in 2005 over Clean Air Act violations, paying $525 million to improve operations at nine refineries nationwide. Assessed a $485,000 fine by the EPA in 2004 for coastal Alaska Clean Water

Act violations, including raw sewage dumping. In 2004, a judge ordered $1.1 million award to a man the company refused to hire, in violation of the ADA. Philanthropy is focused in areas, such as Texas and Oklahoma, where the company has a strong presence. Has a written nondiscrimination policy that does not cover sexual orientation or gender identity. Refuses insurance coverage to employees' domestic partners. www.conocophillips.com

CSK Auto Corporation
No contributions. Paid $11 million in 2000 to settle a wage-and-hour class action suit brought by store managers. Has a written nondiscrimination policy that does not cover sexual orientation or gender identity. www.cskauto.com

DaimlerChrysler AG
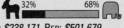
CONTRIBUTIONS: TOTAL: *$739,850* DEM: *$238,171* REP: *$501,679*
Paid $300 million to settle a shareholder class action on the heels of its 1998 merger. Defeated a similar $9 billion lawsuit brought by Kirk Kerkorian, owner of the Tracinda Corporation (p. 204) and a major shareholder. Has a written nondiscrimination policy covering sexual orientation and gender identity. Offers insurance coverage to employees' domestic partners. www.daimlerchrysler.com

Discount Tire Co. Inc.

CONTRIBUTIONS: TOTAL: *$400* DEM: *$60* REP: *$340*
One of two tire companies sued in a 2001 class action for continuing to charge a $2-per-tire recycling fee three years after it was cancelled. www.discounttire.com

Dr. Ing. h.c. F. Porsche AG
No contributions. Foreign owned. Paid $7.9 million in 2004 for fuel economy and safety violations. Recalled a total of 63,000 SUVs in two separate 2004 campaigns for problems with malfunctioning backseat belt anchors and faulty wiring. www.porsche.com

Exxon Mobil Corporation
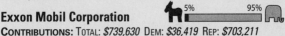
CONTRIBUTIONS: TOTAL: *$739,630* DEM: *$36,419* REP: *$703,211*
Continues to appeal a $7 billion fine ordered by an Alaskan court after the 1989 *Valdez* spill and is spearheading efforts to open the Arctic National Wildlife Refuge to drilling. A 2001 civil suit filed by the International Labor Rights Fund alleged the company knowingly assisted the Indonesian army in perpetrating human rights abuses. Has spent millions funding various think tanks that cast doubt on the link between fossil fuels and global warming. Paid $8.25 million in 2004 to settle allegations of fuel storage violations in southern California; the U.S. State Department in 2002 asked a federal judge to dismiss the suit. Donated $106.5 million in 2004 to higher education, civic and

community organizations, and health research and education. Does not have a written nondiscrimination policy covering sexual orientation and gender identity. Refuses insurance coverage to employees' domestic partners. www.exxon.mobil.com

Fiat S.p.A.

No contributions. Foreign owned. In 2004 the Ethical Consumer Research Association ranked the company eighth of the top ten most ethical car manufacturers worldwide, citing Fiat's commitment to alternative fuels and recyclable automobile components, its noninvolvement in arms manufacture, and its clear labor relations record. www.fiatgroup.com

Flying J Inc.

No contributions. Locations have been assessed fines for diesel fuel spills, sewage ordinance violations, and dumping of petroleum-contaminated water. A 1993 explosion at a Utah refinery, resulting in a worker's death, cost the company $112,000 in OSHA fines for "willful violations" and was one of five fires at that facility in less than a year. www.flyingj.com

Ford Motor Company

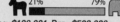 21%　79%

CONTRIBUTIONS: TOTAL: *$662,050* DEM: *$139,021* REP: *$523,029*

Promised then reneged on a commitment to improve fuel economy by 25% in all Ford cars by 2005. Has lobbied against tighter efficiency and emissions regulations, and the company's campaign contributions strongly favor Republicans. In 2005 a U.S. District judge ruled that subsidiary Primus Financial Services Inc. used racially discriminatory lending practices in marking up wholesale loan rates; at press time, dispute was in mediation. Settled a class action racial discrimination lawsuit brought by the EEOC in 2005 for $8.55 million. Settled two class action age discrimination lawsuits, paying $10.5 million to 500 current and former employees in exchange for dropping race and gender claims. Between 1995 and 2000, had 292 "serious" OSHA violations, some repeated and some resulting in worker deaths. A 1999 explosion at a Michigan plant killed 6 workers, injured 14, and got the company a $1.5 million OSHA fine, the largest in state history. Promotes employee volunteerism and works closely with Habitat for Humanity in Michigan, particularly in Detroit. Several locations offer comprehensive, nearly 24-hour, on-site child care. Invests heavily in youth education, especially in science and technology. Has a written nondiscrimination policy covering sexual orientation and gender identity. Offers insurance coverage to employees' domestic partners. www.ford.com

Fuji Heavy Industries Ltd.

No contributions. Foreign owned. www.fhi.co.jp/

General Motors Corporation

27% 73%

CONTRIBUTIONS: TOTAL: *$785,570* DEM: *$210,426* REP: *$575,144*

Maker of the 10 miles-per-gallon Hummer line of vehicles. Has long fought federal fuel economy regulations and in 2004 was named "Public Polluter #1" by the Union of Concerned Scientists. Has lucrative military contracts. Former African American managers at an Ohio plant filed a pending $4 million racial discrimination suit, alleging, among other offenses, hangman's nooses displayed in their workplace. Voluntarily reports environmental information. Recently invested $1 billion into research into hydrogen fuel cell vehicles and has taken some steps toward reducing emissions and using alternative energy at its plants in the United States. Supports community improvement, with donations to cultural, environmental, educational, and societal concerns. Has a written nondiscrimination policy covering sexual orientation but not gender identity. Offers insurance coverage to employees' domestic partners.
www.gm.com

Goodyear Tire & Rubber Company, The

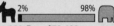

10% 90%

CONTRIBUTIONS: TOTAL: *$243,000* DEM: *$25,038* REP: *$217,962*

Agreed, with five other rubber manufacturers, to spend a total of $19 million on cleanup at an Ohio EPA Superfund landfill. In 2003, a jury awarded a woman employee $3.8 million for her claim that for 20 years the company paid her significantly less than it did men who were her counterparts. Fined $274,000 by OSHA in 2004 for an accident that seriously injured a worker who was trapped for hours up to his neck in coal. Outreach supports the United Way and Ohio community organizations. Supports employee volunteerism and makes in-kind donations. Has a written nondiscrimination policy covering sexual orientation but not gender identity. Refuses insurance coverage to employees' domestic partners. www.goodyear.com

Gulf Oil Limited Partnership

2% 98%

CONTRIBUTIONS: TOTAL: *$80,000* DEM: *$1,600* REP: *$78,400*

In 1997, while transferring fuel from a barge to an onshore facility, a crewperson left the operation unattended, and 30,000 gallons of gasoline were dumped into the harbor of Portland, Maine. Outreach and corporate giving concentrated in Chelsea, Massachusetts. www.gulfoil.com

Harley-Davidson, Inc.

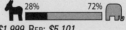

28% 72%

CONTRIBUTIONS: TOTAL: *$7,100* DEM: *$1,999* REP: *$5,101*

Makes no bones about its products' contribution to greenhouse gas emissions and has no programs in place to research alternative fuel sources. Has a strong history of positive union relations, yet donates predominantly to Republican causes through its PAC. Supports high school education programs for low-income students at its facilities in Wisconsin and Pennsylvania.

Offers two college scholarships yearly to participating students. Has a written nondiscrimination policy covering sexual orientation but not gender identity. Refuses insurance coverage to employees' domestic partners.
www.harley-davidson.com

Hertz Corporation, The
See p. 197 in Travel and Leisure.

Honda Motor Co., Ltd.
No contributions. The maker of America's first hybrid car, was named 2004's "greenest automaker" for the third consecutive year by the Union of Concerned Scientists. In 1998, American Honda Motor Co., Inc., paid a $330 million settlement to more than 1,400 plaintiffs, upon allegations that new cars had been diverted to large dealers who paid kickbacks; a 1996 ruling determined that defrauded dealers had the right to sue the Japanese parent company, and more than 50 suits ensued. Among its environmental initiatives are the introduction of water-based paints, research into alternative and more efficient fuels and engines, and recycling up to 80% of automobile components. Has also been praised as the leading maker of hybrid and low-emission vehicles for meeting and often exceeding national emissions and fuel efficiency standards. Also a leader in research into hydrogen fuel cell cars. Community activities include reforestation in Mongolia, environmental cleanup, and ecology education for children. Has a written nondiscrimination policy that does not cover sexual orientation or gender identity. www.world.honda.com

Hyundai Motor Company
3% ▬▬▬▬▬▬ 97%
CONTRIBUTIONS: TOTAL: *$1,300* DEM: *$40* REP: *$1,259*
Foreign owned. The vice chairman received a suspended two-year prison sentence for embezzlement and improper political contributions during the 2002 Korean presidential race. Fined $2.4 million in 2003 for illegal intersubsidiary transactions. Outreach supports community improvement endeavors.
www.hyundai-motor.com

Isuzu Motors Limited
0% ▬▬▬▬▬▬ 100%
CONTRIBUTIONS: TOTAL: *$4,000* DEM: *$0* REP: *$4,000*
Foreign owned. Paid $307,000 with General Motors Corporation (p. 215) in 2005 to settle allegations that the company violated clean air laws in Massachusetts. Has developed natural gas vehicles, 5,000 of which are already on the road in Japan. Environmental initiatives include creating cleaner-running diesel engines and researching alternative fuel sources.
www.isuzu.co.jp

Jaguar Cars Limited

No contributions. Subsidiary of Ford Motor Company (p. 214). Has a written nondiscrimination policy covering sexual orientation and gender identity. Offers insurance coverage to employees' domestic partners. www.jaguarvehicles.com

Jiffy Lube International, Inc.

No contributions. Subsidiary of Shell Oil Company. A customer filed a suit in 2000 alleging that the company's oil disposal fee violated the Environmental Conservation Law; the company settled in 2005, agreeing to issue $5 coupons to each of 7.3 million customers nationwide. Raises funds for the Muscular Dystrophy Association, the Dana-Farber Cancer Institute, and St. Jude Children's Research Hospital. Parent company has a written nondiscrimination policy covering sexual orientation but not gender identity and offers insurance coverage to employees' domestic partners. www.jiffylube.com

Kawasaki Heavy Industries, Ltd.

No contributions. Foreign owned. A 1999 class action suit filed by former World War II prisoners in Japanese camps sought reparations from the company for forced labor that ultimately benefited those businesses. Human Rights Watch has reported that though Japanese law prohibits exporting military products, Kawasaki Heavy Industries, Ltd., has supplied the Indonesian army with light-transport helicopters. www.khi.co.jp

Kia Motors Corporation

No contributions. Foreign owned. Has been the target of a significant number of "lemon law" complaints including a class action suit brought in 2003 by 10,000 Kia owners whose new cars had mechanical difficulties that were not covered by the company warranty. Introduced the first electric vehicle in South Korea in 1986, and current research focuses on alternative fuel sources, such as solar energy. Supports disaster relief and sponsors charity events such as Kia Motors UK's 259-mile bicycle race raising funds for vascular and heart disease research. www.kiamotors.com

Land Rover

No contributions. Subsidiary of Ford Motor Company (p. 214). To circumvent EPA emissions standards and NHTSA requirements, the company attempted in 2003 to import its Defender—U.S. sales of which ceased in 1997—in pieces, as a "kit" to be assembled upon delivery. Announced that for every Land Rover sold, a $1,000 donation would be made to the Gay and Lesbian Alliance. Sponsors Biosphere Expeditions, wildlife charity the Born Free Organization, and the China Exploration and Research Society. Has a written nondiscrimination policy covering sexual orientation and gender identity. Offers insurance coverage to employees' domestic partners. www.landrover.com

Les Schwab Tire Centers

CONTRIBUTIONS: TOTAL: *$700* DEM: *$0* REP: *$700*

Has a written nondiscrimination policy that does not cover sexual orientation or gender identity. www.lesschwab.com

Lincoln Mercury

CONTRIBUTIONS: TOTAL: *$1,000* DEM: *$0* REP: *$1,000*

Subsidiary of Ford Motor Company (p. 214). Has a written nondiscrimination policy covering sexual orientation and gender identity. Offers insurance coverage to employees' domestic partners. www.lincolnmercury.com

Marathon Petroleum Company LLC

CONTRIBUTIONS: TOTAL: *$287,100* DEM: *$46,512* REP: *$240,588*

Ohio River Pipe Line subsidiary was ordered to halt construction in 2003 of a highly controversial 140-mile gas pipeline through Ohio and West Virginia, after the Army Corps of Engineers found improper disposal of fill in waterways. Paid a $3.8 million EPA fine for Clean Air Act violations in 2001, pledged $6.8 million for improvements in affected communities, and agreed to make $265 million in emissions systems improvements at seven refineries. Its Canton, Ohio, plant was the site of two 2001 accidents: cars and homes in a three-mile radius became coated in oil vapor after a tank blew open, and a sulfur dioxide release was severe enough that residents were confined to their homes by firefighters. Settled a class action suit brought by neighbors of a Minnesota refinery in 2000, paying only $39,000 of the $52 million sought for declining property values due to emissions violations, but also agreed to establish a $5 million fund for residents having problems securing mortgage financing. Supports local charities and raises funds for the United Way. Supports employee volunteerism. Has a written nondiscrimination policy covering sexual orientation but not gender identity. Refuses insurance coverage to employees' domestic partners. www.marathonpetroleum.com

Mazda Motor Corporation

No contributions. Ford Motor Company (p. 214) holds a controlling 33% stake in the company. Subsidiary Mazda Motor North America Inc. settled Federal Trade Commission (FTC) charges for $5.25 million in 1999 for false advertising. Introduced cars with 75% lower emissions than required in 2005. Outreach has included fund-raisers at its research and development facility and wheelchair donations to social organizations. www.mazda.com

Meineke Car Care Centers, Inc.

CONTRIBUTIONS: TOTAL: *$11,600* DEM: *$1,441* REP: *$10,159*

In what was then the largest class action franchise litigation in U.S. history, in 1997 a judge tripled the jury award, ordering $601 million in damages paid to franchise owners for breach of fiduciary responsibility relating to the use and distribution of advertising fees paid by franchise owners. www.meineke.com

Mercedes-Benz USA, LLC

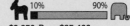

CONTRIBUTIONS: TOTAL: *$1,000* DEM: *$1,000* REP: *$0*

Subsidiary of DaimlerChrysler AG (p. 213). Outreach supports diversity initiatives and women's issues. Donates to Big Brothers/Big Sisters and Teach for America. www.mbusa.com

Michelin North America, Inc.

CONTRIBUTIONS: TOTAL: *$28,250* DEM: *$2,850* REP: *$25,400*

Foreign owned. The French company successfully appealed a precedent-setting ruling in Canada that insomnia caused by shift work constitutes a workplace injury, called "shift-work maladaption syndrome." Has a written nondiscrimination policy covering sexual orientation but not gender identity. www.michelin-us.com

Midas, Inc.

No contributions. Foreign owned. The internationally franchised company, perhaps best known for its mufflers, is now branding itself as a total auto maintenance destination. www.midas.com

Mitsubishi Motors Corporation

No contributions. Foreign owned. Publicly endorses its commitment to the Universal Declaration of Human Rights, the International Labor Organization (ILO) Core Labor Standards, and the Voluntary Principles of Security and Human Rights. Offers insurance coverage to employees' domestic partners. www.mitsubishi-motors.co.jp

Monro Muffler Brake, Inc.

CONTRIBUTIONS: TOTAL: *$36,000* DEM: *$36,000* REP: *$0*

Fined $56,000 by OSHA for 10 safety violations at its New Hampshire facility in 2005. Was cited for similar hazards a New York facility earlier in the year. www.monro.com

Nissan Motor Co., Ltd.

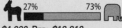

CONTRIBUTIONS: TOTAL: *$17,500* DEM: *$4,690* REP: *$12,810*

Agreed to offer preapproved loans to 675,000 black and Hispanic potential buyers after a class action suit argued successfully that it charged blacks and Hispanics more than comparable white buyers. Produces and sells ultralow-emission vehicles in Japan and is launching the Altima hybrid in the

United States in 2006. Hydrogen-powered fuel cell vehicles, whose only byproduct emission is water, are still in development. Has a written nondiscrimination policy covering sexual orientation but not gender identity. Plans to offer insurance coverage to employees' domestic partners. www.nissan-global.com

PDV America, Inc

CONTRIBUTIONS: TOTAL: *$500* DEM: *$0* REP: *$500*

Foreign owned. American subsidiary of Venezuela's state-owned PDVSA and part owner of the CITGO Petroleum Corporation (p. 212). Venezuela has the largest proven petroleum reserves outside the Middle East and sells 60% of its oil to the United States, making it the fourth largest importer. Workers in Venezuela have gone on strike against Venezuelan president, Hugo Chavez, who redirected $4 billion of PDVSA's profits into social programs annually. www.pdvsa.com

Penske Corporation

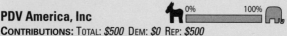

CONTRIBUTIONS: TOTAL: *$93,500* DEM: *$23,571* REP: *$69,929*

Cited repeatedly for allegedly dumping lead-tainted garbage in public landfills and other hazardous waste violations subject to up to $3 million in fines. Supports five NASCAR and Indy racing teams. www.penske.com

Pep Boys—Manny, Moe & Jack

No contributions. Lost two lawsuits alleging fraud and deceit; then lost a third case seeking to obtain indemnity for fraud and deceit charges through its insurer. Founded the Motorist Assurance Program to promote fairness in the auto service industry by curbing superfluous repair and overcharge. www.pepboys.com

Precision Auto Care, Inc.

CONTRIBUTIONS: TOTAL: *$52,400* DEM: *$40,318* REP: *$12,083*

www.precisionac.com

Royal Dutch/Shell Group of Companies

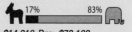

CONTRIBUTIONS: TOTAL: *$86,500* DEM: *$14,318* REP: *$72,183*

Operations in Nigeria have led to complaints by human rights groups. Activists called a general boycott after nine protestors were killed by the Nigerian military. Recently withdrew from the most controversial of its projects in Cameroon, Pakistan, and Nigeria. The family of the late author Ken Saro-Wiwa filed a suit alleging the company's complicit role in his 1995 execution in Nigeria. Campaign contributions favor Republicans three to one, but the company's chairman has been relatively outspoken about the dangers of global warming and has taken steps to diversify the company's holdings into wind and solar energy. Foundation supports small enterprise and entrepre-

neurship in Africa. Has a written nondiscrimination policy covering sexual orientation but not gender identity. Offers insurance coverage to employees' domestic partners.
www.shell.com

Ryder System, Inc.

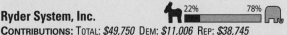
22%   78%

CONTRIBUTIONS: TOTAL: *$49,750* DEM: *$11,006* REP: *$38,745*

A suit brought by 46 truck drivers from two unions alleges wage and contract violations. A 2003 suit brought by a former employee alleging age discrimination was settled for an undisclosed sum. Has a written nondiscrimination policy covering sexual orientation but not gender identity. Offers insurance coverage to employees' domestic partners. www.ryder.com

Saab AB

No contributions. Subsidiary of General Motors Corporation (p. 215). Has a written nondiscrimination policy covering sexual orientation but not gender identity. Offers insurance coverage to employees' domestic partners. www.saab.com

Saturn Corporation

No contributions. Subsidiary of General Motors Corporation (p. 215). Has a written nondiscrimination policy covering sexual orientation but not gender identity. Offers insurance coverage to employees' domestic partners. www.saturn.com

Sinclair Oil Corporation

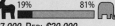
19%   81%

CONTRIBUTIONS: TOTAL: *$37,000* DEM: *$7,000* REP: *$30,000*

A pending EPA investigation was handed over to federal prosecutors in December 2004 following violations of the Clean Air Act standards since 2001. Has accumulated more fines from the Oklahoma Department of Environmental Quality than any other Oklahoma entity. Has refused to dismantle its Arkansas River refinery despite state revitalization plans, Oklahoma Department of Environmental Quality violations, and a class action suit claiming harmful toxic emissions.
www.sinclairoil.com

Sunoco, Inc.

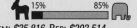
15%   85%

CONTRIBUTIONS: TOTAL: *$239,330* DEM: *$35,816* REP: *$203,514*

Paid $3.6 million to settle a federal lawsuit for a 192,000-gallon crude oil spill in a wildlife refuge in Pennsylvania and agreed to over $300 million in environmental improvements to its refineries. Paid a $475,000 fine for violating sulfur dioxide emission limits one year after a $200,000 fine for the same violation. Litigation is still pending on its liability for MTBE groundwater contamination. Paid $175,000 in OSHA fines for safety violations following a hexane fire resulting in an employee being seriously burned at a manufacturing plant in Texas. Eliminated the gasoline additive MTBE following a ban on the additive in New York state. The first Fortune 500 company to endorse the

Coalition for Environmentally Responsible Economies (CERES) Principles (formerly the Valdez Principles), a 10-point code for environmental conduct established by a coalition of environmental groups, investment funds, and public interest groups. Has a written nondiscrimination policy covering sexual orientation but not gender identity. Refuses insurance coverage to employees' domestic partners. www.sunocoinc.com

Suzuki Motor Corporation
No contributions. Foreign owned. www.globalsuzuki.com

TBC Corporation
No contributions. TBC Corporation, one of the largest providers of discount tires in the United States, announced in the fall of 2005 that it would be acquired by Japan's Sumitomo Corporation. www.tbccorp.com

Toyota Motor Corporation
11% — 89%

CONTRIBUTIONS: TOTAL: *$6,000* DEM: *$665* REP: *$5,310*

Foreign owned. Owns a controlling 51% stake in Daihatsu Motor Co., Ltd. Subsidiary Toyota Motor Credit Corporation involved in a pending class action suit alleging violation of the Equal Credit Opportunity Act for discrimination against African Americans. Faces industry-wide environmental impact issues. Outreach supports environmental preservation, education, arts, and culture in communities where the company does business. Has a written nondiscrimination policy covering sexual orientation but not gender identity. Offers insurance coverage to employees' domestic partners. www.toyota.co.jp

Triumph Motorcycles Limited
No contributions. Foreign owned. Sponsors various charity events in Britain. www.triumph.co.uk

Valero Energy Corporation
13% — 87%

CONTRIBUTIONS: TOTAL: *$812,000* DEM: *$104,052* REP: *$707,949*

Agreed to a settlement negotiated under a lawsuit brought by the Justice Department to bring its U.S. refineries into compliance with the Clean Air Act. Outreach supports United Way and children's charities and encourages employee participation. Has a written nondiscrimination policy covering sexual orientation but not gender identity. Refuses insurance coverage to employees' domestic partners. www.valero.com

Valvoline Company, The
No contributions. Subsidiary of Ashland Inc. (p. 210). www.valvoline.com

Volkswagen AG
No contributions. Foreign owned. Has supported the United Nations Global Compact since 2002, voluntarily committing to upholding its nine principles relating to human rights, labor

standards, anticorruption, and environmental protection. Established a humanitarian fund on behalf of the forced laborers compelled to work at the company during World War II. Support and development of women employees is a company focus, as is alleviating unemployment in Germany. www.volkswagen.de

Volkswagen of America, Inc.
No contributions. Subsidiary of Volkswagen AG (p. 222). Outreach supports young artists with disabilities and programs to encourage driving safety. Has a written nondiscrimination policy covering sexual orientation and plans to offer policy covering gender identity. Offers insurance coverage to employees' domestic partners. www.vw.com

Volvo Car Corporation
No contributions. Subsidiary of Ford Motor Company (p. 214). Has a written nondiscrimination policy covering sexual orientation and gender identity. Offers insurance coverage to employees' domestic partners. www.volvocars.com

Yamaha Motor Co., Ltd.
No contributions. Foreign owned. Outreach supports environmental preservation. www.yamaha-motor.com

The Blue Pages Index

"John Sperling has brilliantly exposed the truth about Retro Republicans using fear to marginalize America's quest for fairness and social justice. Yet, as the book shows, there is a real Metro progressive majority in the country that can create a 'more perfect union'. It needs to speak up and take action. It can't happen soon enough." **Arianna Huffington, columnist, political commentator and bestselling author of** *Pigs at the Trough: How Corporate Greed and Political Corruption are Undermining America*

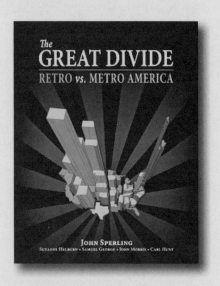

The Great Divide:
Retro vs Metro America

By John Sperling, Suzanne Helburn, Samuel George, John Morris, and Carl Hunt

ISBN: 0-9760621-0-0

$19.95

Available at booksellers everywhere.

Visit us at PoliPointPress.org

"With insight and clarity, Joe Conason shows how the longstanding conservative antipathy toward Social Security has morphed into a lavishly funded and breathtakingly dishonest conservative PR campaign… In untangling spools of GOP propaganda, The Raw Deal sets the record straight and shows what's really at stake for all Americans in the current battle." **David Brock, President and CEO, Media Matters for America, and author of** *Blinded by the Right: The Conscience of an Ex-Conservative*

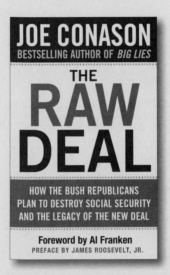

The Raw Deal: How The Bush Republicans Plan To Destroy Social Security And The Legacy Of The New Deal

By Joe Conason. Forward by Al Franken.
Preface by James Roosevelt Jr.

ISBN: 0-9760621-2-7
$11.00

Available at booksellers everywhere.
Visit us at PoliPointPress.org